# BEYOND
# SODOM
# AND
# GOMORRAH

**Journeys of Faith®**
1-800-633-2484
www.bobandpennylord.com

**Bob and Penny Lord**

## Other Books by Bob and Penny Lord

THIS IS MY BODY, THIS IS MY BLOOD
Miracles of the Eucharist Book I
THIS IS MY BODY, THIS IS MY BLOOD
Miracles of the Eucharist Book II
THE MANY FACES OF MARY, A LOVE STORY
WE CAME BACK TO JESUS
SAINTS AND OTHER POWERFUL WOMEN
IN THE CHURCH
SAINTS AND OTHER POWERFUL MEN
IN THE CHURCH
HEAVENLY ARMY OF ANGELS
SCANDAL OF THE CROSS AND ITS TRIUMPH
MARTYRS - THEY DIED FOR CHRIST
THE ROSARY - THE LIFE OF JESUS AND MARY
VISIONARIES, MYSTICS AND STIGMATISTS
VISIONS OF HEAVEN, HELL AND PURGATORY
TRILOGY BOOK I - TREASURES OF THE CHURCH
TRILOGY BOOK II - TRAGEDY OF THE REFORMATION
TRILOGY BOOK III - CULTS, BATTLE OF THE ANGELS
SUPER SAINTS BOOK I - JOURNEY TO SAINTHOOD
SUPER SAINTS BOOK II - HOLY INNOCENCE
SUPER SAINTS BOOK III - DEFENDERS OF THE FAITH
BEYOND SODOM AND GOMORRAH

### ISBN 1-58002-136-0

Cover Art     *"Destruction of Sodom"* - J. M. W. Turner
from Genesis 19:15-26

# Table of Contents

# Dedication

Dear brothers and sister, more than ever before, we wish to thank and dedicate this book to you and to special people who have played a key part in our lives, their courage and love for Mother Church, in the face of overwhelming odds, has been our strength to forge on.

*Pope John Paul II*--The Lord has given us our Vicar, our sweet Christ on earth who, through his endless urgency, has guided us and inspired us to bring the children of God from all over the world home to Christ's true Church.

*Mother Mary Angelica of Our Lady of the Angels Monastery* - True Defender of the Faith, Mother has taken as a personal mandate the passage from the Book of Revelation 14:6. *"And I saw another Angel flying in mid-heaven, having an everlasting Gospel to preach to those who dwell upon the earth, and to every nation and tribe and tongue and people."* She has dedicated her life to fulfilling that mandate. We thank Our Lord Jesus for letting us be part of that fulfillment.

*Mother Teresa of Calcutta*--Now gone to her reward, this selfless woman has left an indelible mark on the world and the Church. Her saying, *"You don't have to be successful; you only have to be faithful"* has given our Ministry the courage to bring the joy of Jesus and His Word to the whole world.

*Brother Joseph and Luz Elena* - They have given up their lives to serve the Lord unselfishly in our Ministry. They truly believe, as we do, that we have been given an opportunity by Our Lord Jesus and Our Mother Mary to touch the hearts of their children, you our brothers and sisters in Christ, that you might know Him, love Him and serve Him.

*Rob and Andrea Ziminsky and Matthew* - Our grandson Rob has always been a constant source of love and affirmation. When he married, he gave us a beautiful grand-daughter to love, and now they have both given us a reason why we want to change the world, a precious great-grandchild.

*We thank You, Jesus, for the gift of life and the gift of love.*

# Should we apologize to Sodom and Gomorrah?

*"Yet know this; the Kingdom of God is at hand. I tell you, it will be more tolerable for Sodom (and Gomorrah) on that day than for that town."*[1]

We have always stood for the Good News, and have had a distaste for gloom and doom, forecast of disaster. We have always related to the *God of Mercy* and avoided thinking of the *God of Justice*. But, as has been said,

*"Anyone who cannot see we are living in the time of the Third Secret of Fatima, is either deaf, dumb or blind."*

The moral decay in our world, has hit an all-time low. There may have been a time when moral values were as non-existent as they are today, but there are times now, we feel we should apologize to Sodom and Gomorrah.

*God said: 'The outcry against Sodom and Gomorrah is so great, and their sin so grave, that I must go down and see whether their actions fully correspond to the cry against them that comes to me. I mean to find out."*[2] In the Bible, the footnote to this verse states that "the sin of Sodom was homosexuality which is therefore also known as sodomy."

We look back on the biblical Sodom and Gomorrah, in which the Lord could not find any good men other than Lot and so, He sent Angels disguised as men to save Lot and his family from the destruction that was going to rain down on the city. The evil men in Sodom wanted to have their way with the Angels, who were strong and handsome. They said to Lot:

*"Where are the men who came to your house tonight? Bring them out to us that we may have intimacies*[3] *with*

---

[1]Lk 10:12
[2]Gn 18:20
[3]Homosexual relations

Left:
*Lot leaves Sodom and Gomorrah*
*"As dawn was breaking, the Angels urged Lot on, saying, 'On your way! Take with you your wife and your two daughters who are here, or you will be swept away in the punishment of the city.'"*

Above:
*Destruction of Sodom and Gomorrah*
*"The sun was just rising over the earth as Lot arrived in Zoar; at the same time the Lord rained down sulphurous fire upon Sodom and Gomorrah. He overthrew those cities and the whole Plain, together with the inhabitants of the cities and the produce of the soil."*

*them.' Lot pleaded with them, but they were going to attack him when the Angels reached out the door, pulled him in and then they struck the men at the entrance of the house, one and all, with such a blinding light, that they were utterly unable to reach the doorway,"[4]*

*"As dawn was breaking, the Angels urged Lot on, saying, 'On your way! Take with you your wife and your two daughters who are here, or you will be swept away in the punishment of the city.' When he hesitated, the Angels, by the Lord's mercy, seized his hand and the hands of his wife and his two daughters and led them to safety outside the city. As soon as they had been brought outside, he was told 'Flee for your life! Don't look back or stop anywhere on the Plain. Get off the hills at once or you will be swept away."[5]*

*"Lot replied: 'Look, this town ahead is near enough to escape to. It's only a small place. Let me flee there - it's a small place, isn't it? - that my life may be saved.'*

*"The Angel replied, 'Well then, I will also grant you the favor you now ask. I will not overthrow the town you speak of. Hurry, escape there! I cannot do anything until you arrive there.'*

*"The sun was just rising over the earth as Lot arrived in Zoar[6]; at the same time the Lord rained down sulphurous fire upon Sodom and Gomorrah. He overthrew those cities and the whole Plain, together with the inhabitants of the cities and the produce of the soil. But Lot's wife looked back, and she was turned into a pillar of salt."[7]*

When we compare the wicked behavior of the people of Sodom and Gomorrah, which precipitated such an action by the Almighty, to the sins of the modern world, not only in our

---

[4]Gn 19:5,10-11
[5]Gn 19:15-17
[6]means "small" in Aramaic
[7]Gn 19:20-26

country but particularly in our country, we find ourselves apologizing to them!     For this generation, with the wholesale *perversion* and *legalized immorality* running rampant throughout our society, it has plummeted far lower than that of Sodom and Gomorrah!     And then as *the punishment befits the crime*, we can at the least, expect that which God meted out on the evil men and women of these cities.

What has become legal and is now the law of our land, not too long ago was *against* the law and *punishable* by prison up to twenty years ago.  When we consider the legalization of Abortion, Homosexual actions, same-sex marriages, Euthanasia, assisted suicide, sterilization, cloning, choosing who has the right to live - refusing life support and/or imposing death on those whose quality of life is judged below the standards prescribed by insurance statistics, approving or disapproving operations and transplants based on age, and on and on, it makes Sodom and Gomorrah seem like a high school prom which got out of hand.

When has the *Culture of Death* equaled that of the last days of the Twentieth Century?  We seem to be on a course of outdoing every decadent society before us, striving to top the perversions of Sodom and Gomorrah and go beyond those of the Roman and Greek civilizations.  Homosexuality and sexual permissiveness ran unrestrained, completely out of control in the Greek and then in the Roman empires.  In every society gone mad, the citizens drunk with the elixir of the pagan gods of permissiveness, promiscuity, depravity, and human sacrifice, those civilizations perished!  Did they have a government helping to finance and police forces[8] enforcing depravity?  In any event, we do and we all know

---

[8]who justify their actions by saying they are just following orders, like the Nazis at the Nuremberg trials

what happened to those civilizations, and so, unless we can change men's hearts, what can we expect?

In those times, there were not organized women's groups *(financed by our tax dollars)* dedicated to the murder of unborn children, under the banner of woman's choice over her body and the woman's right to freedom from the heels of a male-dominated society. Even during the great movement of women to be freed from the oppression of men's laws, the foundress of that outstanding Woman's movement in this country, Susan B. Anthony, maintained that the murder of a pre-born child was a deplorable crime. She stated, *"I deplore the horrible crime of child-murder (referring to abortion), no matter what the motive, love of ease, or a desire to save from suffering the unborn innocent. The woman is awfully guilty who commits the deed (abortion)."* The feminists of her day considered abortion acts of *"desperate savageness"* and *"the slaughter of the innocents."* Susan B. Anthony, foundress and spearhead of the feminist movement in the United States, would most likely be drummed out by the current gurus of the movement. It would not be convenient for them to support their mother-in-faith.[9]

Maybe the Renaissance period, the great rebirth of art and culture, and the downfall of spirituality and morals, which was famous for its *secular humanism*, its debauchery, its attempt to recreate the orgiastic flavor of the Roman Empire at its worst, comes close in sinfulness and wickedness to this, the last decade in the second millennium. Renaissance was broken up into two philosophies, Secular Humanism and Christian Humanism. Whereas one philosophy's intention was to explore the beauty of the languages, the sculptors, the artists, the philosophers, in an effort to glorify God through the advancements of His

---

[9]Information courtesy of CRNET, Mannassas, VA 1994

creation, another stronger philosophy's focus was to delve into the subculture, the perversion of ancient Rome and Greece, with its open sex, permissiveness, radical homosexual activity, materialism, self gratification and personal advancement, a philosophy of, *if it pleases you, go for it!* We may have said it before, but just looking at what began in mid-Fourteenth Century Italy, and then spread over all of Europe, the parallels are frightening with what's going on today. But again, we seriously doubt that at their very worst, they equaled the wickedness of these (last?) days.

We've seen it coming for years. In the last ten years or so, as we have traveled around the country giving talks at Marian and Eucharistic Conferences, Days of Recollection and Parish Missions, we have made statements like, *"We have to apologize to the people of Sodom and Gomorrah. Our behavior makes them look like choir boys and girls."* Since the scandal of Abortion came upon the scene in 1973, and the subsequent legalization of the ghoulish practice of taking body parts from aborted babies, which are then used for experimentation and ingredients in the manufacture of skin creams for aging men and women, for human growth hormones to make old men feel younger, *all for fun and profit*, we've had to take another look at our attitudes towards the Nazi butchers and their atrocities at Auschwitz.

We went to Auschwitz and Birkenau to videotape documentaries on man's inhumanity to man as displayed in the vile genocide of Edith Stein[10] and St. Maxmilian Kolbe. We taped one segment outside the death cell of St.

---

[10] When she was brutally murdered by poison gas, the Nazis had just begun using this method of annihilation. It had not yet been perfected. The prisoners were supposed to die within fifteen or twenty minutes. Edith Stein and her sister languished, their throats and lungs torn apart from the cyanide gas for over twenty-four hours. She was Canonized on October 11, 1998 by Pope John Paul II as St. Teresa Benedicta della Croce (St. Teresa Blessed by the Cross).

Maxmilian Kolbe, where prisoners were taken by the Nazis, lined up against a wall and shot after first having all their clothes removed so that they could be used for other prisoners in a cost-cutting effort to maintain economy in the camp. We noticed that all the windows in the building across from St. Maxmilian Kolbe's death cell were boarded up. None of the other buildings in Auschwitz were boarded up. So we asked our guide what had gone on in that building. We were told that was where experimentation was done on pregnant women and aborted children. Genetic study began in that condemned building. But how has history judged them and how will history judge us? In the light of the legalized murder of over a **billion unborn children** worldwide through Abortion, will our generation be found guilty of massive genocide, or will they say that the butchers at Auschwitz were perhaps just slightly ahead of their time?

**Consider this:**
†Except for the possibility *that maybe*, and that's a *big maybe*,
    better sanitary and operating conditions exist today in
    abortion clinics, *but probably not*,
    considering those dying of infections today due to
    unclean instruments and damaged uteri,
    or as a result of the use of inferior operating conditions,
    and apathy of the untrained, uncaring personnel
    performing operations,
    all a part of the subterfuge that women should be
    afforded the right to have safe abortions, another part
    of the lie,
†what was so different about the butchery performed in that
    boarded-up building in Auschwitz,
    which was later condemned at Nuremberg as
    outrageous crimes against humanity, and still echoes the
    screams of the victims tortured and killed there,
†and the silent screams of what is practiced in abortion mills

---

and subsequently various medical and cosmetic laboratories throughout the country and the world today under the guise of science and commerce?

†Will there be another Nuremberg trial during our lifetime?

†Will there be another Sodom and Gomorrah, only due to a nuclear holocaust, or will God's vengeance be wrought on Judgment Day, when everything which was done in darkness, will be put to the test of the brilliance of the blinding light of the presence of Jesus?[11]

We are so sure the Lord is ready to hit us with a lightning bolt, to get our attention, we find ourselves turning to Scripture and prophecies of the Saints to determine what signs the Lord is giving us in these, the last few years of the Second Millennium. While we have always read Scripture, and the particular passages we feel are of the utmost urgency to bring to your attention, we were never aware of how apocalyptic they really are, until we read them in the light, not of things to come, but chastisements and tribulations happening and on the verge of happening.

*We're not doomsday people, my brothers and sisters.* You know us. You've read many of our books and seen our television programs. We're Kingdom people; we're Alleluia people. But a truth has to be acknowledged. There are crimes which cry out to Heaven for vengeance. Vengeance is the Lord's, and we believe we are aiming headlong into a time of God's Justice, which can also be termed God's Vengeance.

We believe in the God of Mercy. We don't like to think about Three Days of Darkness,[12] and yet we know they will come. We don't like to go to the Scripture passages which talk about the end times, and yet we know the Lord is going to fulfill those Scripture passages in Chapter 21 of Luke's

---

[11] *cf* Lk 12:3

[12] Read chapter in this book on Y2K - Three Days of Darkness

Gospel.[13]  Although no one wants to get anywhere near the prophecies in section four of the Book of Revelation, dealing with *The Seven Seals, Trumpets and Plagues*,[14] much less section five, which deals with *The Punishment of Babylon* and *the Destruction of Pagan Nations*, we know that these days are coming!

We don't want to explore the deeper meaning of these passages, nor do we really want to know the time frame, but we can't keep our heads in the sand.  We can't ignore the prophecies, when they're staring us smack in the face.  We believe the Lord has given us these signs as means to help us repent of our sins, change our ways, and try to bring back those who have become swallowed up in the Twentieth Century super *glitzy* expanded version of Sodom and Gomorrah.  Remember, the Lord tells us in Scripture that if our brother sins, we have a responsibility to tell him about it and try to convince him to change his ways.  If we do that, and he doesn't change, we have done all we can and we do not share in the punishment.  But if we see our brother sinning, and we don't do anything to try to change him, we are as accountable as he.[15]

There are many signs the Lord has been giving us, down through the centuries.  What is in Holy Scripture should be enough to make us fall to our knees, repent, convert and pray for God's Mercy.  We are going to walk through Scripture passages and see how they relate to the present days.  In the Book of Revelation, most everyone thought St. John was writing about Nero and his cohorts, and the great whore of Babylon was the Roman Empire.  They were convinced that those predictions were for those people and that time.  But that's not necessarily so.  In the light of what

---

[13]Read chapter in this book on Y2K - Three Days of Darkness
[14]Read the chapter on the Sign of the Angels in this book
[15]*cf*Ez 3:18-20

has been going on in these last days, we may discover that some or all of those predictions were for this time in history.

In addition, the Lord has spoken often to prophets who have lived since the end of the Book of Revelation. Now, we're not required to believe these private revelations. However, keep in mind that these prophecies were proclaimed by different prophets from different locations at different ends of the globe, over a period of centuries. The means of transportation and communications in those days was primitive, at best. If these many prophets were given messages which clearly point to people or events of these last days of the end of the second millennium, and if these prophecies do not contradict Scripture, but possibly affirm what we read in the Word of the Lord, it would be folly to disregard them. We will bring you a number of these prophecies. The goals, or the desired results are that we will all take the messages to heart, and convert our lives. And not only our lives, but those of our loved ones and friends.

We know the end of the story. It's no great mystery. *Jesus triumphs!* It's in the Bible. But how many dead bodies will we leave behind? We used to have great difficulty with the following Scripture passage:

*"Two men will be out in the field; one will be taken, and one will be left. Two women will be grinding at the mill; one will be taken, and one will be left."*[16]

Penny could not understand how our loving Jesus could take one and leave the other. That was not like the Merciful Savior we have known. And then the Lord spoke to our hearts. *"You're right, I would not take one and leave one. The ones who will stay behind are the ones who do not know Me, and so they will not come."*

Brothers and sisters, If Jesus were coming today to bring us to the Kingdom, who do you know who would not

---

[16]Mt 24:40-41

be coming with us? We know we're going; we might have a stop off at Purgatory, but we know we're going eventually to Heaven. Think about it. Who do you know, *husband, wife, mother, father, brother, sister, cousin, aunt, uncle, daughter, son, friend or neighbor*? As we mentioned these categories, someone came into your mind's eye. There is someone you know who would not be coming with us. And whose fault would it be? That person who came into your mind is the first person you should try to bring back to the Lord.

My brothers and sisters, if this book serves to make you or a loved one, look at life and *become aware* of what's going on around us, then we have done God's Will, as we understand it. We must counteract what Satan has been industriously going about trying to accomplish - his two greatest goals for the end time, and they are:

First, he wants people to believe there is no Satan, and there is no sin, that people's actions are just "*different strokes for different folks*," and that it's okay for you to do the things you always thought were evil; because there is no such thing as right or wrong, sin or remorse; everything goes!

Secondly, he wants you to believe that you have all the time in the world to convert and return to the Lord.

You know that we love you. More than anything else, we want to be together in the Kingdom. We don't want to put fear into your hearts, unless it's fear (awe) of the Lord. We want you to love the Lord so much, your desire is to be in the Kingdom with Him, more than anything else in your life. We don't want any of us to wish our way into hell. Remember, the gates of hell are locked from the inside; but once inside no one asks to leave. Jesus was born and died that we might be with Him in Heaven. We want you to be in that great number in Heaven, when the Saints come marching in. *But more importantly Jesus wants you with Him in Heaven. Praise God!*

# God cries out through the Prophets

*"...it was not enough for them to err in their knowledge of God, but even though they live in a great war of ignorance, they call such evils peace!*

*"For while they celebrate either child-slaying sacrifices* (abortion) *or clandestine mysteries, or frenzied carousals in unheard-of rites,*

*"They no longer safeguard either lives or pure wedlock; but each either waylays and kills his neighbor, or aggrieves him by adultery.*

*"And all is confusion - blood and murder, theft and guile, corruption, faithlessness, turmoil and perjury,*

*"Disturbance of good men, neglect of gratitude, forgetfulness of God, defiling of souls, unnatural lust, disorder in marriage, adultery and shamelessness.*

*"For the worship of infamous idols is the reason and source and extremity of all evil.*

*"For they either go mad with enjoyment, or prophesy lies, or live lawlessly or lightly forswear themselves.*

*"For as their trust is in soulless idols, they expect no harm when they have sworn falsely."*[1]

Why did the Lord lead us to this prophecy from wise King Solomon, written about a hundred years before the birth of Our Lord Jesus? What was the Lord trying to warn us about in these, the last days of the Second Millennium?

At a time when our entire moral structure is under collapse, and we seem to be flying to our destruction as a people of God, as a country, and as a world, we look to God for warnings, for advice on how to avoid the cataclysmic course looming ahead of us. Turning to the Old Testament, we find a faithful God patiently waiting for His unfaithful children to convert and live fully the life He had planned for them. But our brothers of long ago chose false idols and

---

[1]Wis 14:22-29

pagan religions, along with momentary carnal pleasures which did not satisfy. Now, in our time, do we not choose false idols and pagan religions, only often because of *economy*, how it lines our pockets, how it fills our stomachs? The parallels of these the last days of the horrific Twentieth Century and those of the past are frightening! The Lord is speaking to us clearly, not in veiled words, all we need do is open our hearts and minds to Him, that we understand.

We read in the book of Baruch:[2]

*"Justice is with the Lord, our God; and we today are flushed with shame, we men of Judah and citizens of Jerusalem, that we with our kings and rulers, and priests and prophets, with our fathers, have sinned in the Lord's sight and disobeyed Him. We have neither heeded the Voice of the Lord, our God, nor followed the precepts which the Lord set before us. From the time the Lord led our fathers out of the land of Egypt until the present day, we have been disobedient to the Lord, our God, and only too ready to disregard His Voice. And the evils and the curse which the Lord enjoined upon Moses, His servant, at the time he led our fathers forth from the land of Egypt to give us a land flowing with milk and honey, cling to us even today. For we did not heed the Voice of the Lord, in all the words of the prophets He sent us, but each one of us went off after the devices of our own wicked hearts, served **other gods**, and did evil in the sight of the God."*

We do not need to have a doctorate in theology or in history, for that matter, to know that the Word is alive and has no time limitation, not solely for one period, one place, one people. Is this reading from the Old Testament not for us? My father was a student of history, preferring Ancient to Modern History, insisting if you know Ancient History you will not only know Modern History but can prophesy the

---

[2]Bar 1:15-22

History of ages to come.  His face would grow serious, as he shared, "*Sadly History repeats itself, with man paying the price, over and over again, often with his body and soul, to satisfy the hunger instilled in him by Satan for things of this world - the innocent manipulated by offers of fame and fortune.*"

The Word of God tells us that because the Jews, who had been released from captivity, "*did not heed the Voice of the Lord, in all the words of the prophets He sent them, but each one of them went off after the devices of their own wicked hearts, served **other gods**, and did evil in the sight of the God,*" because they were disobedient to God, and refused to listen to His Voice, they suffered one disaster after the other, *and were made to wander aimlessly in the desert for forty years, searching for the Promised Land.*  Are we doing less or more, and what will be God's answer to us?

Throughout the Old Testament, we hear of man trading in the one True God for false gods, forsaking all God has given them and all He has planned for them, worshiping pagan idols, relying on diabolical powers to fulfill empty desires with false promises.  All we have to do is study the History of the past to realize that the enemy of God is a liar and never keeps his promises; he betrays the happiness he guarantees, even while we are still alive; for the joy he provides is temporary, at best, using creations such as diamonds which will distract us for a time by their glitter and then pale in the light of the Creator, and either lose their value to us or be taken away from us.

When you read in the preceding passage from the prophet Baruch, "*we with our kings and rulers, and priests and prophets, with our fathers, have sinned in the Lord's sight and disobeyed Him,*" we have no need to wonder who the "*we*" is; **the we is us!**  *But,* if *we* just ask the Lord to remove the scales from our eyes, which are blinding so many to the wages of sin, we can see the Word is referring to not only the *kings and rulers, prophets and priests* of that time, but of our time, and time *in memoriam.* Do we not know leaders of nations, statesmen, and sadly even priests and ministers, who have gone against all they vowed to uphold and, snapping at the tempter's bait of fame, recognition, wealth and power, have forsaken their God?

[I will never forget when we were students, and had little money, Bob took his income tax refund and treated me to a dinner in a fine chinese restaurant. As we were eating, we only had eyes for each other; but we could not help noticing an older couple (probably all of 30 years old) across from us. She was wearing an engagement ring whose diamond blinded us a good twelve feet away; we had never seen anything quite like it. Suddenly we noticed something which took the glitter out of the diamond; they were not looking at each other; he was looking in one direction and she in the other. I still remember us praying, *Lord do not allow us to have so much wealth that we stop looking at each other.* Little did we know the wealth that the Lord had in store for us; and it was not diamonds mined out of the mountains but Himself and His Church.]

**God always sends us prophets**

*Who are the Prophets and why did God send them?*

Benedict XIV wrote:

*"The recipients of prophecy may be Angels, devils, men, children, heathens or gentiles; Nor is it necessary that a man should be gifted with any particular disposition, in order to receive the light of prophecy, provided his intellect and senses be adapted for making manifest the things which God reveals to him. Though moral goodness is most profitable to a prophet, yet it is not necessary in order to obtain the gift of prophecy."*

A prophet is one who speaks for God under Divine guidance or inspiration. The prophet has been called by God to serve Him, and by and large does, even though he may be reluctant, as in the case of Jonah and Jeremiah. In the Biblical sense, a prophet is one who hears the Word of God and brings God's Word to men. He is an inspired speaker. Prophecies come in the form of visions, inner locutions, ecstasies and mystical experiences.

Prophets have been given to us down through Salvation History, much as Angels have, to help us through the Pilgrimage of life, to keep us on the straight path back to the Kingdom of God, from whence we came. They are messengers of God, like the Angels, only prophets have always maintained human form.

In the Old Testament, we find prophecies relating to the Jewish people and their walk toward and away from the Lord, and signs pointing to the coming of the Messiah. But as Jesus warned, there are those with eyes but do not see and with ears but do not hear. When prophets and prophecies did not fill their immediate needs and aspirations, they killed the prophets and ignored the signs. The Messiah came, but the Israelites did not recognize Him and so they wait still for Him to come.

For the purposes of this chapter, we want to delve into revelations in the Old Testament in which we can see apocalyptic forewarnings of events which will precede the final days. As we research these prophecies, we can't help but realize they are becoming more and more evident, as well as coming closer and closer to pass. Mother Nature is venting her anger against man's outrageous disregard of God's and her laws. Never before in the history of mankind has the world experienced physical upheavals and natural disasters of such cataclysmic magnitude as those striking the world, today. And what is man's answer - turn to man for solutions! Turn to man who is the cause of this crushing holocaust? A philosopher once said, "*God always forgives; man sometimes forgives; nature never forgives.*"

†††

We begin with the Old Testament prophets speaking about the endtimes, the latter days, which we translate to mean *these times,* the end of the Second Millennium.

The prophet Isaiah was given extraordinary glimpses into the future. He spent almost his entire book warning us of things to come, and for these last 2000 some-odd years, these prophecies have been staring us in the face, and still we don't listen to them. Keep in mind as you read Isaiah's prophecies of the last days, that he lived in the Eighth Century *Before Christ.*

*"Behold the Lord shall lay waste the earth, and shall strip it, and shall afflict the face thereof and scatter abroad the inhabitants thereof.*

*"And it shall be as with the people, so with the priest, and as with the servant, so with his master; as with the handmaid, so with her mistress; as with the buyer, so with the seller; as with the lender, so with the borrower; as with him that calls for his money, so with him that owes it.*

*"With desolation shall the earth be laid waste, and it shall be utterly spoiled; for the Lord has spoken this word. The earth mourned and faded away, and is weakened; the world faded away, the height of the people of the earth is weakened.*

*"...therefore a curse shall devour the earth and the inhabitants thereof shall sin; and therefore they that dwell therein shall be mad, and few men shall be left.*

*"...There shall be a crying for wine in the streets: all mirth is forsaken; the joy of the earth has gone away. Desolation is left in the city and calamity shall oppress the gates."³*

†††

*"Howl, for the day of the Lord is near, as destruction from the Almighty comes. Therefore all hands fall*

---

³Is 24:1-12

*helpless, the bows of the young men fall from their hands. Every man's heart melts in terror. Pangs and sorrows take hold of them, like a woman in labor they writhe. They look aghast at each other, their faces aflame.*

*"Lo, the day of the Lord comes, cruel, with wrath and burning anger; to lay waste the land and destroy the sinners within it! The stars and constellations of the heavens send forth no light; the sun is dark when it rises and the light of the moon does not shine.*

*"Thus I will punish the world for its evil and the wicked for their guilt. I will put an end to the pride of the arrogant, the insolence of tyrants I will humble. I will make mortals more rare than pure gold, men, than gold of Ophir.*[4] *For this I will make the heavens tremble and the earth shall be shaken from its place. At the wrath of the Lord of Hosts on the day of His burning anger."*[5]

✝✝✝

*"Now, come, write it on a tablet they can keep, inscribe it in a record; that it may be in* **future days** *an eternal witness: this is a rebellious people, deceitful children, children who refuse to obey the law of God. They say to the seers, 'Have no visions:' to the prophets, 'Do not descry* (discern) *for us what is right; speak flatteries to us, conjure up illusions. Out of the way! Out of our path! Let us hear no more of the Holy One of Israel.' Therefore thus says the Holy One of Israel: Because you reject this Word, and put trust in what is crooked and devious, and depend on it, This guilt of yours shall be like a descending rift bulging out in a high wall, whose crash comes suddenly, in an instant."*[6]

✝✝✝

---

[4]Ophir's gold: Rare and only worn by princesses as in Psalm 45:10
[5]Is 13:6-13
[6]Is 30:8-13

We go to the Four Gospels, where we hear Jesus relating to the Last Days.

In Matthew 23:37, we hear Jesus crying out, not only to the people of His time, but of all time:

*"Jerusalem, Jerusalem! you who kill the prophets, and stone those who are sent to you! How often would I have gathered your children together, as a hen gathers her young under her wings, but you would not! Behold, your house is left to you desolate. For I say to you, you shall not see me henceforth until you shall say, 'Blessed is He Who comes in the Name of the Lord.'"*

Jesus stands by the door to our hearts and knocks! As He preordained that the doorknob be only on our side, He patiently waits for us to let Him in, as He said - to allow Him to gather us and our children in His loving Arms, under the shelter of the wings of His Love. And whom do we choose? The false god of things, material things which will perish at best with time and more often through boredom and lack of satisfaction. For, as St. Augustine said, *Our hearts are restless until they rest in Him.*

The disciples showed Jesus the Temple and He foretold its destruction: *"Do you see all these things? Amen I say to you, there will not be left here one stone upon another that will not be thrown down."*[7] And in the year 70 A.D., the temple was destroyed, with not one stone left upon another.

Jesus is sitting with His disciples on the Mount of Olives, when they turn to Him and ask when will the end of the world come to pass and what will be the signs. Jesus warns them to not be led astray by those claiming to be Him. He cautions them to beware of those who say that they are the Christ, for they will surely lead many away from Him and to hell.[8]

---

[7] Lk 19:41

[8] read about a New Age guru who claims to be the Messiah- *Lord Maitreya* in chapter: *Apostasy and the Antichrist.*

Each day, we see more and more signs pointing to the Lord's *Second Coming* and hear more and more modern day prophecies. But when we do, as Jesus before us, we cry out to those warning us - revealing the circumstances, the time and the place of the Last Judgment, and those taking them seriously, that no one knows but the Father and His Son. Jesus reassures them and us, that although we hear of "*wars and rumors*" we are not to be afraid, that this has to come to pass before the Son of Man is to return; but it is not an indication that it is the end of the world.

Jesus prophesies, that there will be nation against nation and kingdom against kingdom. When I have heard this Scripture, I have wondered, *Lord which kingdom do You speak of today?* Was Jesus speaking of the kingdom of man fighting the Kingdom of God? Was he warning us against those who tickle our ears and give us all we think we want, rather than that which we need?

As parents we would never think of allowing our children to eat only ice cream, cake and candy, but is this not what we are doing today, asking for the sweets which the enemy of God holds out to us, irresponsibly insisting *I want what I want and I want it now*, regardless of the consequences? And as too much sweets leads to an upset stomach, too much self-love leads to an upset soul.

Today, we see people going from conference to conference, from book to book, trying to ascertain the time and place of the end of the world, listening to anyone who comes up with an alleged message from God, the more sensational the better. In trying to remain faithful to the Lord and the mission He gave us, we have stuck strictly to the Word of God and that which He generously sent to us through His Mother and the Saints. You want to know about the present times, how you should prepare for His Second Coming, read the Bible; it's no secret; it's all there.

Jesus warned us to be prepared - He spoke of the ten virgins and the oil lamps;[9] He spoke of two men in bed and said one would be taken, one left behind, two women grinding together, one would be taken and the other left behind, two men in the field and how one would be taken and the other left behind.[10] When the Lord comes, will we be running to the Mall to buy just one more thing? When He comes, will we reject Him and refuse to follow Him like His chosen people, the Jews, did the first time He walked the earth? Will He say, *Is My Way too hard for you to bear?*

Do we believe in Jesus? Do we ask ourselves, *What would Jesus do, what would Jesus say?* Do we believe that we are united with Jesus every time we receive Him, His Body, Blood, Soul and Divinity in the Holy Eucharist? And if our answer is Yes! then how accountable we are for every unkind word we say to one another, for every scandal we spread, for every sin of calumny we commit against our brother and sister! If we believe in our precious Lord, then we know that when we gossip, when we spread scandal, we are breaking the Fifth Commandment, *Thou shall not kill.* When the Lord comes, will He ask us how many times we gossiped about Him, we bore false witness against Him by spreading rumors false (or otherwise) about Him, acted against Him, judged Him? And when we ask, *When did we do these things against You, dear Lord?* will He walk us through our lives and show us how every time we did this to the least of His children, we did it to Him? Instead of the person we offended, will we see instead Our Lord?

Are we like the pharisee, who was in the Temple, busily telling God how great he was because he fasted and tithed beyond the required, prescribed amount? Or are we the taxpayer who sat in the back of the Temple, feeling unworthy

---

[9]*cf* Mt 25:1-13
[10]*cf* Lk 17:34

to be in the House of God, but wanting so much to be reconciled with Him?  Do we need to go to confession?

I can still remember one time, on a Saturday afternoon when a man did a terribly unkind thing to one of my dogs, frightening him, and I lost my temper!  When I cooled down, I ran to church to ask the pastor to hear my confession.  I began with, *I was feeling so good.*  The associate pastor who was hearing my confession, said, *Oh no!  You were feeling pretty good, were you?  Well that's just when the door is wide open for the enemy to walk in.*

And then there was another time, when I ran to confession because I felt so unworthy to receive Our Lord, and my confessor's response was, with tears in his eyes, *How close you are standing to Jesus on the Cross.*  When he saw that I did not understand, he explained, *How can anyone stand before the Lord on the Cross, Our Lord Who gave up His Life for sinners, and feel he was anything but a sorrowful sinner in His Presence?*

Do we believe Jesus is truly present in the Eucharist?  If we do, how can we receive Him without going to confession at least once a month?  For if I say that I am not a sinner, am I not calling Jesus a liar?  When He comes, like a thief in the night,[11] will I be ready to go with my Lord?

✝✝✝

Paul spoke of the gifts of the Holy Spirit, one of which was Prophecy.  Down through the 2000 year history of our beloved Church, we have had Saints and Mystics who have had the gift of Prophecy!  But although they have been proclaimed Saints, which proved their sanctity, we are not obliged to believe in the authenticity of all their revelations.  For even the Mystics questioned, *Was it the Lord, was it the devil or was it a manifestation of their minds?*

---

[11]*cf* 1Thes 5:2

When the Cause for Beatification is opened, all the writings of the candidate are carefully investigated to ascertain the holiness of the Servant of God and to determine there are no serious errors, contrary to the teachings of the Church. But this is in no way, a proclamation declaring the prophecies authentic; nor are the faithful obliged in any way to accept all the prophecies as Gospel truth. Not all private revelations have come to pass, and there are instances where even the Saints made mistakes, and in other instances where one Saint's prophecy contradicted another Saint's. Jesus plainly said that only the Father knows the time and the place.

St. Paul as well as others, thought the Lord was coming for the Second Time in their day. Then St. Vincent Ferrer who lived in the late Fourteenth Century and early Fifteenth Century predicted Christ would come in *his* time. When we wrote *Scandal of the Cross and Its Triumph* and went through all the attacks on the Church and how she narrowly survived, I can see how the faithful, like those of these mad days, thought the end of the world was at hand.

One thing is consistent, no matter how dire the prophecy, true Prophets spoke of hope, if man turns away from his sinful ways and returns to God. The title of this chapter is God cries out through the Prophets. Are we listening, or when Jesus comes will He say, - *I sent you My prophets, but you chose to follow those false prophets who tickled your ears?*

Left:
***God the Father***
***Ceiling of Sistine Chapel***
***painted by***
***Michelangelo***
***God the Father gave us***
***the promise of a Messiah,***
***a Redeemer, who would***
***be Christ the Lord.***

Right:
***Part of the Creation***
***scene showing the***
***expulsion of Adam and***
***Eve from Paradise***
***painted on the ceiling of***
***the Sistine Chapel by***
***Michelangelo***
***Then the Lord God said***
***to the serpent: "Because***
***you have done this, you***
***shall be banned from all***
***the animals and from all***
***the wild creatures and***
***dirt shall you eat all the***
***days of your life. I will***
***put enmity between you***
***and the woman and***
***between your offspring***
***and hers. He will strike***
***at your head while you***
***strike at His heal."***
Gen 3: 14-15

# First God the Father
# and then the earthly father

You may be wondering what God the Father has to do with *Prophecies and Promises of the Final Days.*  Sometimes we get so intrigued about the newest and latest prophets and their prophecies and promises, we forget the first, the greatest promise made to us, by God the Father.

*"Then the Lord God said to the serpent:*
*'Because you have done this, you shall be banned*
  *from all the animals and from all the wild creatures;*
*On your belly shall you crawl*
  *and dirt shall you eat all the days of your life.*
*I will put enmity between you and the woman*
  *and between your offspring and hers;*
*He will strike at your head while you strike at His heel."*[1]

With that prophecy, God the Father gave Lucifer his future role, and gave us the promise of a Messiah, a Redeemer, who would be Christ the Lord.  He also prophesied that the Savior would come from the woman, our Mother Mary.

God the Father, the ultimate Prophet, gave us another powerful prophecy--through His promise to Noah.

*"See, I am now establishing My covenant with you and your descendants after you, and with every living creature that was with you; all the birds, and the various tame and wild animals that were with you and came out of the ark.*

*"I will establish My covenant with you that never again shall all bodily creatures be destroyed by the waters of a flood; there shall not be another flood to devastate the earth.*

*"God added, 'This is the sign that I am giving for all ages to come, of the covenant between Me and you and every living creature with you.*

---

[1]Gn 3:14-15

*"'I set My bow in the clouds to serve as a sign of the
covenant between Me and the earth. When I bring clouds
over the earth, and the bow appears in the clouds, I will
recall the covenant I have made between you and Me and
all living things, so that the waters shall never again
become a flood to destroy all mortals beings. As the bow
appears in the clouds, I will see it and recall the everlasting
covenant that I have established between God and all
living beings - all mortal creatures that are on earth.* "[2]

††† 

Those who do not love God the Father, have never
studied the Word and the traditions of the Church. There
you will find a treasury of love that the Father has always
had for his children.

**The Word of God attests to God as a Father.**

In the Old Testament, we read: *"Have we not all one
Father? Has not One God created us? Why then are we
faithless to one another, profaning the covenant of our
fathers?"*[3] It was this covenant which bound Israel together
as a family, with God as the Head and *Father*, God Who had
delivered them from slavery and bondage of Egypt. Do you
recall how they reacted when they had to sacrifice a little,
how they soon forgot the miraculous parting of the Red Sea?
Yes, no different from our civilization today, they began to
worship the golden calf!

Now, as God is a Father, a tender loving Father, Who is
always a personal and unconditionally faithful Father, He
did not take back His promise to send them a Messiah. But
also, as a loving Father, He punished them for their own
good, that they might learn and convert their unfaithful
hearts to Him. When His children rebelled, choosing to
compromise the Love He had for them, just as any good

---

[2]Gn 9:9-16
[3]Mal 2:10

father on earth, he did not take away the Promise and Hope of a Promised Land, He merely had them wander aimlessly, going in circles for forty years in the desert, their dream a heart beat away.

We go to the New Testament, and we hear Jesus calling His Father, *Abba* or *Daddy*, a very personal, intimate name for a very loving and endearing Father, a name a little boy would use instead of the grownup term--Father.  God the Father was Jesus' *Daddy*, His *Abba*, the Daddy Who sent Him, the One He would obey, right to death on the Cross. Jesus knew the Father and trusted the Father.  He put His Life in the Father's Hands.

Both in the Old and New Testaments, God is seen as a Father Who has made a covenant with His people -- a contract He promises never to break.  This bond between God and His children is more powerful than that of an earthly father, in that He always remains faithful, the door of His Heart open to receive His prodigal sons and daughters, always forgiving, always prepared to give us one more chance.  As I write about our *Father Who art in Heaven*, my eyes fill with tears!  How can anyone hurt Him!  It must be they no longer have the Grace to know Him.

Even more far-reaching than the part God plays in the Old Testament is His relationship with Jesus His only begotten Son.  Throughout the New Testament we hear Jesus speaking of the Father; we learn of that *eternal* Father and Son relationship God the Father has had with Jesus the Son, from before the beginning of the world.  As we believe in the Holy Trinity, Who is, was and always will be, so we believe that God the Father, and His Son Jesus, in company with the Holy Spirit were all there, when God lovingly formed the earth and placed all the creatures we so enjoy on the earth.  God, our Father as Creator brought Adam and Eve into the world.  How eternally loving is the Father!  As our first parents, the first to fall for the enemy's lies, were betraying Him, selling Him out, the Father, always with that open door, was planning the salvation of their children, those who would come after.

I believe, as you read on, you will see that the attack is not simply on God, our Heavenly Father, but as well, on our *earthly fathers*; the aim--the dissolution of the family of God-- the Church and the human family. Just as God is the Head of the Universe, and through Jesus--the Pope is the Head of His Church on earth, so the human father must be the head of the human family.

### God the Father will allow us to go to hell

God gave us Free Will. He loves us so, He will not take our Free Will away from us. Jesus said we are no longer slaves but His friends and, as friends and brothers, He desires we love His Father *freely*. In order for us to remain as God has created us, to love Him with all our hearts and souls, we must have Free Will. God has come to us, through Holy Scripture and the Traditions of the Church, and taught us how it will be for those who desire Him and *eternal life* with Him in Heaven. It is up to us; we can choose God and His Kingdom-Heaven or the devil and his kingdom-hell. God *will not* force us and the devil *cannot* force us!

We fall and God picks us up; generous Father, He forgives us and gives us chance after chance. But as His Son said, no one knows the time and the place and we are to be prepared, or like the master who left his house unprotected and a thief broke into his house,[4] the Son of Man will come and claim us, at an hour we least expect,[5] with no more time to repent. Jesus also taught us the Father's ways, with his parable of the virgins who were prepared and allowed to enter the banquet and those who were denied entry because they had not made provision for the Bridegroom's coming,

---

[4]Lk 12:39
[5]Lk 12:40

with Jesus saying "*I do not know you.*"  Again, He forewarns us, as He did those virgins, "*Therefore, stay awake, for you know neither the day nor the hour.*"[6]

When Jesus became Man, His goal was to reconcile the children of God with their Heavenly Father.  As the final Sacrifice, all that was required of Him was to carry the Cross, heavily ladened with our sins, up to Calvary and ransom us with His death, death on that same Cross.  He thereby had only to die for the sins of the world, that through this, His Sacrifice, we might know the salvific love of God.  But for the three short years He had left on earth, He tirelessly taught the people about the Father, that they might know the gift that was awaiting those who adored Him (the Father).  But as they did to the landowner's son, so they killed God the Father's Son.[7]

Now, in these dire days, once again, God the Father is talking to His children.  As He did in the Old Testament, He is sending us *Prophets* to warn us; as in the New Testament, the Father is sending us modern day *John the Baptists* heralding the coming of the Lord: Pope John Paul II, Mother Teresa, Mother Angelica and other evangelists spreading God's Word.  Their message is no different than that of John the Baptist, *Repent and be saved!*  You read in our chapter on Mary, *If only my children will convert.*  What are we doing?  Are we fearlessly passing on the Father's message to His children?  We do not have much time, I fear; God will not allow this depravity and wholesale murder to go on.  This is the hour of the prince of darkness.[8]

**Why is God the Father so under attack?**

God the Father made many promises to them and to us. We believe one of the most important was when He told the

---

[6]Mt 25:1-13
[7]Mt 22:33
[8]Lk 22:53

Israelites "*You will be My People and I will be your God. You will know that I am your God when I deliver you from the hands of your enemies.*"[9]

When the Old Testament begins in the first chapter of the book of Genesis, we immediately see the Father as Creator of the heavens and the earth. However, in the last book of Malachi, we hear God chastising His children, warning of His wrath:

"*I have loved you, says the Lord;*
*but you say, 'How have You loved us?'*

*Was not Esau Jacob's brother? says the Lord:*
*yet I loved Jacob, but hated Esau;*

*I made his mountains a waste,*
*his heritage a desert for jackals.*

*If Edom says, 'We have been crushed*
*but we will rebuild the ruins,'*

*Thus says the Lord of hosts:*
*They may indeed build, but I will tear down,*

*And they shall be called the land of the guilt,*
*the people with whom the Lord is angry forever.*

*Your own eyes shall see it, and you will say,*
*'Great is the Lord, even beyond the land of Israel.'*

*A son honors his father,*
*and a servant fears his master;*

*If then I am your Father,*
*where is the honor due to Me?*

*And if I am the Master, where is the reverence due to Me?*

*So says the Lord of hosts to you, O priests who despise His Name.*

*But you ask, 'How have we despised Your Name?'*
*By offering polluted food on my altar!*[10]

---

[9]cfEx 6:7

[10]Could that be interpreted as a parallel for today, the use of *illicit leavened* bread being used instead of *unleavened* bread, as was used by Jesus in the Last Supper?

*By saying the table of the Lord may be slighted!"[11]*

*"So now if you implore God for mercy on us,*
*when you have done the like*
*Will He welcome any of you?*
*says the Lord of hosts."[12]*

*"...this commandment is for you:*
*If you do not listen,*
*And if you do not lay it to heart,*
*to give glory to My Name, says the Lord of hosts,*
*I will send a curse upon you*
*and of your blessing I will make a curse."[13]*

*"...you have turned aside from the way,*
*and have caused many to falter by your instruction;*
*You have made void the covenant of Levi[14]*
*says the Lord of hosts.*
*I, therefore, have made you contemptible*
*and base before all the people."*

*"Have we not one Father?*
*Has not One God created us?*
*Why then break faith with each other,*
*violating the covenant of our fathers?"[15]*

**Why have women turned against**
**not only their Heavenly Father, but their earthly fathers?**

Is this not prophetic of the last days?  Rather than progressing, as they insist, becoming a brave new world, are we not being pushed back into the days of the Amazons?

---

[11]Mal 1:2-7 [could this be referring to the Altar being placed in the midst of the congregation, resulting in the people becoming the focus, rather than the Eucharist?]
[12]Mal 1:9
[13]Mal 2:1,2
[14]*one of life and peace*
[15]Mal 2:8-10

Do we not hear feminists insisting: "*We do not need men; we will harvest their sperm and have children without them.*" As a woman, I need to ask these sisters, "*Why the anger! What is going on and how did it start?*"

We have to stop here and give you a little history lesson. The feminist movement had failed; women were tired of opening their own doors, driving trucks and being knocked down on football fields; cigars did not agree with them; and in spite of all this freedom from the yoke of their fathers, and the fathers of their children, they were not happy.

They began missing meetings of feminist front organizations, which were in reality lesbians trying to push an agenda. Attendance and support dropped drastically. The feminist movement was sounding out its death knell. These angry women had to do something to find a way to discredit God the Father. They came up with a brilliant, and also despicable plan--go after the largest organized group of women in the world--destroy those most beloved of Him, His Brides, the women religious! And put the blame squarely on the shoulders of the male-oriented, chauvinistic Church, and its leader, God the Father.

Knowing our Sisters have been our teachers for time *in memoriam*, and that we are prone to believe anything and everything they say, just as we did in school, these feminists not only got them to spread their anarchist, anti-male ideas, these women religious who had taken the vows of obedience, began disobeying the teachings of the Church and passing on *their teachings* (the teachings of the feminist movement) by filling key positions in schools, universities, chanceries and etc. Their artillery in place, they first infected and affected the hierarchy, and then much of the laity.

This only brought about confusion, with the laity not knowing what and who to believe. Being trained by some of the world's shrewdest propagandists, they employed the tactic *"the best defense is a strong offense;"* they attacked quickly and put down decisively any hint of opposition!

Dissidents, broadcasting seeds of disharmony cried out indignantly, accusing those who did not go along with their diversionary tactics of creating *"disunity and division!"* This was merely a weapon to bring the laity, who defended the Magisterium, under compliance and ultimately submission. And as a final death blow to opposition, they removed anyone not with them and placed those who were, in important positions in the churches.

Then these dissenters built a modern Tower of Babel, a blockade in which no *outsider* understood anyone or anything anyone on the *inside* was saying; a unique club of psychobabble took form and confusion was the key word. As in the case of the Emperor's clothes, many women *and men*, refusing to look ignorant, began dancing to the dirge they were playing, but hadn't an idea of what they were doing. Expressions like *Wicca Witch, Starhawk,* and ceremonial rituals like *Spiral dances* infiltrated the women's religious orders. Tree hugging and dancing around trees were prevalent practices. As they gathered strength, they built up false courage. In an effort to try to appease a series of complaints which were orchestrated by the gurus of the feminist movement, the official Church gave in to so many demands that pretty soon, Mother Church was considered weak, and Father God was being replaced by Creator God.

As there was no foundation for their wild theories and diversionary tactics, and their design to delude the women of the world began to crumble, they came up with the mythical invention that God is a woman! Now, since they were unsuccessful in their attempt to twist the Word of God, they did battle on another front: sneak through changes in Holy Scripture, on the pretext that they wanted to eliminate the overpowering male element in the wording of the Mass. This would serve their agenda; for if you *leave out* one word or *change* one word, you will change the entire meaning. Wasn't that what it was all about?

Thank God, for our strong Pope who has done battle against great opposition from within, and they have not been able to cry *Victory!* as yet. I do not believe this is the work of these once holy Brides of Christ; I believe the enemy of God has a plan to destroy the Church and the world, through this willful strategy to create dissension and ultimately - division. Our Lord said, "*If a house is divided against itself, that house will not be able to stand.*"[16]

**God always balances the scales.**

God always raises Powerful Men and Women to defend the Church. At this most crucial time in our Church, He gave us one of the most powerful men the Church has ever known, our Pope John Paul II. To counteract all the infidelity prevalent in the world and the Church, He raised up two powerful women--Mother Teresa and Mother Angelica, women who would be that sign in the world of obedience and faithfulness! Mother Teresa has gone to her reward; plans are being made for the Pope to forsake the waiting period and open up the Cause for her Canonization, making it possible to declare her a Saint in his lifetime. She said, "*We do not need to be successful, we need only to be faithful.*"

Like her powerful sisters of the past, Mother Angelica is a strong woman, who dares to be unpopular (although not to her millions of viewers). Like Joan of Arc, she is a soldier blazing a trail of Truth, the *Eternal Word* according to the Magisterium. Unafraid, courageous, undaunted by the slings and arrows of the enemy, we see and hear Mother Angelica defending the Church, never counting the cost. A strong woman, she has no need for God to be a woman; she has no

---

[16]Mk 3:25

need to be anything but a faithful Bride of Christ and daughter of the Church.

## You shall honor your father and mother

Having problems with going after God the Father? Go after earthly fathers (and mothers). But how, how can you get someone to go against their own parents? Use Psychology; it doesn't matter if it's renegade psychology, which has not been approved by the American Psychiatric Society; if it's novel, innovative, sensational, it will fly! It's amazing how attractive sin and scandal are to the human species, how ready we are to accept the worst. Names of phobias were either made up, or resurrected from dead theories, long ago discarded by their own inventors.[17] Many without approval or accreditation began spouting any psychological sludge they could dredge up from the swamps of a mix-upped society from the past.

Young people, vulnerable because they had problems, were fair game for a new attack by Satan to destroy the family. Those who survived the scourge of illegal drug-taking, were being prescribed equally dangerous *legal*, hallucinogenic drugs. So-called therapists, many of whom had no credentials in Psychology, used hypnosis as well as dangerous, unorthodox brainwashing techniques to feed ideas into young people from varied backgrounds, inducing them to alienate themselves from their families--the therapists becoming the new family, the patient completely under their control (very like the modus-operandi of dangerous cults). Youngsters, particularly from sound religious upbringing, began accusing their parents of horrible, bizarre behavior, of belonging to satanic cults, of engaging in satanic cult rituals; no one was excused; the older the parents the easier the target; the wealthier the

---

[17]Freud for one

more appetizing; insurance companies were fleeced for millions. It was truly a Twentieth Century *Salem witch hunt.*

Movies, television, and books whetting the appetites of those seeking the sensational, were written and began making best-seller lists; the hate program was on, and the living out of Jesus prophecy began: "*a father will be divided against his son (only now daughter as well), a mother against her daughter (those mothers who did not go along with the lunacy became estranged from their daughters), and a daughter against her mother...*"[18] And God the Father wept once again for His children of this new Sodom and Gomorrah.

Some parents became so distraught, they took their own lives; others aged prematurely--their hearts broken--they would never reach their children; families split apart; it looked as if this nightmare would overtake the land like a pestilence, never to end and then....thank You, dear Jesus, not all the parents were damaged beyond repair; some fought back, a foundation was formed, of respected psychologists[19] to fight this scourge on the human family; many victims were helped to return to family and friends; some of the victims, parents and children, brought suits against many of those perpetrating this abomination on the family and won judgments against them in court. Criminal charges were filed for insurance fraud; convictions began coming out of the courts. But how many dead bodies were strewn over the earth?

**"Whoever has seen Me, has seen the Father..."**

When they asked Jesus to see the Father, Jesus said, "*Whoever has seen Me, has seen the Father...*" Then Jesus prophesied: "*...whoever believes in Me, will do the works I do, and will do greater ones than these, because I am going to the*

---

[18]Lk 12:53
[19]False Memory Syndrome Foundation
3401 Market St., Philadelphia, PA 19104-3315

*Father. And whatever you ask in My Name, I will do, so that the Father may be glorified in My Name.*"[20] Jesus did not say, so *He* could be glorified, but that the *Father* may be glorified. Jesus speaks of the *Father* being glorified! Those who would diminish and belittle the Father's role in our lives, those who portray Him as an ogre Who abuses women, who condemn and malign Him, whom do they glorify? Listen to them; you will hear them pointing to themselves, to *their* word, *their* findings, *their* truths! Do they not glorify themselves? Is this not another indication or prophecy of the Last Days, or the end of our civilization--as in the days of the Roman Empire where self-glorification ran rampant, and along with it degradation of every kind?

Like Mother Mary, who always points to her Son, Jesus always deferred to God His Father: "*Jesus answered and said to them, 'Amen, amen, I say to you, a Son cannot do anything on His own; but only what He sees His* **Father** *doing.*"[21]

Then again giving all credit to the Father, Jesus tells the Jews, "*It was not Moses who gave you the bread from Heaven; My Father gives you the True Bread from Heaven.*"[22]

At the end of His life, as He was struggling with His last breath, He cried out -- not to mortal man, but to His Father in Heaven. "*...about three o'clock, Jesus cried out, 'My God, My God, why have you forsaken Me?'*"[23]

Jesus knew that mortal man would betray Him, and although He knew He was being asked by the **Father**, to do sacrifice for the sins of the world, to die for those who were rejecting Him, taunting Him, crucifying Him, he knew that only His Father in Heaven could be trusted with His Spirit: "*Jesus cried out in a loud voice, 'Father into Your Hands, I*

---

[20] Jn 14:12-14
[21] Jn 5:19
[22] Jn 6:32
[23] Mt 27:46

*commend My Spirit' and when He said this He breathed His last.*"[24]

When Jesus was asked when the world would end, He referred them to the Father, and He promised:

"*For this is the will of My* **Father**, *that everyone who sees the Son and believes in Him may have eternal life, and I shall raise him (on) the last day.*"

Jesus tells Nicodemus of God's love for the world and his plan for us: "*God so loved the world that He gave His only Son, so that* **everyone who believes in Him might not perish but might have eternal life.**" And on the other hand, He prophesies*: "but whoever disobeys the Son will not see life, but the wrath of God remains upon him...*"[25]

**First the earthly father; then our Heavenly Father**

A couple of years ago we were at a Catholic Book Conference or at least what we thought was a Catholic Book Conference. We had paid for tickets to two luncheons; so you can imagine our indignation when we discovered that we had little or no choice as to the speakers who would be addressing us during the luncheons. Each day you had the choice of one of two dining rooms in which you could eat. Well, Day 1, both rooms had speakers well-known for their lack of respect for the Pope and the Magisterium. Forget going to a luncheon that day! The next day did not prove much better with one an outright out-spoken dissident and the other a woman. Now, forgive me, we usually do not mention who is writing at any given time in our books; but I must now identify myself, to make sure there are no misunderstandings. I am a woman and I am not proud to admit, because of a few women who have openly attacked our Church, I usually avoid talks or books by women, unless

---

[24]Lk 23:46
[25]Jn 3:36

I know beforehand that I am not going to be offended by them maligning our Pope and/or the Church I love.

As we knew pretty much the sentiments of the male speaker, we opted to try the luncheon with the female speaker. We sat near the door, in the event my darkest fears were to materialize, and we had to leave in the middle of our lunch. She would soon not disappoint us. She began railing against her father, how abusive he had been and how she had feared him and on and on until she discovered who she was and how she was empowered, and a lot of mumbo-jumbo, clicky words I did not understand, nor did I desire to. I was poised; I closed my eyes; I just knew what was coming next. Then she started in on God the Father and that's when we and half the tables got up and left. God the Father! Oh, Father in Heaven, forgive those who out of ignorance malign You. We love You!

**I love God the Father!**

St. Paul writes, *"When I was a child, I used to talk as a child, think as a child, reason as a child; when I became a man, I put aside childish things."*[26] I love God the Father! I must admit that it was not always so. Ignorance only serves to keep people apart; and if your lack of knowledge is of God, you are dangerously apt to turn against the One Who not only created you, but never stops loving you, even when you are speaking out against Him, rejecting Him and committing acts against Him. I am not talking down to anyone because I was one who did not know my Heavenly Father.

At age six, my grandmother died, and along with her my link with the Church. My father had been a victim of the Depression. He, along with other white-collar workers, was among the first to lose his job. Consequently, it became necessary for my mother to go to work sewing pants in a

---

[26]1Cor 13:11

factory.  Nana not only acted as my Mother during the day, she formed me and my love for Jesus and Mary and all the Saints, through the stories she told me about them.  But too soon that would come to an end.  I can still see my beloved *Nana* on her deathbed, her children all around her, turning to my mother and saying the only sadness she felt was that her body would not be cold before my mother would leave her little baby (that was me) and return to work.  My mother remained home for a year; but soon finances required she return to work in the factory; my father was now employed, but his job, although prestigious, did not pay enough for our family to survive.

Both parents having to work, when I came home from school, a lady who lived in our apartment house would baby-sit me, until my parents came home from their jobs.  Now, she was a very kind lady who had three children of her own, with whom I played and at times, fought.  I remember still-- every Wednesday afternoon, she would bring me to Bible School along with her own children; the only problem was it was a *Protestant* Bible School.  Although it was there I learned about the Bible and fell in love with the Word of God, lacking the guidance to truly understand Holy Scripture, especially the Old Testament, I grew to dislike God the Father.  I loved Jesus Who was plainly a God of Mercy Who preached, healed, forgave men their sins, brought the dead back to life; but not His Father Who seemed to always be punishing His children.

Now as I had an earthly father who was more a lover than a disciplinarian, leaving a lot of the scolding to Mama, it was hard to relate to a Heavenly Father Who appeared to be more a judge and executioner than a defense attorney.

But when we came back to Jesus and His Church, and started to study the Bible with the aid and wisdom of the Church who chose the books of the Bible--the Roman Catholic Church, I became aware of a Heavenly Father Who unconditionally, patiently loved His children, warning them, chastising them at times for their own good--His focus their souls more than their bodies which He lovingly created.  It was then I came to love Him, as I had loved His Son; only now loving the both of Them with head and heart knowledge.

I discovered, it was not that He did not love, and does not love our bodies, but knowing more than we that this shell we call our body is a temple of the Holy Spirit, a *temporary* temple wherein the soul dwells; and when the flesh and its demands overpower the soul, then sin forces its way into this temple and we are led away from God.  This is why the Father scolds and sometimes answers our prayers with a No! Just as a holy, but imperfect, earthly father, Our God Who is perfect sees the bigger picture, and although He risks our not liking Him, out of unconditional love He continues to do all in His Power to save us from ourselves.

I have a *Heavenly* Father, just as I had an *earthly* father and they both loved me and taught me how to love.  I have a *Heavenly* Mother, Mother Mary, and I had an *earthly* mother. My earthly mother always respected my father and taught us to do likewise; our Mother Mary obeyed the Father and through her example we are called to do so, as well; both never needed to take away from the head of the family. They ran the house because they were the heart of the house, Mother Mary always interceding with the Blessed Trinity on our behalf, just as our earthly mother interceded with our earthly father.  Now just as this does not in any way demean Mother Mary, neither does it belittle the mother of the family who is its heart!

### A Promise and a Prayer

Through His only begotten Son, Jesus, God the Father gave us a way of talking to Him, reaching out and putting ourselves in His Presence.  When Jesus was asked how we should pray, knowing how important God the Father is in our lives, He taught the first disciples and, through them, us how to pray the perfect prayer to *His Father* - calling Him *Our Father!* In this prayer, we hear Jesus showing us the Father as more than the Creator; He introduces Him as a merciful and loving Father.

**That we might know Him, It was the Lord Himself**
**Who gave the Disciples the Lord's Prayer, the *Our Father!***
†
### *Our Father Who art in Heaven...*

Here, Jesus tells us that *His* Father is *Our* Father, God having made us His children, when He sent His only Son to become Man and, in so doing, joined our *earthly* family to His *Divine* Family. *When we say these words do we mean we will adore and revere You, respect You, Father as our Heavenly Father, before all men?*

### *Hallowed be Thy Name...*

Jesus gives us the opportunity to acknowledge before all mankind that our Father is *holy* (and this we do every time we pray this perfect prayer). When we pray these words, we are proclaiming God *alone* is holy, not the false gods the world puts before us to worship each day. Is this one of the reasons that those, who would have us worshiping false gods or goddesses, want the words of the Lord's prayer changed, especially the male image of God as our Father?

### *Thy kingdom come...*

Are we aware that every time we pray these words, we announce to the world that we are looking forward to the day Jesus returns and God will reign on earth--God will reign, not poor sick creatures who think they are gods.

### *Thy will be done on earth as it is in Heaven...*

As we repeat this next part of the Lord's Prayer, let us reflect on what we are saying to the Father: We are *petitioning* God to take over! Do we really mean, *Father we accept Your Will in our lives; do with us as You deem best; we trust in You?* This is a perfect act of faith which most of us do not understand fully, until the day, we really have to give up our will and turn everything over to God the Father. Do we mean *I accept whatever it is You judge best?* Are we turning our lives over to the Father? I remember the first time we said the Lord's Prayer, after having been away from Jesus and the Church for three years; I thought:

*"'Your will be done...' was I ready for that? After all, hadn't it been His will that my son die? Would I give Him that much trust? I knew that what He wanted for me had always been best; but I still have a problem with that much surrender because I do not know how much I can handle."*[27]

I still choke a little, when I pray that beautiful prayer of total abandonment and trust to the Father.

### Give us this day our daily bread

*"Give us this day our daily bread..."* It's all up to You; give and take as You please.[28]

Now here is the truly hard one, which although it gets easier, it's inch by inch, day after day. Are we truly saying, Give us the security to be insecure, to place our lives and the lives of our families in Your Hands, Lord? Dear Father, give us a sense of the true values You desire to instill in us.

### And forgive us our trespasses,
### as we forgive those who trespass against us...

*"Am I ready to forgive those who turned my son and the hundreds of thousands, no, millions of sons and daughters on to drugs and death? We said to Him (the Father) and to one another, this prayer of total surrender; and have been trying to*

---

[27]*There's a New World Somewhere*...from Bob and Penny Lord's autobiography, *"We Came Back to Jesus."*

[28]*There's a New World Somewhere*...from Bob and Penny Lord's autobiography, *"We Came Back to Jesus."*

*live it ever since, falling seven times and getting up the eighth.*"[29]
On our Marriage Encounter weekend, with tears pouring
down our faces, we made a commitment to forgive others as
God had forgiven us.

Was God saying, I will forgive you, as you forgive one
another; and to the degree you show mercy, I will show
mercy?  Was not Jesus trying to reach us, in the parable of
the master of the household and his servant--the servant who
after his master had forgiven all his debts, demanded that his
fellow servants pay the smaller debts due him?  Was not
Jesus speaking of Purgatory through the master's words:

*"You wicked servant!  I forgave you your entire debt
because you begged me to.  Should you not have had pity on
your fellow servant, as I had pity on you?  Then in anger, his
master handed him over to the torturers until he should pay the
whole debt.  So will My Father do to you, unless each of you
forgives his brother from his heart."*[30]

### And lead us not into temptation...

The world is crashing in on us, more than ever before.
Everything we see on television and hear on radio (except
EWTN), all the secular newspapers we read, are
methodically attempting to lead us to sin, and to our final
destination--hell.  Knowing how weak we are, and how
devious the enemy is, Our Lord gave us this plea to the
Father, *Please Father, lead us not into temptation, or in other
words, do not put us to the test.  Send Your Holy Spirit upon us
that we might know the Truth and follow the Truth.*  Each day,
we are more and more amazed at the recklessness of the
world, people running after and embracing more and more
temptation, believing the devil's lie that they can handle it!
It is as foolhardy as an alcoholic who takes a job tending bar.

---

[29]*There's a New World Somewhere*...from Bob and Penny Lord's
autobiography, *"We Came Back to Jesus."*
[30]Mt 18:32

### *But deliver us from all evil...*

If ever we were in need of this prayer and especially this last invocation, it is today, at the end of this millennium, where we are living in a topsy-turvy world gone mad, with laws being distorted to deceive, tainted beyond recognition, misquoted, misread, misinterpreted, spiraling this way and that, so that laws no longer protect us. As never before, we either turn to the Father for His Mercy or we will surely experience His Justice. In the Old Testament, the Father was not past punishing us, by using our enemies to mete out His retribution.

On our first Marriage Encounter weekend, *"we were asked to face each other, and say to one another, Our Lord's Perfect Prayer, the prayer I swore I would never pray again, once I realized the ramifications of the prayer."*[31] Now, almost twenty-five years later, we dare to pray this prayer, each day at Mass, looking in each other's eyes, pledging as a couple, our *Yes* to the Father and His Will.

The next time you pray the Lord's Prayer, reflect on why Jesus left this to us, what *He* is saying today, what *you* are saying, and then slowly make these petitions and promises to the Father. As the Bible tells us, God will not be outdone in generosity, so although you tremble a little, as you make this oath, walk in the confidence that the Father does not trick His children and rewards even the reluctant giver. If we live this prayer, can we change the world? We're betting on it!

†††

We thank You, Father, for loving us; and as long as we have a breath in my body, we will love You and try to share that love You have always shown us with Your children.

*Amen*

---

[31]*There's a New World Somewhere*...from Bob and Penny Lord's autobiography, *"We Came Back to Jesus."*

**The Last Judgment by Michelangelo - Sistine Chapel**
*On this painting we see both the Good News of the Final Triumph of good over evil, and the bad news of the judgment of the damned being dragged into hell by the fallen angels.*

# Sign of the Angels

*We have good news and we have bad news.*

The best way to actually envision the prophecy of good news and bad news, we talk about in this book, is to study very closely Michelangelo's "**Last Judgment**" on the back wall of the Pope's Altar in the Sistine Chapel in the Vatican. We see both the Good News of the final Triumph of the Cross, with good overcoming evil, the good being rewarded by Jesus; and the bad news of the judgment of the damned, who screaming and kicking, are being dragged down by the fallen angels and cast into a boat, which carries them across the River Styx to the gates of hell. It is a fearsome sight. It is a true *prophecy* of the Last Days. It is a *promise* of things to come.

†††

**The Good News is that Jesus is coming, Praise God!** He will come as he prophesied, on a cloud with the Archangel Gabriel blowing the horn[1] announcing *this* Good News, as he announced to Mary the Good News that she would be the Mother of God. All those whose bodies have been in the ground, waiting to be united with their souls, will rise up from the dirt and take on the glorified bodies, Jesus promised us through the teachings of St. Paul.[2] God will triumph; He will bring all those who have been washed in the blood of the Lamb[3] with Him to the Kingdom.

**The Bad News is He's very upset with us!** We, the people of God, have taken the gifts He has given us so for granted; we have stood by and allowed our Church and our world to be brought down to the level of the animal world. Excuse me, I must apologize to the animal world. They would not kill their own. We've sunk to a lower level than the animal world; we kill our own. As part of our moral

---

[1] *cf*Lk 21:27
[2] Phil 3:21
[3] cfRv 7:14

decay, this country founded under God, has given Favored Nation Status to a country who often uses child labor, paying below living standard wages (even for China). And this is the law of that land. Should that make it acceptable?

We stress the concept of hiding behind the law of the land as justification for our actions because during a program of Crossfire on CNN, just prior to the November 1998 elections, Pat Buchanan, the conservative host, had a guest on who was pro-life. Bill Cross, the liberal host, had on a gay guest who was a gay advocate. They were talking about gay bashing and killing of a young homosexual male in Wyoming. The pro-life guest tried to equate that with the lack of respect of life for the unborn, i.e., abortion. Bill Cross, who was very sympathetic with the plight of *the gay community*, and this young man's murder in particular, stopped him with "*Let's not go down that road. Abortion is the law of the land, protected by the Constitution.*"

Well, Bill, China, the country we mentioned (above), forces murder of unborn children as the natural course of things, imprisons, tortures and murders those whose philosophy differ from the official party line, and *that is the law of the land*; just as the annihilation of the Jews was *the law of the land* in Nazi Germany;[4] and the slaughter of Christians was *the law of the land* in ancient Rome. How do you feel about that? Can you just slough off the slaughter of the marginalized, disenfranchised and those with different opinions as okay because it's the law of the land? Or are those just...different situations?

You cannot buy a pair of running shoes, or an appliance, or a little gift item, or for that matter, much of anything today in stores in our country that is not made in China. God forbid we should ask for a product made in the

---

[4]During the Nuremburg trials after World War II, the defense of many Nazi officers for their crimes against humanity was that they were following orders, which were the law of the land.

United States. That's like an endangered species. When we complained to our stores that we wanted to buy a product made in a country other than China, we were told that was almost an impossibility these days. And this *favored nation*, is the same one who was given the technology to produce nuclear missiles, which are now aimed at American cities; a result of which is that North Korea, using that technology, which they got from China, and China got from the United States, launched a missile which exploded off the coast of Alaska in the fall of 1998. They have abused the rights of their own citizens, and we foolishly ask how they can abuse gifts the United States gave them, and continues to give them, and get away with it?

Because we are weak, we are wishy-washy; we are apathetic. What has happened to the John Wayne Americans, the Ronald Reagan Americans of our country? My brothers and sisters, I fear we've eaten too many cheeseburgers, french fries, onion rings, nachos and chocolate shakes. We've become obese;[5] our arteries have become clogged with cholesterol; our brains have become fried with too much beef lard from the french fry machine; we're dying. We've become a nation of *oinkers*; a world of apathetic fast-food freaks.

It's a fact that the Japanese took over China, prior to the Second World War, by feeding them opium, making them a nation of junkies. While we're also being fed drugs, we're also becoming victims of our own cravings, which we not only can't control, we really ***don't want to control***. We're a nation of getting all that we want when we want it, no matter the consequences. *"Pilate ...washed his hands in the sight of the crowds, saying 'I am innocent of the blood of this just man. Look to it yourselves.' Whereupon they shouted in*

---

[5]Statistics tell us that 1/3 of our nation is obese.

reply, **'His blood be upon us and upon our children.'"**[6] There
will be consequences, my brothers and sisters, and they will
be upon us and upon our children.

### Prophecies of the Last Days

There have been so many prophecies of things to come,
most of them unpleasant. Let's begin with the prophecies
given us by the Lord Jesus Himself in Scripture.

*"Take care not to be deceived, because many will come
using My name and saying 'I am He' and 'The time is near
at hand.' Refuse to join them. And when you hear of*
**wars** *and* **revolutions,** *do not be frightened, for this is
something that must happen but the end is not so soon.'
Then He said to them,* **'Nation will fight against nation,
and kingdom against kingdom.** *There will be great*
**earthquakes** *and* **plagues** *and* **famines** *here and there;
there will be fearful sights and great signs from heaven.
But before all this happens, men will seize you and
persecute you; they will hand you over to the synagogues
and to imprisonment, and bring you before kings and
governors because of My name - and that will be your
opportunity to bear witness.'"*[7]

Our Lord is speaking of the days we find ourselves
living in, and it sounds pretty grim. But He is speaking of a
glorious time, as well--a time of martyrs, those willing to give
their lives for the Faith. *"They will bring you before kings..."*
Are not our brothers and sisters being dragged off to prison,
because they did not sit apathetically by and let millions of
Americans die, only not on a normal cruel battlefield but a
battle being waged and lost by so many holy innocents--in
the battlefield of their mothers' wombs! And we believe that
the same Angels who were beside Jesus, as He was giving
His last breath to the Father, withholding their anger, until

---

[6]Mt 27:24-25
[7]Lk 21:8-14

at the moment He expired, when the rage would not contain itself, and the mountain split in two. Are these same Angels standing by as with each day we spit and mock their Lord and King? And how long do you think Mother Mary can withhold their righteous anger?

If the words of the Lord do not bring us to change our lives and help change the lives of others, let us reflect on what John is saying in the Book of Revelation. There are many prophecies of the Last Days in the Book of Revelation, it's hard to choose which one to share. We have chosen some of the accounts of the seven Angels with the seven seals, in that there are those who believe these prophecies have already begun to come upon the earth. We'll summarize them as much as possible, but we pray you and your loved ones, get the full impact of the Word of God.

*"Then I looked, and I heard around the throne and the living creatures and the elders the voice of many Angels, numbering myriads and myriads and thousands of thousands, saying with a loud voice, 'Worthy is the Lamb who was slain, to receive power and wealth, and wisdom and might and honor and glory and blessing.'*

*"And I heard every creature in Heaven and on earth and under the earth and in the sea, and all therein saying, 'To Him who sits upon the throne and to the Lamb be blessing and honor and glory and might forever and ever!' And the four living creatures said 'Amen!' and the elders fell down and worshiped."*

Here we have a picture of how it may be when the Lord comes a Second time! It is a time of rejoicing; but like today, man is not heeding the warnings and we, of necessity, will hear the fury of the retribution beginning!

*"Now I saw when the lamb opened one of the seven seals and I heard one of the four living creatures say, as with a voice of thunder, 'Come!' And I saw, and behold, a*

*white horse, and its rider had a bow; and a crown was given to him and he went out conquering and to conquer.*

*"When he opened the second seal, I heard the second living creature say, 'Come!' And out came another horse, bright red; its rider was permitted to* **take peace from the earth,** *so that* **men should slay one another;** *and he was given a great sword."*

If the following is not a picture of what is happening today, we don't know what is!

*"When he opened the fourth seal, I heard the voice of the fourth living creature say, 'Come!' And I saw, and behold, a pale horse, and its rider's name was Death, and Hades followed him, and they were given power over a fourth of the earth, to* **kill with sword** *and with* **famine** *and with* **pestilence** *and by* **wild beasts** *of the earth."*

The God of Justice has summoned His Angels to bring Justice to those who have been slain proclaiming His Name, martyrs of every size and color from the four corners of the world.

*"When he opened the fifth seal, I saw under the altar the souls of those who had been slain for the word of God and for the witness they had borne; they cried out with a loud voice, 'O Sovereign Lord, holy and true, how long before thou wilt judge and avenge our blood on those who dwell upon the earth?' Then they were each given a white robe and told to rest a little longer, until the number of their fellow servants and their brethren should be complete, who were to be killed as they themselves had been."*

Never in the history of the world have we had such horrendous calamities, nature rebelling against man, seeking retribution for all he has done to the Creator and His Creation.

*"When he opened the sixth seal, I looked, and behold, there was a great* **earthquake;** *and the sun became black as sackcloth, the full moon became like blood, and the stars*

*of the sky fell to the earth as the fig tree sheds its winter fruit when shaken by a gale; the sky vanished like a scroll that is rolled up, and every mountain and island was removed from its place. Then the kings of the earth and the great men and the generals and the rich and the strong, and every one, slave and free, hid in the caves and among the rocks of the mountains, calling to the mountains and rocks, 'Fall on us and hide us from the face of Him Who is seated on the throne, and from the wrath of the Lamb, for the great day of their wrath has come, and who can stand before it.'"*

All those kings of the earth who have mocked Him and persecuted His lambs will now stand before the Throne of God and He will mete out His Justice.

*"When the Lamb opened the seventh seal, there was silence in Heaven for about half an hour. Then I saw seven Angels who stand before God, and seven trumpets were given to them. And another Angel came and stood at the altar with a golden censer; and he was given much incense to mingle with the prayers of all the Saints upon the golden altar before the throne; then the Angel took the censer and filled it with fire from the altar and threw it on the earth; and there were peals of **thunder**, loud noises, flashes of lightning and an **earthquake**."*

Are our waters not polluted, our fish poisoned?

*"The third Angel blew his trumpet and a great star fell from heaven, blazing like a torch, and it fell on a third of the rivers and on the fountains of water. The name of the star is Wormwood. A third of the waters became wormwood, and many men died of the water, because it was made bitter."*

Then we hear the angels heralding the three days of darkness! Will they be the enforcers, those who have always defended us, protected us, even as we were abusing them and their God?

*"The fourth Angel blew his trumpet and a third of the sun was struck, and a third of the moon, and a third of the stars, so that* **a third of their light was darkened**; *a third of the day was kept from shining, and likewise a third of the night.*

*"Then I looked, and I heard an eagle crying with a loud voice, as it flew in midheaven, 'Woe, woe, woe to those who dwell on the earth, at the blasts of the other trumpets which the three Angels are about to blow.'*

*"And then the fifth Angel blew his trumpet and I saw a star falling from heaven to earth, and he was given the key of the shaft of the bottomless pit; he opened the shaft of the bottomless pit and from the shaft rose smoke like the smoke of a great furnace and the sun and the air were darkened with the smoke from the shaft.*

*"Then from the smoke came locusts on the earth, and they were given power like the power of scorpions of the earth; they were told not to harm the grass of the earth or any green growth or any tree, but only those of mankind who have not the seal of God upon their foreheads; they were allowed to torture them for five months, but not to kill them, and their torture was like the torture of a scorpion when it stings a man.* **And in those days men will seek death and will not find it; they will long to die, and death will fly from them.**

*"Then the sixth Angel blew his trumpet, and I heard a voice from the four horns of the golden altar before God, saying to the sixth Angel who had the trumpet, 'Release the four Angels who are bound at the great river Euphrates.' So the four Angels were released, who had been held ready for the hour, the day, the month and the year, to kill a third of mankind.*

*"...The rest of mankind, who were not killed by these plagues,* **did not repent** *of the works of their hands nor give up* **worshiping demons and idols of gold and silver**

**and bronze and stone and wood,** *which cannot either see or hear or walk; nor did they repent of their* **murders** *or their* **sorceries** *or their* **immorality** *or their* **thefts.**

*"Then I saw another mighty Angel coming down from Heaven, wrapped in a cloud,* **with a rainbow over his head,** *and his face was like the sun, and his legs like pillars of fire. He had a little scroll open in his hand. And he set his right foot on the sea, and his left foot on the land, and called out with a loud voice, like a lion roaring; when he called out, the seven thunders sounded.*

*"And when the seven thunders sounded, I was about to write, but I heard a voice from Heaven saying, 'Seal up what the seven thunders have said, and do not write it down.' And the Angel whom I saw standing on sea and land lifted up his right hand to Heaven and swore by Him who lives forever and ever, who created Heaven and what is in it, the earth and what is in it, and the sea and what is in it, that there should be no more delay, but that in the days of the trumpet call to be sounded by the seventh Angel, the mystery of God, as He announced to His servants the prophets, should be fulfilled.*

*"And the voice I heard from Heaven was speaking with me again, and saying, 'Go take the open scroll from the hand of the Angel who stands upon the sea and upon the earth.' And I went away to the Angel, telling him to give me the scroll. And he said to me, 'Take the scroll and eat it up,* **and it will make thy stomach bitter,** *but in* **thy mouth it will be sweet as honey.'** *And I took the scroll from the Angel's hand, and ate it up, and it was in my mouth sweet as honey, and when I had eaten it my stomach was made bitter. And they said to me,* **'Thou must prophesy again to many nations and peoples and tongues and kings.'"**[8]

---

[8]Rv 6-10

The deceit of the world often *tastes sweet in the mouth*, pleasing to the palate, but soon turns sour when it hits the stomach. We did not want to dwell on this particular prophecy in the Book of Revelation, but it was so powerful and so intense, we had no choice but to include this section in its entirety. Everyone should take time to read the Book of Revelation.

We shared some parts of the prophecies of the seven seals and trumpets. We believe we have to take these prophecies seriously, or we'll find ourselves like the people during the days of Noah, who were eating and drinking, marrying, buying and selling, when the great flood came. They were not prepared and so they perished.[9]

We don't want to become obsessed, nor are we called to be haunted by the prophecies of the *Chastisement* and *Final Judgment*. As followers of Christ, we are to live our lives as Jesus instructed us, expecting the Master to come at any moment. But be prepared, in the event that the following Scripture passage comes to pass, where Our Lord warns us to "*Stay awake. For you do not know on which day the Lord will come.*" "*..be prepared, for at an hour you do not expect, the Son of Man will come.*"[10]     And if that does not provide a strong enough motivation, read Matthew's Chapter 24 *where It relates to the trials and tribulations, the destruction of Jerusalem, the signs of the Last Days, and the end of the world.*

Family, the Lord is speaking to us; He has been speaking to us for the last two millenniums. Our job now is to listen to what He's been telling us and to act on His Word.

*Jesus loves you!*

---

[9]*cf*Lk 17:26-27
[10]Mt 24:42-51

# A Cry in the Desert

We are in serious times, but not in impossible times. God is still in charge; He is always in charge; and we hold on to what His Mother Mary said in Pontmain, France, when she appeared in 1871, *"But pray my children. God will soon answer your prayers. My Son allows Himself to be touched."* Is not Our Lady saying, Our Lord is listening; He loves us and will keep us out of harm's way, if only we pray?

Saint Augustine tells us that the sin of Adam was *Pride* and *Humanism*, the desire to be independent of God and His Grace and dependent on no one but himself.

Unlike the Angels, who were given one chance--to choose Heaven or hell, their choice irreversible, man is given options; he can elect to either follow man's first father Adam or Our Lord and Redeemer Jesus Christ; through one, the gates of Heaven were closed to man; and by the Sacrifice of the Other they were opened! Likewise, when we choose, are we not making a choice between God and the devil, between the pursuit of Heaven or hell?

St. Augustine said, when God created man, God also created a bridge which connected Adam (and humanity) with God. When Adam sinned against His Creator and Father, he lifted his side of the bridge cutting himself off from God; and then because of Adam's disobedience and defiance, God lifted His side of the bridge, leaving Adam and man to himself. When Jesus suffered and died for us on the Cross, He lowered the bridge on both sides, on one side as God and on the other as Man. As Adam had sinned, a new Adam had to suffer to bring about reconciliation with the Father; and Jesus said Yes!

When we are baptized, through the waters of Baptism, we are cleansed of the stain of sin resulting from the sin of our first parents.[1]  When *we* commit sin,[2] as with our first parents, we alienate ourselves from the Father, lifting up our side of the bridge estranging ourselves from God.   By sinning, we are saying we do not need God, we are self-sufficient and able to find our own happiness.   But St. Augustine says that man is created with a longing for God which only God can fill; this inner desire struggles to be reunited with God, restless till it rests in Him Who created man.  And so, because of sin, man is blind to the truth, and cannot see Who it is he is hungering for; therefore, he goes on a relentless trip seeking fulfillment.

Man has, through the *father of lies*, been falling to the lowest form of beast of the animal world, in a useless endeavor to satisfy that which he cannot, that void in life which only God can fill.  But God never gives up on us.  Just as we as parents grieve, when our children go astray, but keep the door open awaiting their return, so God our faithful Father does not close the door but stands ready to forgive and welcome back the repentant sinner.

According to St. Augustine when we sin, we "*deform the image of God*" within us.  But God in His Mercy is always ready to remold and renew the soul which has wandered from Him, once again into His image, the Image God imprinted on his heart, before he was born. Although by his choice, man shuts out God, devoted Father that He is, God never forgets the child He created.  No matter how soiled his soul is with sin, God recognizes the sinner and loves him.  No depravity too grave, no estrangement too permanent, God's Arms are opened wide, as on the Cross, ready to embrace the sinner.  God never stops loving His children, no matter how much they sin against Him, how much they malign Him, how much they ignore Him, how much they trade Him in,

---

[1]Original Sin
[2]Actual Sin

like Adam and Eve, for the false promises of the enemy of God. God will never deny the soul who desires reconciliation.

Why has man turned his back on the *Supernatural*-God, and has chosen to follow the *natural*-man? It doesn't make sense adoring the created rather than the Creator of all that is created. Even without touching upon *eternal life* in Heaven versus temporal or *temporary life* on earth, let us consider how lasting, how rewarding the prizes of this life are. Houses get old, sometimes past repair; and if not, a storm comes and the house you so loved is swept away. You cannot rely on clothes which the world is designing into obsolescence faster than you can wear them out. Most cars are designed to last until your final payment is made. Man relying on self does the best job he can, for the god of materialism--the corporation, and before he can reap the benefits promised, he is *down-sized,* a Twentieth Century word for fired, not because he failed the company but because he invested his life and soul in man, not God, and man betrayed him.

Man is living as if this is all there is. What happens when he finds that less and less brings him the joy he craves? Does he try a little more evil, a little more self-gratification? When man decides for the world, he trades in the most cherished distinction between him and all God's other creatures--the Image of God in him, for the reflection of the most depraved of all beasts, one who wanders the earth stalking the innocent, bent on taking souls with him into his final reward in the bowels of hell.

We are living in a time when we are mocked if we believe in Heaven, Hell and Purgatory,[3] oftentimes from within our own beloved churches. We are told there is no

---

[3]Read about the Church's teaching in *Visions of Heaven, Hell and Purgatory* by Bob and Penny Lord

such thing as sin, only psychosis; and so less and less take advantage of the Sacrament of Penance and more and more are seeking out man's help on a Psychiatrist's couch. Prior to World War II, a small percentage of Catholics (barely 10%) went to Psychologists or Psychiatrists; today the figures are closer to 40% seeking answers to their troubled lives, rather than seeking reconciliation through the Sacrament of Penance. And yet, a survey made by the American Psychiatric Association revealed that it takes at least four sessions before the patient and therapist achieve the trust level that a penitent has the first time he walks into the confessional.

### Pride-the source of all evil

St. Augustine wrote that "*Pride was a draught which the devil gave Adam from his own cup. This pride, 'the head and source of all wickedness and all evil,' lay in Adam's desire to live according to his own will...because he wished to live according to his own pleasure.*"[4] Augustine called *pride* the *head* and *source* of all evil; it is no small coincidence that the Catechism of the Catholic Church calls the *Eucharist* the *source and summit* of Christian life, and the Canadian translation calls the Eucharist the *Heart and summit* of Christian life. Pride is the *head and source* of all evil; the Eucharist the *source and summit*, the very *Heart* of Christian life.

What do we believe? Do we Catholics not believe that the Eucharist is Jesus truly Present in our Church! Do we not believe that the antithesis[5] of Jesus is the devil; and that the sin of the devil, which got him cast out of Heaven, was Pride; and did not the devil use that same sin to lure Adam into sinning against God, resulting in his being banished from God's presence; and is it not our creed that Jesus died on

---

[4]Spiritual Doctrine of St. Augustine
[5]opposite

the Cross, that the devil would not be victorious, and that we would live eternally in the Kingdom?

St. Augustine speaks of Jesus not coming to earth to do His own Will but that of the Father, and assures us Jesus will not cast out anyone who denies himself and his pride, to do God's Will. But one who gives in to the sin of Pride, because it is the source and summit of all evil, will find himself in the dark, the dark which like a black shade, blocks out the Son Who is the Source of all Light.

When God created man, He carefully differentiated between man and animal, giving man a body and soul and animal only a body; in so doing He entrusted man to look after those without a soul--the animal kingdom. When the flesh controls the soul, man falls to a creature below that of the animal world, seeking pleasure in the vilest of fashions, accounting to no one, not even his God.

We lived through the Second World War and saw the inhumane, methodical slaughter of God's people because of greed and jealousy, a madman and a powerful propaganda machine breeding hate and division. Hitler fed on the German people's pride which had been all but completely destroyed as the result of the Versailles Treaty when their country was fragmented into tiny pieces. He fed their egos, boosted their self-worth. He promised them change; many were starving, papering their walls with their life-savings of devalued Marks. They were a beaten people; he charmed them, set their hearts on fire; one woman confessed he seemed to be the only one who cared and had a solution.

He used the Jews as targets. He turned the Germans against the Jewish people, charging the Jews with having dishonestly taken that which belonged to the German people. He promised them a better economy, which he delivered, but at what price? He hypnotized the German people into believing the Jews were animals; they were not human, therefore it was all right to kill them. You have only to visit the Death Camps of Auschwitz or Dachau to see the price, how inhumane man can be to his fellow man. Age was no shield protecting anyone from torture and death, beginning with the very youngest--infants snatched from their mother's arms to the very oldest--wives and husbands screaming as their spouses were led into the gas chambers. Mothers tried to hide their babies under heaps of clothing they were told to remove; the Nazis wanted to waste nothing, so they told everyone to disrobe before going into the *showers* (their cruel joke for what were really gas chambers). We cried, as we passed huge mounds of personal treasures, heaped one upon another--long hair which the Nazis would use for mattresses, combs, tiny shoes, precious items which could have no meaning, except to give those who died so cruelly a name, an identity; they were evidence that someone's children, someone's husband and wife, mother and father had passed this way. No longer numbers in a horrible camp; they were people, families who had been robbed of dignity and hope and then of life; they had been here and we who have been there will never forget! For just as each baby that is aborted is our baby; so each brother and sister who died here is our brother and sister.

The Nazis plowed through one country after the other, conquering, despoiling, torching that which they could not use, dehumanizing, terrifying, torturing and finally annihilating anyone who had what they wanted or posed a threat to them and their regime. German youth of today, ask grandparents who are still alive, how could they have been a party to such monstrous behavior, and they hang their heads and often cry. What will our grandchildren and great-grandchildren ask us?

Does this attack our sensibilities? Is this a tired story and we want to get on with our lives? A sign in Warsaw where Jewish people were herded into cattle cars and taken to Death Camps, reads, "*Those who ignore history are doomed to repeat it."* As we see abortion, the legal, senseless, barbaric annihilation of human beings by their own mothers, do we not hear the Voice of Jesus pleading for these unborn babies He created? Can we not still hear the lament of mothers of the Holy Innocents who were butchered by Herod's soldiers, haunting us, their cries refusing to be stilled, forgotten? For today, the cries come from within mothers' wombs, the holy innocents of today crying, *"Do not kill me, Mommy; I will be good."*

Jesus spoke of these latter days, when He said, *"There will be mother against daughter, and daughter against mother."*[6] Is this not mother against child, performing a selfish criminal act, below that of the animal world, which cries out to Heaven? A female animal will ferociously protect her offspring from all possible harm, even ready to fight the male parent, should he venture too close to her pups, fearing, as in the case of wolves, he attack and eat the cub.

There is no accountability, today! Who will pay for the slaughter of so many innocent babies? As Edith Stein, now proclaimed by Pope John Paul II--Saint Teresa Blessed by the Cross, said, as she and her sister were part of thousands of Jews being carted off to die in a Concentration Camp, *"Someone will have to pay for this."*[7]

[6]Lk 12:53
[7]from *Martyrs, They died for Christ* by Bob and Penny Lord

*Our dear Mother Mary, whom God the Father chose to bring Love into the world, has never stopped bringing that Love to us. She has joined Her Son, His priority, Her priority - to bring about the salvation of the world.*

Left:
*Our Lady of Guadalupe*
*Patroness of the unborn*
*Pope John Paul II consecrated*
*America to Our Lady of Guadalupe.*

Above: *Our Lady of LaSalette, known as Our Lady who wept, appeared to Melanie Mathieu and Maximin Giraud in LaSalette.*

Above:
*Chapel of the Miraculous Medal in Paris where Our Lady appeared to St. Catherine Laboure.*

# Our Lady Saves us
## from Destruction

Our dear Mother Mary, whom God the Father chose to bring Love into the world, has never stopped bringing that Love to us. She has joined Her Son, *His* priority *Her* priority -- to bring about the Salvation of the world. Our Mother Mary has been reaching out to us, prophesying the dire consequences which would result from our disobedience and promising the rewards awaiting us for our obedience.

Mother Mary, carrying that Tabernacle of Love and Hope beneath Her heart, began prophesying to us as far back as her Visitation to her cousin Elizabeth. She brought us great hope, hope that we could hold onto for all generations to come:

*"Behold, henceforth, all generations shall call me blessed...*

*For He who is Mighty has done great things for me and Holy is His Name;*

*His Mercy is from generation to generation on those who fear Him;*

*He has shown might with His Arm,*

*He has scattered the proud in the deceit of their heart,*

*He has put down the mighty from their thrones, and has exalted the lowly.*

*He has filled the hungry with good things, and the rich He has sent away empty.*

*He has received Israel, His Servant, being mindful of His mercy."*[1]

Our Lord left His Mother on the earth for close to twenty years; so that She could guide the Early Church and the children entrusted to Her, to life eternal with Her Son. Our Mother once assumed into Heaven, never stopped being our faithful, loving Mother; She remained involved, as at Cana; She did not stop interceding, only now guiding Her

---

[1]Lk 1:46-55

children and the Church from Heaven. Envision our dear Mother Mary, sitting at the feet of her Son, Our Lord Jesus Christ. Both may be looking down to the earth, at what has been happening to their children over the centuries.

It would be understandable if Jesus was upset with us, if He was even considering some fair, just punishment for the atrocities being committed on earth. His dear Mother, knowing Her Son and wanting to help Her errant children on earth, knows it is time to do something, before it is too late. She knows Him well; their relationship having begun at the moment of her Yes to the Angel Gabriel. She is sad because He is upset, and concerned, how we will fare if She stops holding His arms back. She may ask the Lord if She can come down to earth to speak to us. He most likely doesn't want Her to have to go through all that; but as She thinks man is worth it, in the end, God can't resist Her, and She comes to earth to warn us, to prophesy about things to come if we don't stop mistreating Him and those He created.

She might be thinking how suicidal we are, how we can't believe in the power of God, as people on earth seem to go out of their way to commit horrendous crimes against Him. It's almost like we're daring Him to retaliate. This is where Our Lady comes in, great peacemaker, She comes down.

In all her apparitions down through the centuries, Mary has given us prophecies, warnings and promises. Many of these can be applied to today, if we will just listen to Her. More than anything else, Our Lady has come, either because of her great concern for us, or because we have so deeply hurt her Son. With Her every action, Her every word She is that ever-faithful sign and representation of God working in our lives, here on earth. Because of not only Her love but that of Her Son and Her Heavenly Father, in company with the Holy Spirit, She comes to warn us, to plead with us, to focus us on what our priorities are or should be.

## Mother Mary is truly a prophet of the end times

Saint Louis Marie de Montfort wrote:

*"....towards the end of the world, ....Almighty God and His holy Mother are to raise up saints who will surpass in holiness most other saints as much as the cedars of Lebanon tower above little shrubs.*

*"These great souls filled with grace and zeal will be chosen to oppose the enemies of God who are raging on all sides. They will be exceptionally devoted to the Blessed Virgin. Illumined by her light, strengthened by her spirit, supported by her arms, sheltered under her protection, they will fight with one hand and build with the other. With one hand they will give battle, **overthrowing and crushing heretics and their heresies, schismatics and their schisms, idolaters and their idolatries, sinners and their wickedness**. With the other hand they will build the temple of the true Solomon and the mystical city of God, namely, the Blessed Virgin...*

*"They will be like thunder-clouds flying through the air at the slightest breath of the Holy Spirit. Attached to nothing, surprised at nothing, they will shower down the rain of God's Word and of eternal life. They will thunder against sin; they will storm against the world; they will strike down the devil and his followers and for life and for death, they will pierce through and through with the two-edged sword of God's word all those against whom they are sent by Almighty God.*

*"They will be true apostles of the latter times to whom the Lord of Hosts will give eloquence and strength to work wonders and carry off glorious spoils from His enemies. They will sleep without gold or silver and, more important still, without concern in the midst of other priests, ecclesiastics and clerics. Yet they will have the silver wings of the dove enabling them to go wherever the Holy Spirit calls them, filled as they are, with the resolve to*

*seek the glory of God and the salvation of souls. Wherever they preach, they will leave behind them nothing but the gold of love, which is the fulfillment of the whole law.*

*"They will have the two-edged sword of the Word of God in their mouths and the blood-stained standard of the Cross on their shoulders. They will carry the crucifix in their right hand and the rosary in their left, and the holy names of Jesus and Mary on their heart.*

*"Mary scarcely appeared in the first coming of Christ... But in the second coming of Jesus Christ, Mary must be known and openly revealed by the Holy Spirit so that Jesus may be known, loved and served through her."[2]*

We want to share how Mary has played an important role in Salvation History, as Prophet and Envoy from God.

We begin with Her first apparition to our hemisphere and why it's so important to us, today. Ask yourself the correlation or parallels, between those times and now.

## Our Lady of Guadalupe, Mexico, 1531

Our Lady saw the beauty of the natives of America and that of the evangelists, which Our Lord had sent to bring knowledge of Jesus to this new land; but She also perceived the weaknesses of misunderstanding and differences that promised to destroy them. *Our Lady claimed this land for Her Son!* The emissary, God chose to bring His Word to this land, to bring light into the darkness, was a man called Columbus, *Christ-bearer.* He truly believed his mission was to bring Christ to far off lands. On the voyage across, each morning, a hymn was sung to Our Lord and Savior:

> *"Blessed be the light of day.*
> *and the Holy Cross, we say,*
> *and the Lord of Veritie,[3]*
> *and the Holy Trinity.*

---

[2] from *Visionaries, Mystics and Stigmatists* by Bob and Penny Lord.
[3] *Truth* - Christ Who is the Way, the Truth and the Life.

> *Blessed be the immortal soul,*
> *and the Lord Who keeps it whole.*
> *Blessed be the light of day,*
> *and He Who sends the night away."*

To show the heart of Columbus, the first place in the New World, where he set foot, he named *San Salvador*, after Our Savior, Jesus Christ! He prayed at that spot,

> *"O Lord Almighty and everlasting God,*
> *by Thy Holy Word Thou hast created the Heaven,*
> *and the earth, and the sea;*
> *blessed and glorified be Thy Name,*
> *and praised be Thy Majesty,*
> *which has deigned to use us, Thy humble servants,*
> *that Thy Name may be proclaimed*
> *in this second part of the earth."*[4]

From the time Christopher Columbus first set foot on the New World, a great battle began raging between God and the devil, and it has never stopped. He had truly felt he was coming to evangelize. He had been financed by Queen Isabella, the Catholic Queen, in thanksgiving for having liberated Spain from seven hundred years of Moslem domination. This voyage, which began as a *Mission of Evangelization*, would turn into a mass annihilation of two beautiful cultures, unless Someone interceded.

"Columbus never accomplished what he had set out to do, but he was an instrument the Lord would use. He opened the way for Spain to send evangelists in the form of Franciscan Missionaries. The Lord had a plan for this New World. He had to put up with the frailties and shortcomings of human beings, knowing somehow they would get the job done. For the next thirty-nine years, not much headway was

---

[4] from Bob and Penny Lord's book: *"Martyrs, They died for Christ."*

made in bringing Jesus to the natives. On the contrary to the human eye, things were going downhill in the New World."[5]

For as God has His agenda, Satan has *his* agenda-- sabotage what God is doing. In this case, Satan appealed to the greed and lasciviousness of the people who came over after Columbus; although some had come with the Franciscans Missionaries, their goals were diametrically opposed; the Missionaries' eyes on the conversion of men's souls and the settlers' eyes on gold. *Gold was flowing in Mexico.* There was just so much of it! There was so much of everything, the Spaniards completely lost their perspective of any semblance of the noble values they might have once had, and the reason they were sent. Private interests came and took as much as they could carry out of the country.

The natives, who initially opened their arms to the Spaniards, became suspicious. And as the natives had ways strange to the Spaniards, the colonists were frightened of the natives, and that resulted in a menacing wall of distrust going up, natives and colonists against each other, with a backlash, the encompassment of innocent Franciscan Missionaries, who had no interest in anything but the salvation of souls.

Stories romanticizing the Spanish Conquistadores and their great leader, Hernando Cortez, have been told for centuries; that is not the total truth. But as fictional, is the movement within Mexico today, which, in an attempt to bring about anarchy and division among Mexicans, lays all the blame on the Spaniards, showing the natives completely without any accountability for what transpired.

There are no *good guys* in the world, when it comes to colonization and conquest. In the period between the conquest of Mexico by Cortez in 1521, and Our Lady's appearance to Juan Diego in 1531, there was a mammoth struggle between opposing cultures and philosophies. The

---

[5]from Bob and Penny Lord's book: "*Martyrs, They died for Christ.*"

rulers who took over, after Cortez' decisive victory, became despots. The didn't understand the culture of the people whose lives they controlled, so they treated them as slaves and worse, animals. Sadly, this was one of the darkest periods of humanity, on a par with the atrocities of Adolf Hitler and Joseph Stalin, filled with wholesale massacre, with both sides guilty, and the destruction of two great civilizations, the Aztecs and the Spaniards, in the horizon.

Man had failed; and the consequences, looming in the near future, looked grave. Thirty nine years had passed, since Columbus had landed, Spaniards and natives had agreed to disagree, and there was no hope of peace and reconciliation. Many had died and with them, the realization of Columbus' dream and that of the Catholic Queen Isabella. The situation came to a head just about the time Our Lady chose to appear to Juan Diego on Tepeyac Hill.

Even natives who had initially befriended the Spaniards joined warring tribes and were organizing a revolution, to massacre every European in their land. History tells us that it was almost the eve of the holocaust, when Our Lady came. At the time of Our Lady's appearance, the Aztecs were capable of killing every European in Mexico. There was a great need for God to bring these two people together. Jesus chose His Mother, as the Father had done fifteen hundred years before in Nazareth.

Now, what has this to do with today and our prophetic times? One of the things that had frightened and alienated the Spaniards, was the *human sacrifices* done by the natives to appease their gods, not only using captured warriors from enemy tribes, but young virgins from their own tribes, who had been specially chosen for sacrifice from before they were born. The natives slit open the bodies of those being sacrificed and then ripped their hearts out while they were sill alive! Disgusting? Barbaric? Inhumane? Oh, many descriptive adjectives come to mind, and as they do, suddenly we can see why holocaust was inevitable, before Mother Mary came and brought about reconciliation, and why She is so needed in our continent, in our time. She came and saved Her children from total annihilation!

Now, in our time, has Our Lady of Guadalupe not been given the title: *Patroness of the Unborn*? In addition to stopping the massacre of thousands upon thousands of lives, did She not stop the *sacrifice* of thousands upon thousands of the young and innocent to false gods? Do we not have the horrible sacrifice of the innocents of all ages to false gods today, with birth control, abortion, suicides, deaths due to drug and alcohol overdoses, and euthanasia? And has not our Pope John Paul II consecrated America to Our Lady of Guadalupe? Has She not come to us, at this time, to stop this holocaust which threatens to destroy us? *Because of Her, 8,000,000 conversions came about in a period of 7 years. What can She do, if we all become Juan Diegos and bring her message to the world? Tolle lege!* Take and read!

## Our Lady of the Miraculous Medal Paris, France, 1830

Paris has been given the title of *City of Lights*, because of the many lights that brighten the streets of Paris, at night. But her other title, that of *City of Sin*, was earned by the darkness of sin which had permeated the very souls of her people, nearly extinguishing the Light Who had been their hope and salvation - their Lord Jesus Christ and the Church He had founded. No longer did she boast of being Eldest Daughter of the Church, a title forgotten and thrown away with the traditions and piety of centuries past.

But it had not always been that way. During the Middle Ages, great cathedrals rose up in honor of Our Lady all over Europe, but especially in Paris. The most elegant Lady in the Land, She was called *Our Lady of Paris*. The magnificent Cathedral of Notre Dame de Paris was built in her honor, as was the Cathedral of Chartres, just outside Paris.

Then, the French Revolution came, and cohorts of Satan took particular pleasure destroying the Church and all within it; they wanted to put Jesus and Mary to shame, and with that blot them out of their minds and hearts forever. They took the great Cathedral of Notre Dame and made it into a warehouse, but not before they had performed scandalous, repulsive sexual acts on its Altars.

Now, Our Lady no more her mother and pride, Paris became decadent, depraved, and capable of all that was profanely evil. First a victim of the French Revolution, and then Napoleon Bonaparte; and infected by all that went with the madness, Paris no longer reflected the heritage passed down by the great Saints who had once graced her streets.

When Our Lady came to a little postulant in a tiny out of the way Chapel in Paris, it was at one of the most evil times in the History of France, a period almost as machiavellian[6] as the world is today. It was time for Mommy to get her children back in shape, before it was too late. Our Lady spent much time with a young postulant, who would one day be raised to *Saint* Catherine Labouré. Mother Mary shared the many problems which existed in France and in the world at that time, and prophesied:

*"Our dear Lord loves you very much. He wishes to give you a mission. It will be the cause of much suffering to you, but you will overcome it, knowing that what you do is for the glory of God.*

*"You will be contradicted, but you will have the grace to bear it. Don't be afraid. You will see certain things. You must report them. You will be given the words through prayer.*

---

[6]political principles and methods of expediency, craftiness, and duplicity advocated in Machiavelli's book, *The Prince*; or in other words a period which is deceitful, crafty, etc.

*"The times are evil.    Misfortunes will fall upon France.   The king will be overthrown.   The entire world will be overcome by evils of all kinds, but...*

*"Come to the foot of this Altar.   Here, great graces will be poured upon all those who ask for them with confidence and fervor.   They will be bestowed upon the great and the small."*

She allowed this postulant, little more than a child, who fell to her knees, at the foot of the Altar, to embrace Her knees, the knees of our most exquisite Visitor from Heaven. Mary allowed the young girl to put her hands in the same lap which had held the Baby Jesus.  Mary poured out Her heart to this young girl, sharing the outrages which were in store for France and the Church; Our Lady held back Her tears, as much as possible, but finally broke down and wept.

*"There will be an abundance of sorrows; and the danger will be great.   Yet do not be afraid; tell them not to be afraid.   The protection of God shall be ever present in a special way - and St. Vincent will protect you.   I shall be with you myself.   Always, I have my eye upon you.   I will grant you many graces."*

Our Lady prophesied some of the details of the future:
*"There will be victims...*

*"There will be victims among the clergy of Paris. Monseigneur the Archbishop......"*

In between speaking, the Mother of God cried such hard tears, it forced her to stop in the middle of sentences.

*"My child, the Cross will be treated with contempt; they will hurl it to the ground.  Blood will flow; they will open up again the side of Our Lord.  The streets will stream with blood.  Monseigneur the Archbishop will be stripped of his garments...."*

Our Lady could not continue speaking, She was so overwrought, She cried again, and then continued:
*"My child, the whole world will be in sadness."*

Some of Our Lady's prophecies to Catherine began to occur within a week after She had appeared to the child:

Riots broke out in Paris.

Dead bodies littered the streets.

The King was deposed and fled the country.

There was a three day bloodbath, which the revolutionaries[7] designated as *"The Glorious Three Days"* of the July Revolution. Because the motto of King Charles X had been *"For Throne and Altar,"* the Church was considered to be in collusion with the throne. Actually, because some of the prelates had been born of the nobility, there was a bit of truth to this charge. But what happened against the Church was completely unjust. All priests, bishops and religious were arrested, not just those of the nobility who had lands. Priests and religious were slaughtered. The guillotine was back in use, and working overtime.

This short revolution, just a few days in duration, although it was devastating, turned out to affirm the prophecy of our Lady to Sister Catherine Labouré. Her confessor, to whom she had, under obedience, revealed all these things just before they occurred, was amazed at how quickly they manifested themselves.

Another prophecy, our Lady made at that time was right on the mark. She had been crying, telling Catherine about the devastation which was going to take place in France, when the young postulant thought, *When will all this be?* The immediate answer she received in her heart was *forty years.* The prediction had to do with the persecution of the Church which would begin in 1870, during the uprising of the Paris Commune, following the fall of the Second Empire. The Archbishop of Paris was murdered, and the government turned against the Church officially.

---

[7]political party who took over much of the land of the nobility and the Church for themselves. So much for revolution!

At the end of the apparition, Mary left us with hope. She told Catherine Labouré:

*"The ball which you see represents the whole world, especially France, and each person in particular. These rays symbolize the graces I shed upon those who ask for them. The gems from which rays do not fall are the graces for which souls forget to ask."*

An oval frame formed around Mary, with the words:

*Oh Mary conceived without sin,*
*Pray for us who have recourse to you.*

Then Mary said,

*"Have a medal struck after this model. All who wear it will receive great graces; they should wear it around the neck. Graces will abound for persons who wear it with confidence."*

There was a need for the Mother of God to come and bring the prophecies of doom and the promises of hope. Not only was France in the midst of ungodliness and the willful destruction of body and soul, but the faithful of the entire Church needed to hear the words from Our Lady that She is Our Lady of the Immaculate Conception. The original medal struck, was not supposed to be called the Miraculous Medal but the *Medal of the Immaculate Conception.* But so many miracles and conversions began immediately, the name of the medal was changed to the *Miraculous Medal.* In **1830**, Our Lady appeared to Catherine Labouré as Our Lady of the Immaculate Conception; December 8, **1854**, Pope Pius IX proclaimed the Dogma of the Immaculate Conception; and in **1858**, She appeared to St. Bernadette in Lourdes and identified herself as Our Lady of the Immaculate Conception.

This apparition and that of Lourdes came about to uphold the Dogma of the Immaculate Conception and to dispel *Pantheism, the deadly heresy claiming that man is on a level with God, equal to Him; that God is not a Being, but is manifested in all the forces of the universe.*[8] This heresy began in 1705, in the *exclusive, illuminated* society of the intelligentsia; but then in the French Revolution, like a weed it spread to the poor, unsuspecting common man. Are we today not in days of *Pantheism*, with errors threatening our families, our Church, our very souls, our country, and the world we live in? Is it not time we all began praying to the Blessed Mother and heeding Her words, put on the armor of God, the Miraculous Medal?

**Our Lady cried!**

Despite news of the Miraculous Medal and all the miracles coming about through Our Lady of the Immaculate Conception, in 1846 France was as decadent as if Mary had never graced their land with Her precious presence. Now, although the evil and rampant anti-Church feelings which had begun in the French Revolution, were still contaminating the big cities, they had not reached small villages, especially those hidden comfortably on the high mountain ranges. But there was another deadly enemy--that of apathy and indifference that was eroding the Church, from the bottom up. The churches were empty. Sunday was a work day like the other six days of the week. The Church was just there, like an old shoe, available for *Baptisms, First Holy Communions*, possibly *Confirmations*, hopefully *Weddings* and always *funerals*. Children were no longer taught their prayers; more often than not, First Holy Communion was their last Holy Communion.

Parents were no longer role models for their children. And though they were surrounded by the most breathtaking scenery in the world, they put the Creator of all that splendor on the very outer perimeter of their lives, until He

---

[8]among other serious heresies; for more on this and other heresies, read: *Scandal of the Cross and Its Triumph, Heresies throughout the History of the Church* - by Bob and Penny Lord

barely existed; that is until the last moments of life when even the hardest hearted atheist acknowledges God, if he gets a chance!

Our Lady had to come; for evil spreads and when God is not the center of our lives, the enemy is sure to enter and lead us to hell. Our Lady had to come to two children in La Salette, as Her children in France were in jeopardy; She had to warn them. She cried bitter tears and told the children,

*"If my people will not obey, I shall be compelled to loose my Son's Arm. It is so heavy, so pressing, I can no longer restrain it.*

*"How long I have suffered for you! If I would not have my Son abandon you, I must pray to Him constantly. But you pay no attention to it. No matter how well you act, you will never be able to make up to me what I have endured on your behalf.*

*"You have six days for working. The seventh is reserved for my Son. But no one will give it to Him. This is what causes the weight of my Son's Arm to be so crushing. In addition, the cart drivers cannot swear without bringing in my Son's Name. These are two things which make His Arm so heavy.*

*"If the harvest is spoiled, it is your own fault. I warned you last year by means of the potatoes.*[9] *You paid no attention. Quite the opposite. When you found the potatoes had decayed, you swore; you blamed my Son. They will continue to spoil, and by Christmas time this year there will be none left.*

*"If you have grain, it will do no good to sow it, for what you sow the animals will eat, and whatever part of it springs up will crumble into dust when you thresh it.*

*"A great famine is coming. But before that happens, the children under seven years old will be seized with trembling*

---

[9]Potato Famine of 1845

*and die in the arms of their parents. The grownups will pay for their sins by hunger. The grapes will rot and the walnuts will turn bad."*

THEN OUR LADY GAVE US A PROMISE OF HOPE!

*"If the people are converted, the rocks will become piles of wheat and it will be found that the potatoes have sown themselves."*

She turned to the children, *"Do you say your prayers well, my children?"*

Maximin avoided her eyes, looking down to the ground. The two of them answered, *"No Madam, hardly at all."*

She looked at them so lovingly, *"Ah my children, it is very important to do so, at night and in the morning. When you don't have time, at least say an 'Our Father' and a 'Hail Mary,'* "*but when you can, say more."*

Then She returned to the subject at hand:

*"Only a few old women go to Mass on Sunday in the summer; everybody else works every Sunday all summer long. In the winter, when they do not know what to do with themselves, they go to Mass only to make fun of religion. During Lent, they go to the butcher shop like dogs."* (This is referring to the lack of fasting and abstinence during Lent.)

She turned to them and repeated twice, *"Well, my children, you will make this known to all my people."*

When in La Salette, Our Lady spoke of the potato famine, She was referring to the *Great Potato Famine* that plagued Ireland in 1845, and had reached disaster proportions by 1846. She also predicted further famine, plagues and suffering for France. These were all predictions of things to come, which in fact did occur. Close to a million people died as a result of a wheat shortage in Europe. The grapes of France were destroyed by a pestilence. Children did indeed die in their mother's arms.

But it did not have to happen.  Our Lady gave them a way out: *"If the people are converted, the rocks will become piles of wheat and it will be found that the potatoes have sown themselves."*

Some did respond to Our Lady and returned to Church and the Mass.  Very possibly the chastisement would have been worse if those few had not heeded Our Lady's message and returned to the Mass and the Sacraments.

Our Lady has been warning Her children for centuries, prophesying what would come to pass, in the hope Her children would convert and be saved.  And all She foretold, did indeed come to pass.  Is She speaking to us, today?

†††

**Our Lady prophesies in Fatima**

One of the most powerful prophecies, made by Our Mother Mary, came to us in the Twentieth Century in the little hamlet of Fatima, an out-of-the-way farming village, nestled deeply in the heart of Portugal.  The recipients of the prophecies were very young to be receiving such symbolic prophecies which would have such an effect on the entire world, especially the world of the century in which the children lived.  Lucia, the oldest, was ten years old.  Francisco, her cousin, was just under 9  and Jacinta, her other cousin was barely 7 years old.  The Lord wanted the world to know that it was He, through Our Lady and the Angel of Peace-Michael, and no one else, who was giving this message to His  Children.

Let us focus on the actual words, the prophecies Our Lady made to Lucia, Francisco and Jacinta, **May 13, 1917.**

*"Will you offer yourselves to God, and bear all the sufferings which He sends you, in reparation for the sins which offend Him, and in supplication for the conversion of sinners?"*

*"Then* **you will have much to suffer***, but the grace of God will be your strength."*

*"Say the rosary every day, to bring peace to the world
and the end of the war."*

*"So many sinners are going to hell because no one prays
for them!"*

## July 13, 1917 - Lucia was given three secrets.

These secrets were to cause the children much pain and
suffering.

The **first secret** consisted of the children's vision of hell:

*"Our Lady showed us a great sea of fire which seemed to
be under the earth.  Plunged in this fire were demons and
souls in human form, like transparent burning embers, all
blackened or burnished bronze, floating about in the
conflagration,* [10] *now raised into the air by the flames that
issued from within themselves together with great clouds of
smoke, now falling back on every side like sparks in a huge
fire, without weight or equilibrium, and amid shrieks and
groans of pain and despair, which horrified us and made
us tremble with fear.  The demons could be distinguished
by their terrifying and repellent likeness to frightful and
unknown animals, all black and transparent.  This vision
lasted but an instant."* [11]

Our Lady trusted these little children with a vision of
hell, that would have frightened the strongest adults; Mary
seeing the little innocent souls, petrified, turned to Lucia:

*"You have seen hell where the souls of sinners go.  To
save them, God wishes to establish in the world devotion
to my Immaculate Heart.  If you do what I tell you, many
souls will be saved and there will be peace.  The war will
end,* **but if men do not cease to offend God, another
worse one will begin."**

The **second secret** predicted the Second World War
would be preceded by a sign, the world could not dispute:

---

[10]fire, blaze
[11]*"Fatima in Lucia's own Words"*, Third Memoir, the Vision of Hell

*"When you see a light lit by a strange unknown light, you will know that it is the sign that God gives you that He is going to punish the world for its crimes by means of war, hunger and the persecution of the Church and the Holy Father.  To prevent it, I shall come to ask for the consecration of Russia to My Immaculate Heart and the reparatory Communion of the first Saturdays.*

*"If my desires are fulfilled, Russia will be converted and there will be peace; if not, she will spread her errors throughout the world, causing wars and persecutions of the Church; the good will be martyred, and the Holy Father will have much to suffer, various nations will be annihilated.*

*"....But in the end, my Immaculate Heart will triumph!*

*"The Holy Father will consecrate Russia to me and she will be converted and the world will enjoy a period of peace.  In Portugal, the Dogma of Faith will always be conversed.  You must not tell this to anyone except Francisco."*

*"Come here every month and in October, I will perform a miracle so that everyone can believe."*

**July 13, 1917**, the three secrets were given to Lucia, but she was not allowed to tell anyone, at that time.  It was only after Francisco's death in 1919 and Jacinta's in 1920, that Lucia received permission from Heaven to reveal the first two secrets.  The night of evening of **January 25-26th, 1938** the second secret manifested itself as a sign resembling an *aurora borealis*, but scientists report that the possibility it was an aurora borealis, is most unlikely.  The characteristics of the sign could lead to no other conclusion than, it was miraculously sent from Heaven, as the signs were not indigenous of the known limits of the aurora borealis.

Lest any choose not to believe, this sign was seen throughout Europe, an aurora borealis does not cover so extensive an area.  The *phenomena* as they like to call it, was largely covered in the press, except in the United States where it was relegated to a small insert deeply hidden inside the newspaper. *Phenomena or miracle, all Our Lady said in the first two secrets has come to pass, and now we wait upon the fulfillment of the third secret, and ask, What then!*

On July 13th, 1917, Our Lady gave the children a third secret. Lucia was instructed to write it down and give it to the Pope. Our Lady directed it was to be kept sealed until 1960, at which time it was to be released to the whole world. We are told that Pope John XXIII read it, wept and put it back. We understand, each successive Pope has done the same, although this has never been confirmed.[12]

**October 13, 1917, Mary gave her final message to Lucia:**

*"People must amend their lives, ask pardon for their sins, and not offend Our Lord any more for He is already too greatly offended.'*

That having been said, Our Lady turned from the children, opened her hands at which rays shot out of them in the direction of the sun. The brilliant light emanating from her hand shot up into the sky. As if the clouds were the curtains of a great stage, they parted, revealing the brilliant sun. Lucia shouted *"Look at the sun!"* It turned from a blinding gold to a dull silver. It began to dance in the sky. It twirled uncertainly on its axis. Then it began to descend on the people. It grew bigger and bigger as it came down on them. Streaks of varied colors shot out like sparks from a wheel, covering the people, causing changes of color on their faces and clothes. Reds, yellows, blues, greens hurled down onto the little Cova.

*"It's the end of the world! Forgive me my sins!"*

There were reports of open confessions, shouted at the top of the lungs of the sinners. They thought the Lord was taking His final vengeance on them.

---

[12]Read chapter on Apostasy and the Antichrist

And then it stopped! A command was given from Heaven; the sun moved slowly back, up into the sky, to its proper place in the atmosphere, and at once turned from dull to brilliant. The pilgrims could not look directly into it again. A great hush took place on earth. None of the 70,000, who were there, were harmed; their clothes, soaking wet moments before, were completely dry. The mud which had caked them, was gone. They were clean. Then voices rang out, "*I can walk!!*" "*I can see!!*" The blind opened their eyes; the lame threw down their crutches; others went down on their knees in tears of reconciliation. Mass *miracles, cures and conversions* took place in a period of minutes.

*Oh, Lord that I might see!* Messages have been coming from Mother Mary, who as St. Louis Marie de Montfort said: "*Mary scarcely appeared in the first coming of Christ... But in the second coming of Jesus Christ, Mary must be known and openly revealed by the Holy Spirit so that Jesus may be known, loved and served through her.*"[13]

If you have been listening with your head and heart, you know that what you have been reading are warnings from Our Heavenly Family to convert, to pray and to sacrifice! We must change the course of events; too many lives depend on it! Let the killing stop! Let men and women of good faith rise up and pray for the conversion of the whole world. It is up to us! We are in the days where the forces of good and evil are at war, not men, but powers and principalities.

The Light of Christ must shine and cut through the darkness, so that man, seeing that Light at the end of the tunnel will be free, and being free will free his brother. Jesus loves you; Mother Mary loves you; all the Angels and Saints love you; and we love you! Take our hands; together, with Jesus and Mary in front, we can change the world.

---

[13]True Devotion to Mary #49 - taken from *Visionaries, Mystics and Stigmatists* by Bob and Penny Lord.

# What have you done with my Church?

We are fast approaching the Twenty-first Century. But we must admit, there are times we have difficulty remembering that, especially as we travel around the world and read the newspapers; we feel like we have been dreaming and suddenly have awakened in the Sixteenth Century.

We often wonder, if those who have been stripping our churches of all that points to the Divine and to the worship of the Father, Son and the Holy Spirit, those who have been gutting churches, removing Crucifixes, statues of Mother Mary, the Angels and the Saints, all to the pain and deep sorrow of parishioners, know that they are accomplishing what the Reformation failed to do and that is to destroy every vestige of what it means to be Roman Catholic!

In writing *Tragedy of the Reformation*, we came to understand much of what has been happening over the last four hundred years, the desperate attempts to lead us back into the ancient heresies of Arianism and the like. In the chapter on Henry VIII, you read that although Henry did all he could while he was still alive, to preserve the Catholic Faith, no sooner had he closed his eyes, than there was betrayal and the death of the Catholic Church in England.

Henry wrote a treatise, affirming the Church's Doctrines on the Sacraments and the everlasting Supremacy of the Papacy, which earned him the most treasured award from Pope Leo X - that of *Defender of the Faith*.[1] Henry, right up to his last breath, observed all the tenets of the Roman Catholic Church and insisted his entire Realm faithfully practice the Faith handed down by the Apostles.

---

[1] This treatise was a defense of Mother Church, in response to Martin Luther's 95 theses against Catholic teaching.

Above:

*Saint Peter's Basilica in Rome - During the time this Basilica was under construction, Henry VIII wrote to the Pope: "Luther had declared war not only against Your Holiness, but against your office - against the See and Rock established by God Himself."*

Below:

*Henry VIII's most trusted Archbishop Thomas Cranmer did away with Henry VIII's Six Articles of the Faith, and instituted his own ideas in the new book of Common Prayers and attacked the Sacrifice of the Mass*

Above:

*King Henry VIII Pope Leo X named him Defender of the Faith Later he was excommunicated for his refusal to obey the Pope and declared himself head of the Church in England.*

King Henry's death rang the death knell to all he had defended and treasured. As faithfulness is often rewarded by faithfulness, disobedience results in disobedience. All Henry fought to defend was soon done away with. Protestant preachers came in and taught Calvinism and Lutheranism. During his lifetime, even after he defected from the Catholic Church, King Henry would have put to death anyone in his kingdom advocating Lutheranism. Archbishop Cranmer, his once trusted Primate, soon did away with Henry's Six Articles of the Faith[2] and instituted his own ideas in the new *Book of Common Prayers*. Although the wholesale attack was on the Sacraments and everything Catholic, the most brutal was on the *Sacrifice* of the Mass, the new heretics calling it *idolatrous*.

They removed all mention in their new *services* of the priest as victim-priest; they had to do that, as they were about demeaning the *Sacrifice* of the Mass which is the ongoing *Sacrifice of the Cross* of the *Victim-Priest* Jesus Christ. When the second edition of the Book of Common Prayer was released, it did away with the last vestige of belief in the *Sacrifice of the Mass*; and belief in the Real Presence of Jesus, Body, Blood, Soul and Divinity in the Eucharist, became a crime punishable by death. Those bishops and priests who clung to the beliefs of the Catholic Faith were imprisoned, tortured and put to death, the soil of England, drenched with the blood of Martyrs who died for the Faith.[3]

---

[2]the Dogma of Transubstantiation,
Communion under one Specie,
Masses for the dead,
The Sacrament of Penance,
the taking of vows - such as poverty, chastity, and obedience,
and as is required of all religious - the vow of celibacy.
[3]Read Bob and Penny Lord's books: *Tragedy of the Reformation* and *Martyrs, They died for Christ*.

Altars of Sacrifice were removed from the sanctuary and then replaced by "*decent tables*" which were then situated in the midst of the congregation. The lesson, loud and clear was that this was *not a Sacrifice* but rather a community gathering with a symbolic remembrance of the Last Supper.

Does this sound familiar - with the alterations that are being made today, stripping, modernizing, and refashioning our beautiful churches into buildings resembling gymnasiums, and all in the name of complying to a code? But is there such a code, or has there ever been? Or are we in the days of England 500 years ago? Is Jesus asking, Who will choose Me this time, instead of Barabbas?[4]

Now let us leap forward to the end of the Twentieth Century and prayerfully have this travesty end before the Twenty-first Century!

For the past 30 years or as long as we can remember, we the laity have been grieving, as we have seen our churches defaced and demolished, and replaced by cold looking rectangular buildings which reflect more gymnasiums than Houses of God.

†††

A few years ago, we were in a large city in the midwest. We attended Mass at one of the renovated churches near the airport. The sight we saw as we approached this church was frightening. From the distance, the bell tower had been renovated into looking like the gun towers at the Concentration Camp in Auschwitz, right down to the color, mottled green. We couldn't believe our eyes, but as we entered the renovated church, a shot of fear ripped through us. The entire interior of the church was a replica of the death camp at Auschwitz, including bare walls and pipes painted again with that same mottled green color.

---

[4]These are excerpts from the chapter: *King Henry VIII* in *Tragedy of the Reformation* - by Bob and Penny Lord.

Apparently, there had been some resistance to the "*renovation*" because the chapel where the Blessed Sacrament was reserved, which was some distance from the main Altar, actually, outside the sanctuary altogether, had beautiful remnants of the old church which had been destroyed in order to make room for this monstrosity.

†††

Still they retained the name "*churches*." At first, we grieved, seeing the signs outside many Catholic churches change from "*Roman Catholic Church*" to "Catholic Church" to "*Catholic Community!*" But we must admit, with the removal of the Tabernacle and the Crucifix, the pews, as well as all the statues of Mother Mary, St. Joseph and countless Saints and Angels, they are right; except for the *Sacrifice of the Mass*, which is oft times not very intelligible, it could be a community building. But is this the ruling of the Church?

Doing research for this chapter, we read a revealing article,[5] which we now wish to share with you:

"In July, 1998, His Holiness Pope John Paul II issued *Apostolos Suos*, an apostolic letter regarding the *authority* and *limitations* of national bishop conferences. We have read that the bishops will discuss, later this year the revision of the controversial document issued in 1978, *Environment and Art in Catholic Worship* - a statement of the Bishop's Committee on the Liturgy,[6] which has served as a rationale for the destruction of hundreds, if not thousands, of traditionally designed and furnished Catholic Churches and for the design and construction of bizarre new churches.

"At a press conference, introducing the new apostolic letter, Joseph Cardinal Ratzinger stated that: "*an episcopal conference cannot be considered authoritative unless the*

---

[5]in the Wanderer, January 28th, 1999, by Michael S. Rose
[6]not the NCCB or National Catholic Conference of Bishops

*bishops adopt it unanimously in plenary session or receive prior approval from the Vatican.*"

"*Environment and Art in Catholic Worship* is one such document which has never been adopted, unanimously or by a majority vote, by the National Catholic Conference of Bishops."[7] *For a matter of fact, it has never been brought before the NCCB for approval by the bishops or received prior permission by the Vatican!*

According to the eminent canon law expert Msgr. Frederick Mc Manus the **Environment and Art in Catholic Worship's** "*statement is not, nor does it purport in any way, to be a law or a general decree of the bishops' conference, emanating from the NCCB's legislative power; neither is it a general decree of that body. It remains a provisional*[8] *opinion statement and has no authoritative nature.*"

There is no record of who really drafted this document, only that it has been accepted on face value as one approved by the bishops and the Vatican *(although neither is true)* and has been the architecture of pain for the faithful!

Where could this have possibly come from? We guess no one can ever answer that to anyone's satisfaction; but the book we are about to quote from and the intent of the author may give us a clue, without any other conflicting conjecture presenting itself.

Let us reflect on the following: In 1973, five years before all these architectural innovations began evolving, a Lutheran architect, Edward A. Sovik wrote a book: *Architecture for Worship*, where he expresses his motivation and desired results - his purpose to continue where the Reformation Protestants left off 400 years ago. *Ho horsey!!!!*

Sovik complained, in his book that the Protestant Reformation did not go far enough: "*the destruction of*

---

[7]NCCB
[8]a temporary decision awaiting further authorization

*images[9] and relics and the rearrangement of furniture in the existing buildings, and the sharp contrasts of form that appeared in some of the few new places of worship built in those times, did not effectively bring the minds of churchmen back into harmony with the minds of the early church."*

Time for a comment or two: **First** of all, if he really wants to go back to the Early Church, why does he ignore, as Luther before him, John 6:51-54 where Jesus says,

*"I am the living Bread of Life. Your fathers ate the manna in the desert and have died. This is the Bread that comes down from Heaven, so that if anyone eat of it he will not die. I am, the living Bread that has come down from Heaven. If anyone eat of this Bread he will live forever; and the Bread that I will give is My Flesh for the life of the world."*

The Jews on that account argued with one another, saying, "How can this man give us His flesh to eat?"

Jesus therefore said to them, *"Amen, amen I say to you, unless you eat the Flesh of the Son of Man, and drink His Blood, you shall not have life in you. He who eats My Flesh and drinks My Blood has life everlasting and I will raise him up on the last day."*

How does Sovik come to terms with Jesus' Words, as he sets about reducing them to mere symbolic hyperbole?[10]

**Secondly**, to go back to the Early Church, and discount all the Holy Spirit has done these two thousand years, all the Dogmas proclaimed by Ecumenical councils (which are irrefutable and final) is heresy! Now, we have no quarrel with him; he has his opinion and we have the whole Truth and Tradition, based on that Truth and Tradition which has survived 2000 years of heretical attacks such as his. It is with those who have followed his lead, *within* the Catholic

---

[9]this heresy is called Iconoclasm - for more on that, read Bob and Penny Lord's book: *Scandal of the Cross and Its Triumph, Heresies throughout the History of the Church.*

[10]overstatement

Church, with whom we have a quarrel. But since we know that Jesus is putting His House in order through our Holy Pope John Paul II, we no longer have a quarrel with anyone.

But let us continue, so that in part, although we grieve for what has been done, we can try to understand and now live with the hope it will be rectified. We love our Church and all she contains.

Edward A. Sovik wrote in his book: *Architecture for Worship* that neither Jesus nor the early Fathers of the Church desired a *"house of God."*

Now, that's strange; didn't Jesus throw out the money changers: *"Jesus entered the Temple area and drove out all those engaged in selling and buying there. He overturned the tables of the money changers and the seats of those selling doves. Is it not written:* **'My house shall be a house of prayer; but you are making it into a den of thieves!'"**[11]

The activities in the Temple were not called to be secular but connected with the Temple *worship*. When Jesus threw out the money changers and overturned the tables, He was insisting the Temple be used solely as *God's House of worship*, not for secular purposes. So, Jesus did honor and desire a *House of God*.

Although Sovik speaks of churches as being a *medieval invention*, we believe Holy Scripture contradicts, contests, confounds, and nullifies his point in the **New Testament**:

(1) Mary and Joseph brought Jesus to the **Temple**,

(2) Jesus was found preaching as a boy of 12 in the **Temple**,

(3) In *Revelation*, John spoke of the Seven **Churches** in Asia.

(4) Paul in Corinthians said women should be silent in the

> **churches**, *"But if they want to learn anything, they should ask their husbands at home. For it is improper for a woman to speak in the* **church**.*"*[12]

---

[11]Mt 21:12, Mk 11:15-18
[12]1Cor 14:34-35

(5) Paul spoke of the **churches** *of God* in Romans.

(6) Jesus spoke of "day after day" teaching in the **Temple** (which was the House of God)

(7) We hear of Peter and John going up to the **Temple**.

And many more...

To further confound his theory that churches were medieval inventions, we go to the **Old Testament:**

(1) In the Old Testament, we read of celebrations similar to the present rite (of the Catholic Church) of consecration of a **church** edifice.

(2) After the construction of the **Temple** of Jerusalem, Solomon gathered the Israelites together to witness the entrance of the Ark of the Covenant into the Holy of Holies.

(3) Likewise, when Judas Maccabee regained Jerusalem from the hands of Antiochus IV, he reinaugurated the *Temple worship* with solemn *sacrifice*.

On both occasions (1&2), the dedication of the *Temple* consisted not on a blessing or consecration, but rather in the celebration of **worship within the edifice.**[13]

Now to the History of the Catholic Churches and when the official dedication of churches began:

The first instance of the dedication of a Christian Church edifice was that recorded by Eusebius when he described the dedication of the Basilica of Tyre in **314 A.D.** The church was dedicated simply by the celebration of Mass, without any additional ceremonies. This lustration (or purification) signifies the expulsion of every evil power from the House of God, which is **set aside for worship only.**

In the **Sixth Century**, Pope Vigilius mentioned the placing of relics in the Altar, reminiscent of the practice of celebrating Mass on the tombs of the Martyrs. Now as the faithful congregated there to pray the Mass, right from the

---

[13]edifice refers to a building, or in this context - a Temple or House of God

beginning, when the Church was outlawed by the Roman Empire, you might rightfully say they were the *first churches*, even preceding the one of which Eusebius spoke.

According to Tradition, the Disciples first celebrated Mass in the Church of the Annunciation in Nazareth,[14] shortly after the Resurrection; a document verifies a religious building was built there, no later than the **Third Century**.

In addition there were certain caves that were venerated at even an earlier period. Graffiti with the words, *Holy Place* and *Hail Mary* show not only the continuous ongoing veneration which took place there, but also the Judeo-Christian character of those who traditionally frequented this early church, and that of the visitors.

The Cave of the Nativity was spoken of by Origen (who was ordained in the Holy Land in 231) and by St. Justine Martyr, who died in 155, dating the Cave before that period. When Origen spoke of the Church of Bethlehem, he referred to it as a **church edifice**.

The Basilicas of Bethlehem, and of Calvary were built in the **Byzantine** era. Queen Helena, Emperor Constantine's mother, constructed **churches** wherever there was evidence of Jesus when He walked on the earth. The Chapel of the Loaves and the Fishes at Tabgha are ancient, known to have been erected before the Byzantine period.

The Basilica of St. Mary Major, in Rome, the largest church in the world dedicated to Mother Mary, was built somewhere between **352 and 356**; and rebuilt in **434** A.D.

The Basilica of St. Paul outside the Walls, in Rome, was first built in **380** A.D.

We could go on and on, but there is neither time nor space; the names of churches in the East and the West,

---

[14]It is said - because of this, this is one of the most authenticated places where Jesus walked and lived.

constructed and dedicated before medieval times would fill a book in themselves. So much for the authority of an architect who would use poor information knowingly or unknowingly to deceive and destroy.

[You might be asking, at this point, why the words of this architect who is not even Catholic, are so important. But read on and you will see how they have influenced what has come to pass, across our country and throughout the world, to destroy our beautiful, traditional churches.]

Our architect says he is distressed because the churches built within the last 400 years, in some way still continue to look like *"holy places."* He boldly advocates what he (erroneously) calls the return to the days of the Early Church, to *a "non-church"* or a *"house of the people."* But as you can see through the small former history we have cited of the churches dating back to the Early Church, that this is not so; it is not a return to the Early Church but the realization of every heretic who has been condemned - the demise of the presence of the Divine in our midst.

His churches of utopia would be (and see if this does not sound familiar) *multi-purpose* buildings, *houses for people*, used for a variety of public and secular activities that nourish the human and secular life; and he spends his whole book outlining *how* this can be implemented. Importantly, he stresses **the structure should not be a church!**

He would have us mimic the early Methodists (who no longer do this, thank God), and use whatever convenient barns and lofts are available to get together. Sovik unequivocally states that the *"non-church"* should not be divided into a sanctuary and a nave. And rather than calling it a church, refer to the non-church, as a *"centrum."*[15] He then goes on to describe how this centrum is to be built, so that no one mistake it for a *"place of Worship:"*

---

[15]according to his description - a place for more than one purpose.

(1) Set up a separate room to reserve the "Eucharistic Species," if necessary at all.

(2) Remove any artwork which might be construed as strictly religious in context i.e. religious statues or icons.[16]

(3) Eliminate the traditional sanctuary by bringing the table (he will not call the table an Altar) into the congregation and arranging chairs around the "*table.*" [Sounds like the modern churches which are in the round - with the faithful facing each other, the community the focus, not the Eucharist and the Sacrifice of the Mass.]

(4) Take down the Crucifix and replace it with a plus sign which would only be used in processions and not as a focal point in the "*meeting place.*"

(5) Out with the pews; instead bring in portable chairs that can be removed, to make room for all kinds of activities both spiritual and secular - a meeting place for all religions and persuasions and diverse lifestyles! (*Excuse me, Is this politically correct* enough for homosexuals?) He definitely does not want anyone to mistake this for a church. [This reminds me of a Principal saying they do not have a Crucifix in a Catholic school because to have one, would offend non-Catholic students and their families. Oh, that sounds *politically correct.* The problem is no one has told these misguided educators the penalty for putting human respect before Divine respect.[17]]

He boldly states that since the *people* are really the *focus* of the liturgy, then any very strong architectural focus can subvert the attention of the people. Therefore *remove* the **Tabernacle**, the **Crucifix**, the **Cross** or the **Altar** as the focus in the liturgical service, which we refer to, as the Mass.

---

[16]shades of Iconoclasm - a heresy which was condemned by the Second Council of Nicea in the Eighth Century

[17]for more on that, read Bob and Penny Lord's best seller: *Heaven, Hell and Purgatory*

[Does this sound like priests, who are removing the Tabernacle, claiming it's a distraction during the Mass, taking away from the focus of what is happening on the Altar; but yet are placing the Altar over to the side, on the same level as the lectern, almost out of the church? Is that the reason, Father, or have you been influenced by someone influenced by this architect and his book?]

†††

We went to a *new Catholic Community*, which was once called a Catholic church in the Midwest. The Sanctuary was odd-shaped. They had gold and silver ribbons instead of the Crucifix of Our Lord Jesus. The Altar was a very little table, which would just about accommodate the chalice and ciborium. Instead of walls where you could put paintings or statues, there were stylish French doors, which gave a view of the great outdoors. But, and here's the big thing, to the left of the main Altar (table) there was an **organ!!** It was well over a million-dollar organ. Now, the Altar was on the same level as the congregation. But there were steps around and above the organ, so that the choir dressed in very Protestant-looking robes, actually *surrounded* the organ. *The focus of attention was plainly the organ, the center of worship, not* the Altar, or table which was just there, off to the side! The Blessed Sacrament was no where to be seen. Communion time, a group of Eucharistic Ministers left the assembly and came back some time later, laden with ciboria, filled with hosts. This is one of the few times in our lives when we asked the Lord for a *Spiritual Communion*. We just didn't believe there were Consecrated Hosts in those ciboria.

†††

*Back to Sovik, the Protestant*: Sovik would have us cease kneeling during the Consecration, and definitely while receiving Holy Communion, arguing it is supposed to be a *"celebration"* - it should be joyful, and kneeling is not a posture of joy, not a posture where people can commune.

[Does anyone dare ask what his meaning of commune is?] In both the Canon and the Catechism of the Catholic Church when you look up *Communion*, they refer you to the *Eucharist* - a Communion between you and your Lord - you and the Lord becoming One, or as St. Augustine said, the Lord consuming you.

We differ once again with Sovik with his comment that kneeling is not joyful. The Angels and Saints were joyful as they knelt (and some prostrated themselves) before their God. We believe that kneeling is a posture of adoration, adoration of Our Lord, Who as *Victim-Priest* has been offering Himself to the Father, through His priest who is the victim-priest, supplicating Himself on our behalf; and Sovik does not think this merits adoration? We in the secular world curtsey and bow to earthly royalty, but find it difficult to understand why we should genuflect and kneel before Our Lord, King of kings and of all that has been created in Heaven and on earth. Strange!

Another use of the word Communion is the *Communion of Saints*, which is the Church - *the Church Triumphant, the Church Militant and the Church Suffering.*[18] And the Catechism of the Catholic Church states*: "Since all the faithful form one body, the good of each is communicated to the others. We must therefore believe that there exists a* **communion** *of goods in the Church. But the most important is Christ, since He is the Head...Therefore the riches of Christ are communicated to all the members, through the* **Sacraments**.*"*[19]

Sovik says the *meeting place* would be a good place for cinema, and should make provisions for screens and/or walls where films, slides and filmstrips can be projected, a place where children can run around free. We have no problem

---

[18]*the Church Triumphant*-souls in Heaven, *the Church Militant*-souls on Earth, *and the Church Suffering*- souls in Purgatory.

[19]The Catechism of the Catholic Church #947

with all that in a hall, but the church is where we go before the Lord, to praise and give Him thanksgiving.

Sovik complains that although the Protestant reformers removed the Corpus off the Cross, they did not go *far* enough; by having a Cross, he argues the people are worshiping a means of torture, like that of a modern-day electric chair. Oh, we hope he is that ignorant of the Truth, to make such a weak argument; but we pray that no member of the Roman Catholic Church ever follows suit. We *need* to kneel before the Crucifix and *need* the Crucifix to hold a center place in our churches and consequently in our hearts. The Crucifix is the symbol of the price paid on Calvary; it is the ransom paid for our souls, the freedom purchased for us, from the shackles of sin we inherited from our first parents - Adam and Eve. On that Cross, the Gates of Heaven opened, so that along with Our Blessed Mother, the Angels and the Saints, we would know eternity with God Our Father, Jesus His Son and the Holy Spirit.

Why have we written of this travesty, this conspiracy to rob us of the Divine? So that you do not think you are crazy! You have been right all along! Now, through the prayers and faithfulness of the Communion of Saints, our churches will once again reflect God; they will be Houses of Worship where the faithful worship their Lord and Savior. When we enter this *House of God*, our eyes and hearts will focus on the Altar, its sacristy light burning, welcoming us, telling us Jesus is Home in His Church - waiting to love us, to listen to us, to talk to us in the Tabernacle. As our eyes glance at the no longer bare walls, we will reflect on Jesus' Passion, meditate on His Life so poignantly portrayed on each of the Stations of the Cross.

Back in a place of honor, at the foot of the Cross, adoring Her Son, we will once again pay honor to the Mother of God; we will reverently kneel before Her image and pray for Her intercession. Our churches will all be *holy places* where vocations will grow, holiness begetting holiness. The young and old will be changed by the knowledge that the Real Presence of their God, Jesus alive in the Tabernacle and on the Altar after the Consecration of the Mass, is there in their church. Rather than hard rock stars influencing our children's lives, we will have statues of Saints who put Jesus first and earned a place in Heaven - reassuring youth of that same place, if they will strive like the Saints before them to put God first and lead chaste lives.

When we wrote our book, *Tragedy of the Reformation*, we begged our readers to never allow this to happen again.

**We are in the best of times; we are in the worst of times.**

But we know we are involved, and as no generation before us, we can make a difference! *We will make a difference!* How? Take the Hands of Jesus and His Most Precious Mother, our Mother Mary and following our Pope, our Vicar on earth, our Rosaries in our hands and on our lips, there will be another victory for the Church as there was in Lepanto.

Do not despair! Be of stout heart! We, the Mystical Body of Christ will win the war! Our Church will survive and triumph, once again, because there are soldiers fighting in the trenches for the Mother they love - Mother Church.

*We love you!*

# World War II - Dress rehearsal for the Last Days?

Do you believe in coincidence? Or do you believe in Divine intervention? As we correlate important Feast Days of Jesus, Mother Mary, the Angels and the Saints and their relationship to the events of World War II, well you might say, Our Lord and the whole Heavenly Family of God do not cause war and havoc; and you would be right! But they sure are involved. We are not privileged to know the Mind of God--why He allows certain things to come to pass, why He sends certain signs and what they truly mean, why key moments in the history of the world coincide with those of the Church.

For example:

In the year 1941, the United States of America entered World War II on **December the 8th**, the *Feast Day of Our Lady's Immaculate Conception.*

In the year 1945, World War II ended in Europe and we celebrated V-E Day, on **May 8th**, the *Feast Day of the Apparition of St. Michael the Archangel in the Gargano* in Italy.[1]

In that same year, on **July 16th**, the *Feast of Our Lady of Mount Carmel,* the United States successfully tested the first Atom bomb in New Mexico.

The actual date of the Cease Fire which effectively ended World War II in Japan was **August 14, 1945**, *the eve of the Feast of the Assumption of Our Lady into Heaven.*

What does this all mean? There are facts we know and others we can ascertain, such as those above. What their *greater* meaning is for God to know, and for us to find out; and in so doing, lead us to the truth and a greater awareness of God's place in our lives. It depends *solely* on God. We

---

[1]more on this and the Angels in Bob and Penny Lord's book: *Heavenly Army of Angels*

can only speculate on the reasoning behind the correlation of certain key Feast Days with monumental events which took place during World War II. Is this God's way to let us know He was there by our side throughout the fray, and that He is here now, listening to us, never leaving us alone; we can go forward without fear, but instead with confidence, knowing that, as we had prayed for our loved ones who were defending their country, as we pray for our loved ones now, our Heavenly Family is always listening, for God is with us till the end of the world?

The greatest gift we can receive from knowledge of these events could be to give us confident assurance that God is *active* in every aspect of our lives, in the most insignificant and the most important, always *deeply involved* with the salvation of our souls and with our hearts.

We know that Our Lord has created us with Free will! Now, that is where the problem lies! As with all God's Gifts, we often misunderstand and abuse His Graces, His gifts, His bountiful generosity. God gave us Free Will to love Him freely with all our hearts, minds and soul. We, in our foolishness and pride have allowed the enemy of God to coerce us into believing that our Free Will was our right not to love and obey God, but to use God's gifts against Him. And you ask, *When did we use God's gifts against Him?* Whenever we used them against the least of His children, we did it to Him![2]

We have heard the cries of the wounded--physically and emotionally--victims of World War II. We have walked through the endless rows of graves of the victims, Allied and Nazis, of the Normandy Invasion in France, horrible remembrances, giving witness to man's inhumanity to man. We shook our heads and vowed this would never happen again. Never would the history of the world be tainted by

---

[2]*cf* Mt 25:40

such cold disregard of life! We walked through the different buildings in the death camps of Auschwitz and Birkenau, saw the children's toys, the little dolls, men and women's personal belongings, combs and brushes, razor kits, shoes and suitcases with names on them--hope unrealized. They told them they were going to another life. Sure, they had to leave all they, and their ancestors before them, had known, all they had built, all their friends and often family. There was the pain of separation; but there was the promise, and *that* they held onto--which turned out to be an abominable lie, the dream that still screams out, pleading, *This was not meant to be a nightmare!*

Survivors of the tragic holocaust, those who have suffered for over 50 years, an eternity remembering years lost and love unfulfilled, those who have just gone through the motions of living, trying to fill an empty void which refuses to be filled by any but those who were sacrificed on the altar of infamy of Satan's #1 helper--Hitler, cry out in rage, a rage they could not dare to demonstrate while it was all happening! Now, they want the whole world to know and share their grief! *They want retribution! They demand that someone pay for this!* And because nothing can ever repay them for the atrocity which has haunted them all their lives, they rant; they accuse, often mistakenly pointing fingers at those they judge did too little, too late--putting all Christians into a box, the way Hitler did. And so the hate goes on!

The anger was to hit home, prejudice breeding more hate and hostility! A young man visited our home, with the excuse he wanted us to sign a contract. When we playfully questioned him why he really was there, as we had done business with his company for many years without a contract, he shamefacedly replied he wanted to meet the woman who praised God every other sentence. I insisted, if I did, it was not a conscious thing. Everything was going well, when he noticed all the religious art in our home, the Crucifix, and the statue of Our Lady of Fatima. He began with the comment, he did not know Catholics worshiped Jesus.

Well, we got that straightened out, when he turned to a situation, which had been getting much undeserved coverage in the media, concerning a controversy between a few Jews from New York who had tried to jump the fence of the Carmelite Monastery outside the Death Camp of Auschwitz, and Polish gardeners working on the grounds who tried to keep them out. They had tried to explain that it was private property, a convent of cloistered Nuns and as such, men could not enter without permission from the Abbess. Sadly, misunderstanding heaped on mis-communication and an altercation ensued which naturally got into the papers. What the media, as usual, left out was that this monastery had been the warehouse that had housed Cyclone B, the deadly cyanide gas, used to kill not only millions of innocent victims who were Jews, but Catholics, Priests, Nuns, Professors and leaders of communities, any and all who Hitler considered enemies of the Third Reich![3]

For years, some separated brothers and sisters in Christ have confronted us, accusing our Church of varied and multiple abuses, prejudices, and injustices resulting from our Church's role in the *Inquisition*.[4] Knowing little Church History, we Catholics just hung our heads, wishing the earth would open up and swallow us, relieving us of the shame we supposedly shared but did not understand. But now there was a new form of attack--the issue of the monastery outside Auschwitz. Now, our Pope John Paul II who has been

---

[3]meaning Third Rule or Third Empire, Hitler fashioning Emperor of the new Holy Roman Empire, which was neither Holy or Roman, as it was Germany, under this title ruling most of Europe.

[4]Read more about the Inquisition in Bob and Penny Lord's: chapter on Teresa of Avila in *Saints and other Powerful Women in the Church*, and chapter on Ignatius Loyola in *Defenders of the Faith, Saints of the Counter-Reformation*.

unfairly accused of being prejudiced by a *few* Jews, in an attempt to bring peace and closure to an incendiary situation, ordered the Nuns to vacate the Monastery, they had so lovingly renovated, and move into another building!

The young man asked us what we thought about the entire mess. We replied, *"If you want to know how we feel about the Nuns obeying their Vicar, our Pope, this is in keeping with our Church and her teaching; we are called to obey, as Jesus and Mary before us, without question. But what is the problem with these Nuns having a memorial, a church where they would pray for those who had died as well as those who killed them, and offer acts of atonement in reparation for the sins committed in the concentration camps which cry out for justice and retribution from Heaven, itself."*

Their sister in community, Saint Edith Stein died at Auschwitz, *"as a Jewess and a Catholic Nun, for the Jews who were being persecuted and for the Nazis who were persecuting the Jewish people, saying if she did not pray and make retribution for the Nazis who will?"*[5] These Carmelite Nuns, were merely following in the tradition of their fellow Carmelite, *Saint Teresa Benedicta della Croce* (Edith Stein).

The young man, repeating what he had heard, the objections of a select few, concerning the controversial Monastery, said the Cross reminded the Jews of the Christians who killed millions of Jews in the Death Camp of Auschwitz. When we protested, *"No Christians killed Jews,"* and that he should know, being a Christian, that no follower of Christ, the Prince of Peace, could raise a hand against any of His beloved children, Jews, Moslems or Christians, and call himself a Christian, that Christ loved all His children, right to Calvary where He died for all, those who believe in

---

[5]for more on Saint Edith Stein, read Bob and Penny Lord's book: *Martyrs, They died for Christ.*

Him and those who do not. He was born and died so that *all* mankind would know life eternal with the Father.

We went on, "*Those who perpetrated these atrocities against God's children had chosen a false god, pledging allegiance to Hitler, their Heil Hitler replacing the reverence shown Jesus and Mary when they had formerly proclaimed as Christians, Heil Jesus and Heil Maria.*"[6] Denying their Lord, these poor deluded instruments of a madman no longer believed in the Lord, in Heaven or Hell. The father of Pride had talked them into believing they were a master race, and as such, they only owed allegiance to their new god--Hitler!

Not all Germans were Nazis; there were those who clung to their Faith behind locked doors, afraid to let their own children know they were praying the Rosary or reading the Bible, lest they turn them in, the penalty being internment in a concentration camp with the promise of death not far behind. Hitler made a new family; no more answering to parents, the children became the heads of the families. Parents began to fear their own children, who could turn them in at any moment for acceptance by the party! Is this not like Jesus' prophecy, "*...a son against his father, ...a daughter against her mother*"[7]

The young man, not finished, insisted, "How could Christians be a party to such inhumanity? How could they just stand by and do nothing as cattle cars roared past their homes carrying helpless men and women to torture and finally death? The Germans knew what was happening; and they let their neighbors be taken away to be killed."

"*Oh,*" we asked the young man, "*So then they shared in the guilt because they did nothing?*" He adamantly replied Yes! We then asked him, "*When he had last prayed before an abortion clinic for the express purpose to prevent the*

---

[6] Heil in German means Hail
[7] Lk 12:53

Left:
**Adolf Hitler**
**Leader of the Nazis and**
**the Third Reich**
**and Benito Mussolini**
**leader of the Fascists**

Below:
**Birkenau II - Auschwitz**
**The Death camp entrance**

Above: **Bob and Penny Lord at**
**remains of the white cottage, one**
**of the first gas chambers where**
**Edith Stein was martyred.**

Above: **Saint Teresa Blessed of the**
**Cross (Edith Stein)**
**She was martyred at Auschwitz at**
**the white cottage.**

*annihilation of millions of unborn babies, not by Nazi pagans but by licensed doctors who have taken the hippocratic oath to save and preserve life? How many times had he prayed that the accessories to the crimes, not soldiers in boots and helmets who had blindly obeyed their superiors, but duped mothers obeying inadvertently the prince of the abyss, would open their eyes and hearts and see that the unseen they were carrying were their children, flesh from their flesh, blood from their blood, inescapably one?"* We continued, *"Had he ever tried to counsel any of the women going into an abortion clinic, in an attempt to save the unborn lives being tortured and mercilessly killed in a different type of gas chamber, their mother's womb? In Auschwitz, mothers tried to hide their babies so that they might be spared; the monsters were enemies easily recognizable."*

We maintained that although the horror visited upon the victims of Nazism was one that is reprehensible, and possibly there was little likelihood for escape, unlike these babies being blown apart in their mother's wombs, they had legs to run with, a place to hide, maybe a slim chance to live, but a chance; the enemy was not one they trusted. Oh, when we have looked at sonograms of babies contentedly moving about inside their mothers, we want to cry out, *Will no one speak for those who cannot speak for themselves?*

The young man replied, "Oh, I don't get involved with that." Our reply was, *"Neither did the German people."*

When are we going to realize what is going on? The enemy of God hates the fact he cannot create, and consequently incites others to destroy God's precious creation. You have only to look about you, not far, but within the confines of your own family and you will not see two identical human beings.[8] How carefully God has fashioned with His own Hands each of His creation! How lovingly He has placed His Will and love in each of those He

---

[8]Except in the case of identical twins

entrusted to human parents on earth, on loan, with the privilege and purpose of caring for them, of sharing in the beautiful development of these *innocent* souls into beautiful *holy* souls which will be in time ready to return to the Heavenly Kingdom and dwell with Him and the whole Heavenly Family.

†††

We were children during World War II, and the only link, we had with the war raging in Europe and the Pacific Theater, was our loved ones--brothers and sisters, cousins and uncles, serving overseas in the Armed Services. I can still remember the fear that went through the family every time the door bell rang; we never knew when it would be a soldier telling us our brother had been killed in battle. I still remember my mother crying out, and my father's eyes welling up with tears he could not risk shedding lest my mother fall apart, when a soldier finally did come and advise us our brother had been wounded in action.

It was a war that tore apart families, separated because of loved ones overseas, and divided because of ties members of families had to citizens from countries with whom we were at war. I can remember my father arguing heatedly, and then finally not speaking to an uncle for many years, because he had made a remark lauding Hitler's plan to take over the United States.

†††

On the other side of the world, in Germany, it was a time of illusion and delusion, an insane time, with family people, simple, honest church-going men and women, buying into an infamy they would never be able to live down, turning their backs on their long-time neighbors and lifetime friends, looking the other way when they were rounded up like dangerous criminals and carted away, never to be seen again, because Hitler said they were Jews and Jews were inferior people who had to be relocated in a different place.

Men and women, fathers and mothers, not unlike those who were being singled out for deportation and death (with one exception--they were of the *master race* this maniac, Hitler was fashioning), stooped to a level below that of the animals, justifying inch by inch first prejudice, then violation of their neighbors' rights and finally the taking of lives; all in obedience to a higher force, a new god, a loud mouth renegade and insurrectionist who promised them the world!

The German people had been through the most devastating period in their history after their defeat in World War I. They were near starvation much of the time, eating their pets. Their life savings had been wiped out by the devaluation of the German mark. Hitler took them out of this. He pointed a finger at the Jews and blamed them for all the ills which the people had suffered. When he promised them a better life, they never considered, nor did they inquire *how* he would deliver that which he did not have; and when they realized the price was the persecution, the brutalization, and the inhumane annihilation of those who always considered themselves Germans like them, it was too late. The mad dog who had begun as their protector was out of control. They had bought into temporal reward at the price of their souls; and as the enemy of God had withheld the final outcome to Adam and Eve, his messenger of the Twentieth Century had not told the German people there was no way out of the hell he had planned for them.

We have been studying Hitler and the devastation of World War II, again, because we see so many parallels, today. Brother Joseph has been saying, since 1986, It's 1936, all over again. Little did we fully comprehend the full meaning of his words. We visited Birkenau[9] in 1994, and prayed at the spot where two young Religious were killed, in a little white cottage, one of the first gas chambers of

---

[9]A more advanced section of Auschwitz

destruction. We stood there, mourning the great loss the world will never fully realize, because such as Saint Edith Stein, her sister Rosa, and other innocents met their death, horribly and prematurely, at the hands of men who were no longer men but robots programmed by a monster. Meditating on the signs we see at the close of the Second Millennium, we recall the words of Sister Edith Stein, also known as *Saint Teresa Blessed by the Cross,*

*"When night comes and retrospect shows that everything is patchwork and much one had planned (is) left undone, when so many things rouse shame and regret, then take all as it is, lay it in God's Hands and offer it up to Him. In this way we will be able to rest in Him, actually to rest, and to begin the new day like a new life."*

The well-known publisher, Joseph Pulitzer[10] said, *"If I don't print it, it didn't happen."* In Nazi Germany during the time of Hitler, propaganda machines dictated the mood of the world. We once had the misfortune to meet some news cameramen from a well known major T.V. network. They said, proudly, "We wish the reporters would stay home. We determine the news by *what* we shoot and *how* we shoot it; the *angle* we choose, what we *include* and what we *exclude*." What they did not add was they delivered *their message* rather than the truth. More than 11 million innocent people died at the hand of one monster; and the world is just now discovering (because it is convenient?) genocide of greater numbers at the hands of another monster--Josef Stalin!

We must stop being sheep being led to slaughter. We are a more informed people today than our families during World War II. Let us stop apologizing to the generations coming after us. In this, the last decade of this century, we have had genocides that have reached into the billions

---

[10]Pulitzer was publisher of the New York World newspaper and creator of the Pulitzer Prize for excellence in Journalism.

surpassing those millions of the 1930's and 1940's, and as we end the century, we have another genocide in the Balkans, now called *ethnic cleansing*, which alone is approaching the level of the millions.

Let us begin today to listen to the Word of God, follow God's Law, God's plan for us and for our world.  God created a perfect world for us; our first parents fell victims to the first monster[11] who used propaganda to lead them astray; sin came into the world and has contaminated the world ever since.  The #1 monster[12] has commissioned his monsters[13] to roam the earth without sleeping, to seek the ruin of souls. He has positioned Antichrists in key positions, wolves dressed in sheep's clothing, to delude us and lead us to our damnation.  But God never sleeps, He is always with us, sending us messages and prophecies, to warn us, to give us another chance.

We read about the evil in the world.  We are disillusioned and are being conditioned to believe in no one and nothing.  That is not God's Will, but Satan weaving a web of destruction which can only lead to despair.  We have had alleged prophecies over the centuries, and the end did not come about at the time predicted.  We can choose to believe the prophecies were inaccurate, or we can believe that prayer moved the Heart of God to give us more time, so that we can lead others to *the Way, the Truth, and the Life Who is Jesus*, and eternal peace.  The world is accelerating at breakneck speed on a parallel course towards its final destination.  Heaven has always been God's plan for us; and hell always His enemy's goal.  It's not too late.  Whom and what do you choose?

---

[11]the serpent
[12]the devil
[13]the other fallen angels

# My Country tears of thee, sweet land of liberty; Of thee, I cry!

*My country tis of thee,*
*Sweet land of liberty;*
*Of thee I sing.*
*Land where our fathers died*
*Land of the pilgrims' pride*
*From every mountainside*
*Let freedom ring!*

When did we stop singing this love song to our country? It was so subtle; did it just sort of disappear with many of the other patriotic traditions that our country stood for? How many of us still remember this song, reminding us of the price paid by our fathers--the hopes and dreams of our ancestors, as they struggled in filthy disease-ridden holds of ships bringing them to a new land of promise and **freedom for all**? Writing about Mother Cabrini and the reason she came to our country, we became aware of the struggle, the crosses our families bore to give us a land of promise.

I can still see my father holding his hand over his heart, as he pledged allegiance to the flag and to the country it represented. He was so proud to be an American; his blue eyes filled with tears as his rich tenor voice rang out, singing the National Anthem. He did not take this country, he did not take the flag, for granted; he loved it all. During the Second World War, he died every day, waiting for his oldest son to come home from war, but never cursed the war that could have taken his beloved child from him. His son was fighting to keep this country *free!*

We ask how many remember *My Country tis of thee*; better yet, how many remember the words to our National Anthem, *The Star Spangled Banner?* Has this anthem, which is supposed to be a song of praise and devotion to our country, been reduced to merely a signal that a baseball game is about to begin?    Listen to the echo of voices, American voices, united for the last two hundred years--no longer Jew or Gentile, a people with a heritage and culture of their own, a melting pot no longer divided by barriers of race, color, or creed--a people under God!

   Listen to these words our ancestors proclaimed and the love they had for our country, as they sang our National Anthem and join in!

*"Oh say can you see by the dawn's early light*
*What so proudly we hailed at the twilight's last gleaming?*
*Whose broad stripes and bright stars through the perilous fight,*
*O'er the ramparts we watched were so gallantly streaming,*
*And the rocket's red glare,*
*The bombs bursting in air,*
*Gave proof through the night that our flag was still there.*
*Oh say, does that star spangled banner yet wave*
*O'er the land of the **free** and the home of the brave?*
*O thus be it ever, when **freeman** shall stand*
*Between their loved home and the war's desolation!*
*Blest with victory and peace, may the heav'n rescued land*
***Praise the Power** that hath made and preserved us a nation.*
*Then conquer we must,*
*When our cause it is just,*
*And this be our motto--**'In God is our trust.'***
*And the star-spangled banner in triumph shall wave*
*O'er the land of the **free** and the home of the **brave!**"*
*(emphasis in bold by author, solely)*

†

   The American Revolution was successful because we were a people under God!    The French and the Russian Revolutions failed because they were not.    They persecuted the Church and set themselves up as gods; and *they failed!*

   In *God* is our trust, not in promises made and broken by His creatures, but in *God!*    Have we forgotten we were founded under God and consecrated to the Immaculate Conception of Mary in 1846, by the First Council of Baltimore, declaring the Mother of God: "*Mary in her Immaculate Conception-Principal Patron of the United States?*"

**One nation under God...**

Do tears come to our eyes when our flag is raised and we say our Pledge of Allegiance? *Pledge of Allegiance!*

*I pledge allegiance to the flag of the United States of America,*
*and to the Republic for which it stands,*
*one nation under **God**, indivisible,*
*with liberty and justice for **all**.*

When we made our *Pledge* of Allegiance, we made an *oath* to our *flag* and to our *country*, a country founded under *God*; we made a *promise* to love and protect our country and flag. And many young men and women gave their lives because they believed in those words, and in the flag, and in the nation for which it stood. *Did they die in vain?* Have we so soon forgotten? We have always been a nation which could boast patriots! We were patriotic! We have always loved our country! What has happened to us?

Have we sold out our God for other gods? In the Old Testament, we hear Samuel complaining to God that the people are asking for a king. God told Samuel to give them what they wanted, for it was not Samuel they were rejecting but Him! God said they had been rejecting Him from the time He led them out of Egypt--they had deserted Him and served other gods. The Lord told Samuel to tell them they could have a king, but to be sure to advise them of the price they would have to pay.

"*...he (the King) will make them plow his land and harvest his harvest then make his weapons of war and gear for his chariots. He will also take your daughters as perfumers, cooks and bakers. He will take the best of your fields, of your* *vineyards and olive groves and give them to his officials. He will tithe your crops and vineyards to provide for his eunuchs and his officials. He will take the best of your manservants and maidservants, of your cattle and your donkeys, and make them work for him. He will tithe your flocks and you yourselves will become his slaves. When that day comes, you will cry out on account of the king you have chosen for yourselves, but on that day God will not answer you.*"[1]

The Jews got their king and all the Lord had promised them. Can't we learn by the mistakes of those who have preceded us, before it is too late?

### We want to cry, but instead we write

When we think of our lost innocence, our lost dream, we want to cry and never stop crying; instead we write! We have always believed in our country. Now, we feel like Rip Van Winkle, and we have awakened to find a strange warped world. At times we feel as if we are on a speeding train out of control, and we're crying out, "*Stop the train; we want to get off.*" And no one seems to hear us! We feel as if we are having a nightmare, with everyone around us walking in a daze and only a few are aware of the catastrophe that is brooding on the horizon.

Do we think for one moment that God is going to allow the abuse of His Son to continue? No sooner do they depict Our Lord Jesus as a sinner of one kind, having heterosexual relations in *The Last Temptation of Christ,* than they put on a play *Corpus Christi*[2] presenting the Sinless, Precious Son of God as a homosexual engaging in perverted acts with the Apostles. In all these incidents, they show God Who is Perfect committing mortal sins, breaking His own commandments. *And we do nothing!*

---

[1] 1Sm 8:10-18

[2] In Latin, this means the Body of Christ, what we as Catholics accept as the Lord Present among us in the Eucharist.

What do they have to do for us to speak up! We are told to ignore all they do and they will stop. They have not; they do not; they will not! All that has happened is they have succeeded in de-sensitizing us to blasphemy upon blasphemy against Our Lord, Our Heavenly Mother--the Mother of God, the Priesthood and the Church!

††††

On prime-time television recently, a comedy slipped in a crack about the Host. One of the characters in a sit-com, who plays a bartender, suggested they all go on a treasure hunt. When one of the female characters returned with an Elvis cookie jar she insisted she get points. The bartender said "*I plainly said a Communion wafer.*" She countered with this reasoning, "*You need a priest to have a Communion wafer; priests wear collars; dogs wear collars; 'You ain't nothin' but a hound dog;*'[3] *ergo an Elvis Presley cookie jar.*" The writers fully knew they were making a disparaging remark about the Eucharist, the Catholic Faith and the Priesthood, and they didn't care; *they knew we wouldn't do anything.* We buy their newspapers, frequent their theaters, watch their television programs, endorse their sponsors; and we must ask ourselves, if by so doing, if by our silent endorsement, do we not share in these sins which cry out to God for vengeance?

A vile act took place at Eastertime in 1999 in San Francisco. A gay group, calling itself "Sisters of Indulgence" applied for a city permit to cordon off a one-block area in a largely gay area of San Francisco on Easter Sunday in order to stage an event, in which they desecrate and ridicule every tradition of our Catholic Church, including the Eucharist, Mother Mary and religious orders, especially women's. These people, drag queens, dress as nuns, wearing outlandish habits, with exaggerated make-up and accessories, planned to have a "Hunky Jesus" contest as part

---

[3]a song Elvis Presley made famous

of their lunacy.   Naturally, Catholic groups, including the Archdiocese of San Francisco and the Catholic League for Religious and Civil Rights, campaigned against the city awarding the permit to the group.

In response to the Catholic League pleading with Christian organizations to boycott holding conventions in San Francisco, county supervisor, Mark Leno said, "*This boycott is ill-conceived and ill-fated, like the Southern Baptist boycott of Disney.  No Catholic rights are being violated.*"

†††

God the Father so loved us, He sacrificed His only Son for our salvation.  The Spotless Lamb of God, the Father's Beloved Son, Our Lord suffered, His last words pleading with His Father to have mercy on us, on those who rejected Him, those who spit upon Him, those who had stood by and said nothing as the crowd chose Barabbas over Him.  As I kneel before my Savior's bruised Body on the Crucifix before me, I find myself asking *How much Lord, How much will You take before You come again?*

I have always said I could forgive almost anything but the loss of my innocence.  I feel as if we have lost everything that made us a people set aside, a decent people whose ancestors came here to seek a better life and, yes, *religious freedom.*  A promise was made to the families who left the land of their birth and all they had ever known to come to this land of the free and the brave.  What has happened to all they treasured?  In a country founded under God, Our Lord is blasphemed, pictured as a deviate, a homosexual, the worst of sinners.  Our dear Mother Mary is maligned and held up to ridicule.  It is like we are being attacked by a barrage of rapid-fire artillery.  Nothing or no one is immune from outrageous, trash-filled, public demonstrations, especially if that *one* is Our Lord Jesus, His Mother, the Roman Catholic Church, and the Priesthood!

We were watching the Academy Awards and were particularly impressed with the reverence and honor given to the memory of those who were victims of the Holocaust. But as they were rightfully remembering and mourning the loss of innocent men, women and children, whose only crime was they were Jewish, did not their wounded hearts feel the wounds we have been suffering at *the hands* of these same movie makers, who continue to make blasphemous movies against Jesus, Our Lord and Savior? Are they not as reprehensible as those propaganda machines, which caused the death of so many Jews, as their propaganda breeds hate and division?

When are brothers and sisters going to stop killing one another? Do those who have money and power now, forget that another group had power and money and they were tried at Nuremberg for the atrocities suffered by the Jewish people? When Edith Stein, a Jewess who converted to Catholicism and became *Saint Teresa Benedicta della Croce*, and countless others were going to their deaths, she said *"One day this will have to be atoned for."* When the cattle car carrying them stopped at a station and the doors were opened, a man standing by asked Edith Stein if the others knew they were going to their deaths, she replied, *"It's better for them not to know."* But the time came when the whole world knew and cried.

Let the killing stop; let us stop hurting one another. Stop using the movie and television screen to subject innocent souls to every kind of degradation, perversion, profanity, violence, and brutality, every kind of vile form of behavior imaginable, desecration after desecration demonstrating the lowest regard of God and His Divinity and of man and his dignity as a child of God. The screen, which you dominate can be a vehicle leading to salvation and eternal life with God or a contrivance leading to condemnation and everlasting damnation in hell. The death of souls is as deadly, if not more so, than the death of bodies. Jesus said, "*...do not be afraid of those who kill the body but cannot kill the soul; rather be afraid of those who can destroy both soul and body in Gehenna* (hell)."[4]

He who does not know, is not accountable; but he who willingly leads innocent lambs astray, "*it would be better for him to have a great millstone hung around his neck and thrown into the sea.*"[5]

When one owner of a baseball team made some remarks, deemed offensive to Jews and Afro-Americans in 1993 and again in 1996, she was suspended. Following that, the Major League Baseball executive council required her to sell her team; and in addition take sensitivity training. Now in 1999, we have a situation with someone who has gone to the limit of any Christian's endurance and tolerance.

This founder of a large Cable News Network addressed the *National Family Planning and Reproductive Health Association,* peppering his remarks with insults and crude jokes about Pope John Paul II and the Ten Commandments--to the applause and laughter of the audience. He said: "*If you're going to have 10 rules, I don't know if adultery should be one of them.*" When asked what he would say to Pope John Paul II, he responded with an ethnic joke--"*Ever seen a Polish mine detector?*" and then he showed the audience his foot (according to Marilyn Keefe of the NFPRHA). He further suggested the Holy Father should "*get with it. Welcome to the Twentieth Century.*"

He also called for an international "*one-child*" policy. For his support of the United Nations Population Fund, last year, to the tune of donating $1 billion dollars to the UN for population control programs, this billionaire and his wife, were awarded the group's NFPRHA President Award.

---

[4]Mt 10:28
[5]Mt 18:6

On a roll, he went on, insisting, "*We could do it in a very humane way if everybody adopted a one-child policy for 100 years.*" *Have you visited China, lately, sir?*, we want to shout, where, because they are restricted by law to give birth to only *one child*, parents kill their new-born babies if they are girls, with the justification--they need a boy to help them when they grow old and can no longer work and care for themselves? And even with boys, they are only allowed one. *Is that your idea of a humane way, sir? Where would that put you and your wife, if you had been boy number two and her parents had been Chinese living in the present regime or in your New World Order?*

His crusade against Christianity began in 1990. While still owner[6] of a Major League baseball team, he called Christians "*losers*" and pro-lifers "*loonies.*" Having suffered no chastisement, not even a small reprimand, in 1999 he once again boldly attacked--only now he dares to openly wage "*politically and morally offensive comments about family life and adultery and other verbal insults on Christians.*"

To give you an insight into this man who dictates what comes into our homes via secular T.V., he said that while he was the father of five children, he had them before he was 30 years old, when he didn't know any better; adding, "*Once they were here, I couldn't shoot them.*" He said now he believes an ideal world population would be **2 billion**; it is **presently 5.9 billion**. Now that means the annihilation of two thirds of the world. The New York Times, in referring to the **Demographic Death of Europe**, wrote of Italy's **-0** population growth; saying that in twenty years for every child under the age of five, there will be 25 over the age of 50, and of these 10 will be older than 80.

---

[6]Now, he no longer owns the team; but as Vice Chairman of the parent Corporation, and as an officer of the baseball club, he still has a say in the team's activities.

The birth rate in Italy is .8 (less than 1) whereas in Palestine it is 8.8 per family. At this rate, it is fairly certain that with Italy cooperating with this systematic annihilation of its citizens, they will surely soon terminate themselves through birth control and abortion, and what a loss to the world that will be. It will be like all the birds in the world have stopped singing, as future Pavarottis and Carusos are no longer allowed to be born. How does that sound? Then who would sing for your television programs, Mr. Cable Network owner and who would watch? Or have you that planned, as well?

An editorial in the Cincinnati Enquirer on February 25th noted: "*We'd hate to believe .....[7] gets a free pass from the owners and the media because he is wealthy and powerful and generous to the right liberal causes--but that's how it looks from the stands.*"[8]

After having received objections from the Catholic League for Religious and Civil Rights, the man sent a letter to them, in which he said he "*regrets any offense his comments may have caused...and extends his heartfelt apologies.*" William Donohue, president of the Catholic League for Religious and Civil Rights said," *We certainly accept his apology and this brings closure to the incident.*" But he continued, "*What is disturbing to me is that reportedly, his comments were received with wild applause from the crowd. If he had said the same thing about Indians and blacks, I don't think that would have sat too well with the people there.*" And that my brothers and sisters is the problem!

If it was important to censure and remove one owner from a ball club because of prejudicial language, are we

---

[7]We have eliminated the man's name, because this is not about a man, but a problem! His name is not relevant; for sadly this is not an isolated case and nor a solitary attack.

[8]Thanks to the integrity and courage of the Wanderer who published this story in their March 18, 1999 newspaper.

unreasonable to wonder if there will be equal justice for all? And so, we need ask, *Since he was not reprimanded in 1990, will he be in 1999?* And to go farther, will others who blaspheme and ridicule, malign and spread untrue gossip and slander against Christ and all Christianity, be reprimanded or at least made to stop, affording the followers of Christ the same courtesy and respect shown to our Lord, which they demand for their people!

Jesus was sold out for 30 pieces of silver! How much will we take for the sell-out of Our Lord, our Heavenly Mother, our nation and the tiny unborn citizens of this nation founded under God? Who has the right to life? We're told the unborn do not have the right to live, because there is not enough to eat due to over-population, and yet farmers are being paid by the government to not grow crops, to keep the prices up.

Who is next? The going rate to kill unborn babies seems to be $1 billion dollars (based on the billion dollar donation we spoke of above). If we believe in the Incarnation of Jesus Christ, that life began the moment the Holy Spirit hovered over the Virgin Mother, then we know that at the moment of conception not only Jesus became Man and our redemption began (and this is why, we all ***bow*** when praying the Creed during the Mass, we say, "*By the power of the Holy Spirit He was born of the Virgin Mary and became Man),* but every baby is formed, as with Jesus, with all his or her genes at the moment of conception. And because of this--abortion is murder, murder of a human being with genes which already determine height, color of eyes, hair, skin and etc.! Therefore, if we believe in Jesus' words, *"Whatever you did for one of these least brothers of Mine, you did for Me,"*[9] then we have sold out Jesus again,

---

[9]Mt 25:40

nailed Him to the Cross, only this time in a mother's womb--and the price has gone up!

The prince of darkness has rounded up all the wealth in the world to fight Christ, His Vicar on earth--the Pope and all that we Christians and Jews hold dear, our Judeo-Christian religions, which promote life--not death. It would seem a hopeless situation; we appear outnumbered and outweighed. But we are not! We can make a difference! We, the little people, with our widow's mite[10] built and have supported our majestic, magnificent, glorious Catholic churches.[11] Now, we can dig down deep into the recesses of our hearts and ask ourselves what we can do to stop this holocaust.

Abortion is death of the helplessly entombed in the womb of their mothers, who, when they allow an abortionist to take this life, become a party to murder. We must pass this scientific, as well as theological truth, on to those who are ignorant of the full facts. Not to do so is criminal, and Auschwitz reenacted.

**Where does hate begin and when does it stop!**

Now I have issue with any form of prejudice. When I heard a certain candidate propose, as part of his campaign, sending all minorities to reservations, I asked those who were expressing the possibility that they might vote for him, because he was in agreement with many things close to their hearts, which reservation did they want to go to; for as I further explained: **Prejudice never is satisfied with one set of victims, but devours an entire world, before it is contained.**

We are told that we are to be tolerant and love all our children, to act charitably toward our homosexual brothers

---

[10]Mk 12:42

[11]As a child, growing up in a lower middle-class neighborhood, I saw the old and the poor putting $1.00 bills in the collection, 1/6th of the average weekly pay per household.

and sisters; and I have no problem with that. But to label those who are trying to live according to the Ten Commandments, those who are married and honoring their Sacrament of Matrimony or single people living a chaste and celibate life as abnormal, and *"those who frown on illicit sex, especially homosexual activities, are condemned as being neurotic and psychotic,"*[12] or a new term to harass and intimidate-*homophobic*,[13] brings images to mind of a *topsy-turvy world* where up is down and down is up, right is wrong, and wrong is right.

Sin is no longer preached from the Altar (in those churches which can still boast having an Altar). The Church and the country are catering to the likes and dislikes of the majority (according to what the manipulated Polls are saying--the *alleged* majority is saying); and yet we know that the majority walked away from Jesus, when He gave them the most important mandate--to eat His Body and drink His Blood; and the majority, coerced and manipulated, rejected Him, when Pilate asked the crowd, *Whom do you choose?* Instead, they selected an insurrectionist and murderer over the Spotless Lamb Who had born for them and would die for them.

A long time ago, I heard *"Silence is consent."* I have to qualify, and say *a long time ago*, because there is so much

---

[12]for more on this subject and New Age, read Bob and Penny Lord's book: *Scandal of the Cross and Its Triumph, Heresies throughout the History of the Church.*

[13]There is no reference to this in the dictionary, as yet. It is the rage of New Age and its proponents, as well as those pushing a homosexual agenda on heterosexual men and women. This movement contends that there is nothing wrong with homosexuality; rather it is the problem of those who are really repressing homosexual tendencies in themselves. The Catechism of the Catholic Church states: *Sacred Scripture presents homosexual acts as acts of grave depravity. They are contrary to the natural law. Under no circumstances can they be approved.* #2357

truth being bandied around as *politically incorrect*, and so much deceit applauded because it is *politically correct* and inoffensive, even if untrue.    But when we say nothing, allowing the manipulated, coerced crowd to determine what is right and wrong--using the strictly *humanistic*, totally warped *rationalism* of today, are we not, in essence, saying to the generations who will follow that we believe in sin?

**What have you done with my Lord,**
**                    with my country, my church, my world?**
I can still hear the booming voice of Archbishop Fulton J. Sheen, "*What have you done with my Lord?* I too cry out, but not only "*What have you done with my Lord?* but "*What have you done with my country, with my Church, with my world?* I feel as if someone has invaded our country, raped and pillaged our land, robbed us of all we have always held dear.  You have robbed us of our innocence; someone will have to atone for this.  Wake up!  Before it's too late-- repent!  All of us must face the Lord, whether we believe in Him or we worship false gods; and when that time comes, the invoice becomes due.

In the Name of God the Father, Jesus His Son and the Holy Spirit, the Paraclete, let us love one another.

Speak out!  Share this book with your family, your friends, neighbors, members of your parish.  What can we do?  We can change the world!  We better, before it changes us so, we no longer recognize ourselves.  We love you.  But more importantly, Jesus loves you so much He opened His arms on the Cross and gave up His Spirit that you might have life and life eternal.

# Requiem for the Age of Innocence

*"While the crowds pressed around Jesus, He began to speak to them in these words:*

*'This is an evil age. It seeks a sign. But no sign will be given it except the sign of Jonah. Just as Jonah was a sign to the Ninevites, so will the Son of Man be a sign for the present age. The queen of the south will rise at the judgment along with the men of this generation, and she will condemn them. She came from the farthest part of the world to listen to the wisdom of Solomon, but you have a greater than Solomon here. At the judgment, the citizens of Nineveh will rise along with the present generation, and they will condemn it. For at the preaching of Jonah they reformed, but you have a greater than Jonah here."*[1]

**How did it happen?** *How did we go from faith and fidelity to deception and betrayal?*

*"Those were the days, my friend; we thought they'd never end..."*[2] I still remember those days, *the good old days*, days filled with innocence, love and caring for one's family, friends and neighbors, days where children revered their parents and grandparents, where the family stuck together, days of trust, days of honor, days of patriotism. Yes, we thought they would never end.

My childhood was a simple one, a life filled with awe and wonder, where with other neighborhood children, we would take hours to determine which candies we should buy for the precious penny we had to spend. They were days of dressing up as Mommys and Daddys, the Mommy serving the Daddy make-believe tea and fresh bread my *Nana* had made.

In the heart of Brooklyn, what would be called a ghetto or barrio today, was a *neighborhood*, more like a small

---

[1]Lk 11:29-32
[2]Fiddler on the Roof

village, where everyone knew everyone else, with many aunts and uncles (some really only friends whom we respectfully called Aunt and Uncle). You were never alone; at least one mother or grandmother was hanging out the window, at any hour of the day or night, watching your every move and reporting any mischief you got into, to your parents. We felt safe! It was a world of innocence, with coal stoves and wood-burning stoves warming our bodies and cooking our food. I can still see the dust particles floating up to heaven on the rays of the sun; I can feel the warmth of the sun streaming into our kitchen on the third floor of the apartment house we lived in. I can still feel the warm tears flowing down my cheeks when we moved away from that neighborhood as I waved good-by to everyone and everything I had ever known, and to the Age of Innocence.

†††

*We believed in our country*! We placed our hand over our hearts when we pledged allegiance to the flag of the United States of America. Tears came to our eyes, and our voices choked up a little as we sang the National Anthem of our country. *We were Americans!* When it was time to vote, an electricity filled the air, an excitement, with Daddy explaining the electoral system to us, the importance of casting our vote, and the merits and shortcomings of the different candidates. We were all involved, even those of us who were too young to vote. At four years old, I campaigned clandestinely, while my mother was on duty as one of the inspectors at the Polling Place. Franklin D. Roosevelt badges covering every inch of my favorite red coat, I would find myself being lifted bodily and carted to the other side of the Polling signs, when I wandered too close to the Barber Shop where the voting took place.

Franklin D. Roosevelt was our hero! We would have done anything he asked of us, even die; and many of our loved ones did! It was a time of patriotism and pride--We

Left:
*Franklin Delano Roosevelt*
*President of the*
*United States of America*
*during World War II*

Right:
*Pearl Harbor*
*On December 7,*
*1941 the Japanese*
*attacked*
*Pearl Harbor,*
*Hawaii*
*and destroyed part*
*of our Pacific fleet.*
*This event caused*
*the United States to*
*enter into*
*World War II.*

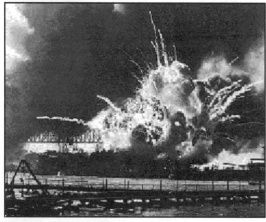

Left: *John Kennedy*
*President of the United*
*States - assassinated in*
*Dallas, Texas on*
*November 22, 1963*
*We were living in*
*Camelot, with a young*
*charismatic President,*
*and a princess occupying*
*the place of First Lady.*

were Americans!  Oh those were days of flags waving and
speeches on the street corners, everyone crowding around
the speakers or hanging out their windows to hear their
platform.  We believed in our country!  We believed we had
a personal interest in the destiny of our nation.  What we
said or did made a difference.  We were important; we
counted!

**When did my world start to fall apart?**

I grew up quickly when at ten years of age, we moved
out of the beloved neighborhood.  *My family moved uptown*
(socially), from an eight-family, four-level apartment house
into a four-family apartment house with only two levels in a
neighborhood of two-level houses.   The smells were
different; the familiar fragrance of Italian sauce cooking,
wafting through the halls into our apartment was missing.
The language was different.    No more Italian music
accompanied by amateur opera singers emanated from open
doors of the apartments across from us.  There *were* no open
doors; our new neighbors stayed to themselves.  They didn't
sing.   I missed the tinkling of banjos and accordions,
neighbors sitting on their stoops, singing along, sometimes to
the wee hours of the morning.  In my new neighborhood,
people sat on their stoops, to beat the sweltering heat of the
summer; but no singing rose to the heavens.   No sounds
filled the halls of our new four family house.  There were no
future Carusos or Lanzas, or Sinatras or Vic Damones.  The
laughing, crying sounds of a passionate people were absent.
I longed for even a tiny touch of the familiar.

There were no more Feast Day celebrations, with
people wearing huge aprons (to match their abundant size),
cooking sausages and peppers, hot chestnuts and other
Italian goodies, their push carts lining the streets.  No more
processions of statues of the Sacred Heart of Jesus, the
Blessed Mother, Saint Anthony or St. Lucy, or some other

important patron Saint being proudly carried high in the air on a litter by the men of our neighborhood, proud to be given the honor of being part of the honor guard.

My friends and cousins were still in the old neighborhood, and although they and my old haunts were just six blocks away, it was like a dream world, long ago and far away. And so I buried myself in practicing my piano and excelling in school. My birthday fell on a Tuesday in 1941. I was thirteen years old, finally a teen-ager. I felt as if I had shed my childhood, and was well on my way to adulthood. But I was not interested in boys. I vacillated between wanting to be a lawyer, defending the poor and downtrodden, or being a missionary in Africa.

Then the war broke out. December was extremely cold in 1941. We were planning for Christmas as best we could, considering we had not fully pulled ourselves out of the Depression financially. But we looked forward to giving some small gift to each member of the family, to show how much we loved one another. My family had the radio on that Monday, December 8, 1941. We had heard about the bombing of Pearl Harbor the day before. We turned the radio to the evening news, when we heard our President, Franklin D. Roosevelt declaring war on Japan. I'll never forget that speech he gave to us on that occasion. *"Yesterday, December 7, is a day which will live in infamy."* My big brother, along with many other fine young men immediately went down to the recruiting office on Tuesday morning and volunteered for service in the military!

Rationing was never really a problem for us; we had learned early to stretch what little we had. Coming out of the Depression, we made everything go a long way. Dainty suppers became the patriotic cry. We ate lots of bread to fill us up, and pasta prevailed. The war news got worse and worse, with the listing of those who had lost their lives for flag and country becoming longer and longer. We resumed going to processions, now supplicating the Lord through His Mother and all the Angels and Saints to bring our brother back home from the war in Europe.

They were hard days; but we survived, because we had a common cause which united us; we were no longer Italians and Jews, Germans and Irish, Blacks and Whites, Browns and Yellows; we were Americans. Rosie the Riveter became a badge of honor as our patriotic ladies donned dungarees (called jeans today) and mens' shirts, rolled up at the sleeve, put their hair in a net, and took up the slack in the defense plants, doing the jobs the men had done before they went overseas to fight the war to keep our homeland safe. Even our movie stars got into the battle. Clark Gable and Jimmy Stewart joined up; Bob Hope and Betty Grable entertained the troops overseas, and the Andrews Sisters became a household name. USO was a haven for our homesick boys, where the average guy and gal could do their part for the war effort to give our fighting boys a little taste of home while they were away from their own home towns.

The war finally came to an end; we were victorious as we knew we had to be; we had God on our side. Our loved ones began to come home; many came back wounded, some physically and some mentally; the common denominator was they were never to be the same. The war had taken its toll on them, and on us. We were proud, but we were tired.

The triumphant G.I.s returned to streets lined with cheering crowds and banners welcoming them. Our boys and girls were home. They had held back the enemy and saved our country and preserved our way of life. They were heroes. As our fighting men and women shared some of the horror stories of war, a little more of our innocence was taken away from us. President Roosevelt was our president; he was our leader! We recall the opening of his first Inaugural Speech: *"We have nothing to fear but fear itself."* Then he brought us through the Depression. In 1941, he brought us through our worst hour of darkness; we almost made him king of America. If he hadn't died in April of 1945, just before the end of the war, *we would have made him king.*

After the war, there were rumors that President Roosevelt knew about the sneak attack on Pearl Harbor a week before it happened, but no one believed any of that. We blamed the Navy for having all those ships so close to each other in port at Pearl Harbor, making them such an easy target for the Japanese. President Roosevelt would never have allowed our soldiers and sailors to be put in such jeopardy and die the way they did during that horrendous attack.

Then, in 1947, as the Cold War accelerated, we became aware of just what had been given away to the Russians at the Potsdam and Yalta conferences. Russia had been given *carte-blanche* in eastern Europe! They didn't declare war on Japan until the day *after* the Atomic bomb was dropped over Hiroshima, and yet they were given territories as a reward, for what? Certainly not for having participated in that war. Most of the spoils of war were given at the Yalta Conference, which dictated pretty much the terms of the Potsdam Conference;[3] the Soviet Union receiving a good chunk of China, as well as great parts of Europe.

By this time, Roosevelt was dead, but the decisions he made at Yalta lived on for decades. However, no one pointed a finger. We speculated that our Allies, mostly the USSR, did not act as ethically as we did. Josef Stalin took advantage of the fact that our President was on death's door and on heavy medication at the Yalta Conference (he died within two months on April 12, 1945) and Harry Truman was just no match for Stalin. The USSR broke the agreements they had made at the conferences. Our friend, the one we

---

[3]Look in back of chapter, for explanation.

were taught in school was our ally, became a dangerous enemy. And we let it happen! Feeling helpless and more than a little impotent, we resumed our lives; but somehow, we lost some of that strong feeling of patriotism.

Nevertheless, it didn't finish us off. The Korean War broke out, which many said was just political. What were we doing in southeast Asia, defending a country and a group of people we didn't even know? We had to look on a map to find out where Korea was. Many Americans felt we had no business being there. But we were still in the age of innocence, where we believed what our leaders told us. In the instance of Korea, they told us we had to defend the world against the spread of Communism, and so our boys were going to Korea to protect the American way of life. But there was an undercurrent of grumbling about minding our own business. Hadn't we adopted a policy of Isolationism somewhere along the line? But with transportation and communications growing in leaps and bounds, it was hard to stay out of another country's business.

In Korea, we would once again be introduced to *jungle warfare.* We had been exposed to it in Guadalcanal, Corregidor and Iwo Jima during World War II; many of our service men returning from that nightmare, having difficulty forgetting the horror of that war. We had been clobbered in the Pacific theater, because we had not been trained for jungle warfare and the total disregard for life shown by the enemy. But we thought the atom bomb put an end to all that. However, here our young men and women were in Korea, and again they were totally unequipped to fight that kind of heartless, inhumane war. What might have been an easy victory dragged on for three years, and ended in a cease-fire rather than a victory. We had had enough of that kind of war, and we just wanted to get out.

Our boys did not return this time to a ticker-tape parade, flags waving. It was as if they were an embarrassment, they did not come home with a victory. The boundary lines between North and South Korea remained virtually unchanged, despite those horrendous years of mortal combat.  It wasn't until some years later that we became aware, it had been a political action by major powers on both sides of the Iron Curtain, flexing their muscles at the expense of the Allied soldiers, most of whom were American, and the people of Korea, whose lives and lands were devastated.

**Where have all the young men gone?**

It was worse with the Vietnamese war which (they say) was not really a war.  Ask those mothers, sisters, wives and children of those who died, those missing in action till today, and those who came back as the living dead, if it was not a war.   There was no cheering for these young men and women of the armed forces, no ticker tape parades down Fifth Avenue in New York or Main Street, USA.  Instead, when they came back home, they were greeted by jeers and ugly signs condemning them, very often being held by draft-dodgers and flag-burners.

The propaganda machine in our own country accused, tried and convicted our boys of being merciless killers high on drugs; and we never asked if that was so, who trained them to kill, and why they were never allowed to put on a real battle, which would have ended in victory in short order. Their hands were tied by politics.  They were treated like the dogs who people had patriotically volunteered to serve in battle, who had to be put away after the battle was over, as they were no longer considered fit to return to society.  We need hang our heads in shame, the way our service men and women were treated by their fellow Americans.

*Is this what started the tragedy of brother against brother?* The spirit of a united nation was fragmented and divided; ignorance and fear filled the air, and we were on our way to chaos and unrest leading to more dissension, and dissension leading to more violence. A war began in our own country, in our streets. Kruschev's prophetic words, *"We will bury you without firing a single shot."* became a reality. The atheistic Communist party of the Soviet Union did not have to use guns to kill us; they infiltrated our schools, our seminaries, our very homes with their godlessness, first to destroy our minds, then our hearts and finally our souls.

## Carol them to Heaven or to Hell

When did the Culture of Death begin? When and how did the agenda to handle the *over population* crisis[4] start? It all began with catchy songs, whose meaning was lost on most of us. The heretic *Arius*[5] in the *Fourth Century* went about spreading errors and division by singing popular ballads, insidiously substituting his deadly message for the original lyrics, divorcing the unaware faithful from all they held dear. Likewise, harmless-looking young men of the *Twentieth Century* led first the young and then an entire generation to drugs and death. Their melodies catching on, parents not knowing that songs like *"Puff the Magic Dragon"* had to do with Marijuana, and *"Lucy in the Sky with Diamonds"* was about taking LSD, sang along with their young ones. We didn't know; no one trained the parents of the youth of America for this onslaught from the enemy in the form of drugs. These Twentieth Century balladiers' message spread, claiming the souls of many of America's finest, leading them from delusion, to despair, to death. And so we see the beginning of the systematic annihilation of a people, the people of the United States.

---

[4]the fallacy being promoted to justify the systematic killing of people

[5]For more on Arius and the other heresies that attacked the Church down through the centuries, read Bob and Penny Lord's book: *Scandal of the Cross and Its Triumph, Heresies throughout the History of the Church.*

**When did the clock stop!**

We were living in Camelot, with a young charismatic President and a princess occupying the place of First Lady. They were beautiful; their children precious--they made an admirable picture in which to mirror our lives. We were so happy, so filled with pride in our country and in our Church. Then one day, I can remember it still. I had an appointment, which I had been trying to get for months, with a buyer from one of New York's finest department store chains. I was browsing, sort of window shopping inside the lady's ready-to-wear department, not buying just looking, when I heard the words that would change our lives, and we would never be the same - "*President John F. Kennedy has been shot!*" The first thing I did was call Bob; he would know if it were true. I do not remember the conversation. All I can recall is getting on the Long Island Rail Road and riding home. The train was filled with people in shock, sleep-walking, staring, tears unashamedly spilling down their cheeks. The train went outside the tunnel, travelling on tracks above busy streets and hustling bodies below. But there was none of the hustle and bustle I was accustomed to. Nothing seemed real! Everything was gray, as if the sky had fallen down. I can't tell you how I got home. We closed down our plant. All I can see in the mirror of the past is the children home from school, and our whole family staring at the television set at home, as if that would make it all go away. We prayed; surely the doctors would come on the screen and say, a miracle had occurred and our President was going to make it. But that didn't happen!

Hours passed into days, and then we, like the millions of Americans beside us, watched a courageous little family--the mother Jacqueline, little daughter Caroline and brave little son-soldier *John-John* process in the streets of Washington, D.C. behind the President's horse, conspicuously poignant because his master was not riding him; even he appeared to be aware and sorrowfully carrying out his last duty to the President who gave us a new Camelot, a day of brave knights and ladies, an eloquence and elegance which died with him. Another picture, engraved on my heart, is the little boy, who weeks before had played with his Daddy on the lawn of the White House, and now was saluting his Daddy, as the horse-drawn carriage was passing by, flanked by an honor guard of soldiers.   The little soldier looked more like a little boy playing at being grown-up, rather than the horrifying truth--this little boy's father had been shot and now was dead.

**Was that when we began to slide toward hell?**

On television, we saw the President of the United States gunned down like an animal.   A nation wept!   Staring in shock, our eyes, minds and hearts glued to the television, we all silently prayed it was a mistake.   We were having a nightmare, praying someone would wake us up.   Then we were treated to another first - *his assassin was murdered live on television*.   It was the beginning of the processing of numbing people against murder on TV.   Then the media, not satisfied we had lost Camelot, went about smearing his name with trash journalism--newspaper reporting at its lowest ebb or another word for ebb-*debasement*.   Had no one told them about the punishment for slander and calumny?   This is a sin against the Fifth Commandment - *Thou shalt not kill*.   For to kill one's reputation is to deal a mortal blow more deadly than that of any weapon forged of steel.   And the wound they dealt killed not only the reputation of John Kennedy, past President of the United States, it killed a nation.

Within one year of the death of President Kennedy, our world exploded.   The hippy generation began with the long hair, rampant use of drugs, the Beatles and other drug-oriented musical groups taking over our young people. Violence came into our living rooms via what has become a deadly medium, initially designed by God to bring His Word to the world, but taken over by the evil one and his cohort. The potential Pauls became instead Judases, selling our God for thirty pieces of silver once again. Children no longer children playing children's games, they turned to games promoted on television, games of violence and death. The answer to the growing problem? Put juveniles (sometimes as young as ten years old) into adult prisons housing hard-core criminals.

College and university campuses were no longer a dream but a nightmare, where either our young were killed by overdoses of drugs, or their souls soiled irreparably by the contagious disease of promiscuity. Nine year-old girls were being raped in the girls' rooms of our public schools. Ten year old boys were being murdered by other ten year olds. Pre-teens were bringing assault weapons to school to take out their fellow classmates and teachers for outrageous reasons, like not giving good marks on a report card. In the fifties, one of the greatest problems facing high school children was getting a date for the prom. In the nineties, it's teen-aged parents trying to juggle child care with school.

One of the first actions of the enemy of God, to bring about his victory, was to estrange the young from their natural family and their Heavenly Family. Knowing we need family, Satan methodically went about using the young against the young, the innocent following unwisely those who were embracing every kind of mind-bending cult as their new family.

**The plagues of deceit and deception filters into the Church.**

Vatican Council II was misinterpreted by some and misused by others. As a result a frenzy began to throw out everything that we had ever held dear. The Rosary was the first major devotion to be thrown out of some churches, the laity being told it was no longer necessary to pray the Rosary. Devotion to Mary was alright, but in small doses--

not too much devotion.  Priests were ripping Rosaries apart from the Altar, throwing them on the floor.  Statues were taken from their places of honor and thrown onto the garbage heap.  A whole new ministry was formed of laypeople mostly, going to churches, to rescue discarded statues and find homes for them.

The rank and file Catholics really didn't know what was going on with Vatican II.  It was in Rome; we were in the United States.  It was a conclave of bishops and cardinals.  It really had nothing to do with lay people.  So we just waited to see what was happening there in Rome.  So, when word came down that Mary was out, we let them throw Mother Mary out of the Church; and we did nothing.  But by taking the Mother of God out of the Church, the enemy of God struck at the heart of the family--the mother.  The Mother of God--out of sight and out of mind, soon our children were being told they had to get away from *Mommy*, their earthly mother, they had to cut the umbilical cord, the old Jewish mother syndrome became the accepted psycho-babble.

The focus of our Mass, the main worship service of our Faith belief, went from Sacrifice to celebration.  No longer did we *pray* the Sacrifice of the Mass;[6] we *celebrated* the Mass.  We were told that we could have the Resurrection without the Crucifixion; we could have Easter Sunday without Good Friday.  Eucharist became *thanksgiving* (which is only part of its meaning) and the faithful were no longer taught to worship their God, their Lord truly Present Body, Blood, Soul and Divinity in the Sacred Species.  The Body of Christ went from being the Body and Blood of our Savior to the Body of Christ being the people of God.

The Tabernacle was placed farther and farther from the center of the church and consequently farther and farther

---

[6]The Council of Trent describes the Mass as "*the continuation of the Sacrifice of the Cross.*"

from the center of the hearts of the faithful.  The Tabernacle was relegated from the center of the Altar, to the side of the Altar, to a separate room off the main Altar, to a broom closet somewhere in the church, to a room somewhere, anywhere where Jesus would not get in the way of what man was doing in the Church.  The enemy knowing that *out of sight, out of mind* would soon become *out of heart*, attendances decreased, as did vocations to the priesthood and the religious life.  They used this as a justification for *married* priests and *women* priests, after all there were not enough vocations coming from men.  No one was willing to pinpoint the reason *why* vocations fell off so drastically, after the changes had come about.

The Word of God was reclassified as merely stories, designed to bring about a point.  No two priests were preaching on the Gospel in the same way; some homilies were in communion with the Magisterium while others did not even remotely resemble the teachings of the Church.  The faithful scattered, first going to other parishes, then to other denominations, and then, finally lost, to none.

No one spoke of sin; and we wonder why there are so many murders.  Not knowing right from wrong, not hearing it from the altars of their churches, their parents confused--not knowing what to believe, children lost a respect for life, often killing other children and then their own families.

We must get down on our hands and knees, brothers and sisters, and pray for conversion, true conversion, major conversion.  We must ask Our dear Lord Jesus for a return of innocence.  Dear Lord, we want You to hold us in the palms of Your Hands.  We don't want a king, Jesus.  We don't want a new Church, a different Church, a modern Church; we want *You* and *Your* Church.  Come, Lord Jesus! Save us! ₁

~ ~ ~ ~ ~ ~ ~ ~ ~ ~ ~ ~ ~ ~ ~ ~ ~ ~ ~ ~ ~ ~ ~ ~ ~ ~ ~ ~

Footnote 3: *Potsdam Conference* - a meeting held near Berlin, from July 17th through August 2nd, included the heads of the major powers: the United States, the USSR (or Soviet Union), and the United Kingdom (Britain), which took place after V-E Day, on May 8th, the unconditional surrender of Germany in World War II. Roosevelt already dead, President Harry Truman represented the United States, Josef Stalin the USSR and first Winston Churchill and after him the new prime minister of Britain, Clement Richard Atlee.

The purpose of the conference was to implement the decisions already reached at the Yalta Conference, and that was principally, but not exclusively the division of Germany, splitting her between the four major powers, with the USSR getting the lion share. Once again a conference stripped Germany and the German people of everything - land, pride, and self-worth.

~ ~ ~ ~ ~ ~ ~ ~ ~ ~ ~ ~ ~ ~ ~ ~ ~ ~ ~ ~ ~ ~ ~ ~ ~ ~ ~ ~

# The Great Battle waged between the Powers of good and evil

## PROPHECIES LEADING UP TO WORLD WAR I

My brothers and sisters, this book is not only about *Prophecies and Promises*, but about how the citizens of the world have gone down to the depths, with outrages *beyond Sodom and Gomorrah*, and how Our Lord Jesus has been sending prophets to warn us, and powerful men and women to save us. In the following chapters, we want to not only chronicle our steady decline as a human race, but also trace the actions of our successors of Peter--our Popes, who, by prophesying, endeavored to protect us--the sheep entrusted to them. As the world has been on a crash-course leading us to hell, our Popes have been battling feverishly to prevent the enemy from winning the war.

Our Popes, especially those of the last hundred years, have been in the thick of the battle. They have not only had to fight the Satan of the secular world, but the Satan trying to infiltrate our Church to destroy it, and by destroying it, not only take over the world, but bring us down into the pits of hell. The Popes, we will be sharing with you in the following chapters, have been stalwart heroes, modern Davids battling Goliath, meeting Satan head-on to shield us from him and his wrath. These Popes are the unsung heroes of our Church and the world. They deserve to be honored! We will not only try to do that, but also endeavor to bring you their tireless efforts to steer the *Ship of the Church*, which read like high adventures.

†††

**"You are rock, and upon this rock I will build My Church."**[1]

Saying this, Jesus handed Peter the Keys to the Kingdom; and in so doing, the helm of the Ship of the

---

[1]Mt 16:16-18

Church to steer His children *Home* to Him and the Father. And for 2000 years, one Peter (Pope) after another, in unbroken succession, has passed on the Keys to the next Peter. Each Pope down through the history of the Church, no matter how weak or strong, filled with the Holy Spirit, led the Church toward Jesus and the Kingdom.

The most prophetic voices we have heard from the time of the Ascension of Jesus until the present day have been those of the successors of Peter, our Popes. It makes perfect sense for the Lord to use them to deliver prophetic statements to His Children. Did He not give them that mandate through our first Pope, St. Peter? Has the Holy Spirit not always protected the Popes from making any doctrines contrary to Church teachings on Faith and Morals? As you can be assured this is all true, come with us as we share some of the *Prophecies and Promises* given to us by Our Lord Jesus through His primary messengers, Our Popes.

In Part I of this series on the Popes and their Prophecies, we are going to walk through the different battles waged between those who love God and those who hate Him, battles fought and won in the last years of the Nineteenth Century which will ultimately affect the Twentieth Century.

In Part II, we will seek, through the tragedy of a Second World War, to understand what has been happening in the world and the Church, yesterday, today and could happen tomorrow.

In Part III, we begin to see the wholesale destruction, planned by Lucifer from the beginning of time, and his next move taking shape. As the enemy of God is a copy cat, without an original idea, we prayerfully will get some idea of the adversary (or adversaries) chosen to lead the innocent to annihilate[2] themselves, the unaware flying toward perdition and finally eternal damnation.

In Part IV, we come to today, and the brave and dauntless Defender of the Faith, our Pope John Paul II and his never-ending campaign to save not only the Church entrusted to him, but the world his Creator has made.

## The Nineteenth Century and the battle for souls.

Before we travel back to the beginning of the *Twentieth Century,* we must, of necessity travel back to the *Nineteenth Century.* If we look carefully at the signs, along our road to understanding, we see the pendulum swinging, as it always does in the Church, from the left to the right, from the right to the left and then finally settling in the middle, that narrow path to the Kingdom, of which Jesus spoke.

The Nineteenth Century was a century blessed by Pope after Pope fighting the apathy that had cropped up among the faithful - an aftermath of the French Revolution. Throughout the history of the Church, *many* Popes battled for souls, but as we have covered much of this in two of our previously written books,[3] we are concentrating on the following:

## Pope Leo XII (1823-1829)

Far from a politician, right from the beginning, Pope Leo XII went about spending his pontificate preserving the sound Catholic Doctrine passed down by his brother Popes for 1800 years. To safeguard the Faith and protect the faithful, he warned the Church to be wary of the *Protestant Bible Societies* who, with their heretical teachings, were leading many Catholics, ignorant of the Catholic Faith, away from the one True Church. To preserve the holiness of the souls in his care, and fight a war against the errors which

---

[2]from the Latin, meaning "To make nothing"
[3]*Scandal of the Cross and Its Triumph, Heresies throughout the History of the Church* and *Treasures of the Church, that which makes us Catholic*

Right:

*Pope Leo XIII - In his encyclical Annum Sacrum, he consecrated the entire world to the Sacred Heart of Jesus. Devoted to the Blessed Mother, he issued nine encyclicals with respect to the Mother of God, Mary Most Holy and the Rosary.*

Left:

*Pope Leo XII went about spending his pontificate preserving the sound Catholic doctrine passed down by his brother Popes for 1800 years. He warned the Church to be wary of Protestant Bible Societies who, with their heretical teachings, were leading many Catholics, away from the one True Church.*

Right:

*Pope Pius VIII continued seeking a solution to a two-fold problem - the lack of spirituality among the religious and the fact that it was trickling down to the laity.*

Left:

*Pope Pius IX would not betray the responsibility he had to his predecessors by conceding the Papal States; he had himself declared a prisoner of the Vatican and never left.*

threatened the Faith, he upheld the Index,[4] urging all his Bishops and Priests to encourage the Laity to abide by it.

His *own man*, true shepherd, his lambs always his priority, and seeing the need of renewal in the Church, he went about establishing communication between himself as the Pontiff and his children throughout the world.  Against the advice of others, he proclaimed a **Holy Year in 1825**, in which he opened his arms wide, reaching out to those who had wandered away, inviting them to return to the Faith.

Pope Leo XII tirelessly fought the indifference toward Jesus and His Church, brought about by the Enlightenment movement.   This movement catered to the egos of the *intelligentsia* who, having made great strides in *Physical* Science, forgot they were the creatures and God the Creator.  They failed to acknowledge *Who* gave them and the world all that is good, and apart from Him there could be no lasting good.  Just as he had done in the Garden of Eden, the enemy of God tricked them into believing they were rulers of their own fate and did not need God.  And so, using this deception, he caused those who could guide many to Heaven,   instead   lead   many   to   hell.    Scientific acknowledgements and discoveries were placed in the forefront, at the cost of the Divine and all that was spiritual and moral.  Dubbed the *Age of Reason*, the world went from centering on the Creator, to the created, turning their hearts and minds to *Naturalism*[5] and *Humanism*.[6]  *Sounds like today!*

The Enlightenment movement had its beginning in the Eighteenth Century.  There it would lay the foundation for *pantheism*, which in turn, no matter how many times it was condemned   by   Ecumenical   Councils,   would   keep resurfacing, like a fast-growing weed, bent on choking out good wheat.    Unable  to  permanently  wipe  out  this

---

[4]Look in back of chapter, for explanation.

[5]Look in back of chapter, for explanation.

[6]Look in back of chapter, for explanation.

pestilence, *pantheism* would again and again covertly crop up in the ensuing centuries, appearing finally in the Twentieth Century sporting a new name: *New Age*.[7]

Aware of the pending, ominous threat to Christianity, Pope Leo XII condemned *Freemasonry*,[8] and along with other Popes, forbid Catholics to join Masonic Lodges, under the penalty of excommunication. Because he favored God, and honoring Jesus' mandate to His first Apostles, over being accepted and well-liked by many of his priests and bishops, the Pope's efforts were blocked by those *within* the hierarchy of the Church, who did not agree with his orthodox approach to guiding the ship of the Church to shore; and so like Jesus before him, he died rejected and unloved by his closest.

## Pope Pius VIII (1829-1830)

Pius VIII ascended the chair of Peter on September 28, 1829. Following in the tradition of his mentor Pius VII (from whom he took his name), and adopting the work begun by his predecessor Leo XII, Pope Pius VIII continued seeking a solution to a two-fold problem--the lack of spirituality among the religious and the fact it was trickling down to the laity. In so doing, he came out strongly, addressing the indifference prevalent among the hierarchy towards Church Dogma. He went about industriously seeking an antidote to the world's unrelenting attacks on the sacredness of Marriage. Because Prussia with its Lutheranism, had gained control of the Rhineland, which had always been a stronghold of Catholicism in Germany, the problem of mixed marriages began surfacing. Pope Pius VIII agreed, the

---

[7]To learn about New Age and other heresies, read *Scandal of the Cross and Its Triumph, Heresies throughout the History of the Church*.

[8]Because of their secret oaths which include the overthrow of the Catholic Church, 8 Popes in 17 different decrees and in different Ecumenical Councils have condemned Freemasonry.

Church would give its blessings on the union, if the couple promised to bring the children up Catholic.

As Leo XII before him had warned, *Freemasonry*, far from dead, was fast infiltrating the schools, spreading its philosophy and pervading influence among highly impressionable adolescents. The decline of morality among an impressionable younger generation was escalating so rapidly, Pope Pius VIII made this an important part of his pontificate. Recognizing, like Pope John Paul II, the importance of our youth, he went about combating this scourge on society and the Church, which could result in a full scale epidemic covering the earth! One short but powerful year and eight months after he had ascended the chair of Peter, Pope Pius VIII died.

### Pope Gregory XVI (1831-1846)

Gregory XVI succeeded Pope Pius VIII on February 2, 1831. Years before he ascended to the Papacy, the Lord was grooming his future Vicar. While still a monk, in 1799, during Pope Pius VI's imprisonment by the French revolutionists, Pope Gregory XVI published a paper upholding *Papal infallibility*, which elaborated on Christ's mandate to Peter, making the Holy See autonomous, and consequently not subject to the laws of the state.

Now as Pope, inheriting many of the same problems as his brother Vicar of Christ, he forged ahead with the same fire and determination to save the sheep and lambs entrusted to him, as his predecessor before him.

Convinced that *modernism*, the companion of *liberalism*, would lead to the infestation and ultimate deterioration of the foundation of the Church and her Dogmas, now as *Pope*, Gregory XVI fought the advancing *socialist* offensive to turn the Church into a *voting body of laity*. Although this may sound, at the outset, like an attempt to bring about a democratic approach to ruling the Church,[9] it's focus was really a devious ploy, a flagrant attempt to sanction the State's interference[10] in the matters of the Church. To combat this, the Pope rallied the hierarchy into a unified religious institution with Christ as the Head.

As part of his fifteen year pontificate, seeing the dire need of reform in existing orders, he not only brought that about, but was responsible for the founding of new orders.

Loyal son of Mary, seeing a growing need, Pope Gregory XVI advanced that which we have always believed from the very beginning - the Doctrine of the *Immaculate Conception of the Blessed Mother*. Although he did not declare it a Dogma of the Faith, his pontificate was noteworthy for having laid the foundation for Pope Pius IX to later declare the Dogma *infallible* in 1854.

Job faithfully done, Gregory XVI vacated the chair of St. Peter's and went to the place reserved for loyal sons and daughters; our brave Vicar left Mother Earth and embarked on his voyage to Heaven. Having accomplished all he could, through love for Jesus and Mary, and the Church which they had entrusted to him, loyal son and Pope - Gregory XVI passed the torch to his successor, and went *Home!*

## Pope Pius IX (1846-1878)

Pope Pius IX followed Pope Gregory XVI. He was at first looked upon as a liberal because as bishop, he had been sympathetic to setting up some reforms in the Papal States, and had been attentive to the faithful in his Diocese desiring the unification of Italy as a nation. So, it was with much celebration that he was greeted as the new Pope. The rejoicing soon quickly waned, when everyone became aware he was not sympathetic with their hopes, at the cost of the

---

[9]Look in back of chapter, for explanation.

[10]more about this and other Martyrs in *Martyrs, They died for Christ*, by Bob and Penny Lord

Papacy. Now Pope, with his holy hands on the *steering wheel* guiding the Ship of the Church, he had no recourse but to insist that the Papal States remain autonomous, in this way enabling the Holy See to continue being independent of outside temporal powers.

Conditions became increasingly worse; people took to the streets; there was hunger. Crowds began to congregate; tempers flared; someone had to be blamed; they killed the Pope's trusted aide Count Rossi, and it was decided it was best the Pope flee Rome. But as Jesus said to Peter, the Pope heard *Quo Vadis*,[11] and Pius IX returned to Rome. The new unified state of Italy offered the Pope certain concessions - he would be allowed to retain the buildings inside the Vatican State, but the rest of the Papal States would be absorbed into the new confederation. The Pope would not betray the responsibility he had to his predecessors by conceding; he declared himself a prisoner of the Vatican and never left.

The Bishops rallied around the Pope; they joined in his quest to establish a close working arrangement; and in so doing brought about the unity which Jesus had commanded of his first Apostles. This was important, as it dealt the final death blow to the heresies of *Gallicanism*[12] and *Josephism*,[13] which had gained new meaning with bishops, more or less, once again establishing National churches autonomous of the authority of the Papacy. Not only was his Pontificate famous for dispelling this heresy and bringing about the unity Jesus prayed for to the Father,[14] under Pope Pius IX's

---

[11]Wither goest thou, Peter?

[12]Look in back of chapter, for explanation.

[13]Look in back of chapter, for explanation.

[14]"*I pray not only for them, but also those who will believe in Me through their word, so that they may be one, as You Father are in Me and I in You, that they also may be in Us, that the world may believe You sent Me.*" John 17:20-21

influence, the world-wide missionary role of the Church expanded greatly.

But possibly he is most well-known for proclaiming on December 8, 1854, *The Dogma of The Immaculate Conception of the Blessed Mother*. Through this Dogma, the Pope irrevocably dispelled the deadly heresy of Pantheism, which erroneously taught man could be God.

Judging that the warped principles, resulting from the French Revolution, were leading to the destruction of traditional values in the social, moral, and religious order, Pope Pius IX issued a document condemning the most deadly errors *sadly* still prevalent in our times.

"Pope Pius IX came against major heresies which had found their way down to the rank and file, from as early as the Renaissance, then to the Age of Reason and the Age of Enlightenment. He wrote an Encyclical against them on December 8, 1864, on the tenth Anniversary of his Dogma of the Immaculate Conception. It was entitled *Quanta cura*, which means "With Great Care." With this document and the *Syllabus of Errors*, which became a part of it, Pope Pius IX systematically dealt with ten major categories of concern, either wreaking havoc on the Church or separating us:

1.    *Pantheism,[15] Naturalism,[16] Absolute Rationalism[17]*
2.    *Moderate Rationalism*
3.    *Indifferentism,[18] Latitudinarianism[19]*
4.    *Socialism, Communism, Secret Societies,[20] Bible Societies and Liberal-Clerical Societies*
5.    *The Church and Its Rights*
6.    *Civil Society and Its Relation to the Church*

---

[15]Look in back of chapter, for explanation.
[16]Look in back of chapter, for explanation.
[17]Look in back of chapter, for explanation.
[18]Look in back of chapter, for explanation.
[19]Look in back of chapter, for explanation.
[20]the Freemasons, for one

7.    *Natural and Christian Ethics*
8.    *Christian Marriage*
9.    *The Temporal Powers of the Pope*
10.   *Modern Liberalism*[21]

"Two days after he published this, he announced to the Cardinals in his Curia that there would be an Ecumenical Council; knowing that the only way this encyclical and its Syllabus of Errors would have the strength necessary to be enforced in the Church, would be through a Council.

"It's almost as if he could predict what was about to happen to the strength of the Church in its relationship with the secular world. In an effort to protect the Church against the eventuality of losing its lands and much of its temporal power, he added some things to the Encyclical dealing with the relationship between the Church and the secular government, emphasizing the Divine Foundation of the Church and its full independence from all secular authority."[22]

He convened Vatican Council I in 1870, where he proclaimed the *Dogma of the Infallibility of the Pope*, called *Pastor Aeternus*. At this Council, he also defined the doctrine, *Dei Filius*, **Son of God**, considered possibly the most important work of Pope Pius IX.

"*His issuing of Dei Filius, reaffirming the teachings of the Church, was a brilliant move by the Pope to slow down the tide of Modernism which had already found its way into the Church on a major scale. We believe this dear Pope was given discernment about the tide of blasphemy which would be precipitated by the rise of Secularism and the dreaded Modernism movement which Pope St. Pius X would come against and condemn at the beginning of the Twentieth Century.*"[23]

---

[21]Look in back of chapter, for explanation.
[22]*The Holy Spirit in the Councils* chapter, in *Treasures of the Church*
[23]excerpt from *Treasures of the Church* by Bob and Penny Lord

Something we discovered, when writing of St. Dominic Savio, was a desire most dear to the Pope's heart - the return of the separated brothers and sisters of the Church of England to the Roman Catholic Church.

"He (St. Dominic Savio) kept telling Don Bosco he wished he could speak to the Pope, before dying. When Don Bosco asked him what he wanted to tell the Pope, he replied, *'If I could speak to the Pope, I would tell him that in the midst of all his troubles he must not stop taking special care of England. God is preparing a great triumph for the Catholic Church there.'* When Don Bosco pressed him to tell him how he knew of this, Dominic begged Don Bosco to tell no one, so that they would not make fun of him. He said, he had a vision (he called it a distraction), one morning after Communion, when he was making his thanksgiving. He saw an enormous plain with people covered by a thick blanket of fog, confused, floundering, lost. When he inquired who they were, he was told this was England. Then Dominic saw Pope Pius IX, as he had seen him in pictures. He walked toward the people carrying a flaming torch. As he approached an area, the fog lifted, and in its place was a clear bright day filled with rays of sun, streaming down from Heaven. Then Dominic heard, *'This is the Catholic religion which must enlighten the English.'* When Don Bosco recounted this to Pope Pius IX, in 1858, he said that it just confirmed his desire to continue striving vigorously for England."[24]

The Good News is that more and more, our brothers and sisters in the Church of England, the Anglican Church and the Episcopalian Church are coming back to the Church of their ancestors--the Catholic Church, whole parishes converting along with their pastors.

But the bad news is that when Queen Elizabeth steps down, and Prince Charles, receives the crown as King of

---

[24]*Holy Innocence* by Bob and Penny Lord

England, it has been said, he will not carry on the over four hundred year old tradition, passed down by Henry VIII, that of assuming the title of *Defender of the Faith*; but will instead declare himself Defender *of faith*. Further breaking with tradition, he will not have the religious ceremony of all the monarchs before him, in Westminster Abbey, but instead will have an ecumenical service with all religions represented - Buddha, Islam, Hinduism, Confucianism and on and on. His further plans are for the Archbishop of Canterbury *not* to preside, proclaiming his desire for *one Church* in the world, encompassing *all* religions. Now, if that does not sound like ancient prophecy, I don't know what does.

Loved and respected by most, *"Pio Nino,"* as he was affectionately called, like all who speak the truth, had his enemies. The day his body was being processed from St. Peter's to *San Lorenzo fuori i Muri,*[25] anti-clerical Romans tried to hold up the funeral procession and throw his body into the Tiber river. Although stripped of temporal power, he left a legacy of renewed strength and a foundation of spirituality upon which the Church would continue to build.

**Pope Leo XIII (1878-1903)**

Pope Leo XIII succeeded Pope Pius IX in February, 1878. He continued the work instituted by his predecessor, promoting devotion to the Sacred Heart (begun by Pius IX). In his encyclical *Annum Sacrum*, Pope Leo XIII consecrated the entire world to the Sacred Heart of Jesus. Devoted to the Blessed Mother, he issued nine encyclicals with respect to devotion to the Mother of God, Mary Most Holy and the Rosary.

We believe that Pope Leo XIII was a prophet. Did he have an apparition of Jesus, in which He told him that the devil was to be loosed on the earth, and to consecrate the world to the safety of that burning furnace of Mercy and

---

[25]St. Lawrence outside the walls

Love - His Sacred Heart?  Did Jesus tell His Apostle--Leo XIII to turn His children over to His Mother for Her loving, compassionate intercession, that She might cover Her children with Her mantle?  Did the Pope, knowing the disaster that faced the world at this time and in the future years of the Church, direct his children to be strengthened by the Rosary, which is nothing less than the *Life of Jesus and Mary*?[26]

One thing we know; Pope Leo XIII had a vision of St. Michael driving Satan back into hell, whereupon he instituted the recital of the prayer to St. Michael the Archangel to be prayed at the foot of the Altar, at the end of Mass.

*"St. Michael the Archangel, defend us in battle, be our protection against the wickedness and snares of the devil. May God rebuke him, we humbly pray, and do thou O prince of the Heavenly host, by the Power of God, thrust into hell Satan and the other evil spirits who roam through the world seeking the ruin of souls."*

Striving to keep the priesthood holy and unblemished, free from the evil of secularism prevalent in the politics of the world, their hearts and minds focused on the Design of the Father, he banned the participation of the clergy in politics and the holding of office in the State.

He appointed the first Apostolic Delegate to the United States in 1892.  But when he saw the danger of a movement of *"Americanism,"* escalating among the clergy, in 1899 Pope Leo XIII condemned the movement, asserting strongly the universality of the one True Church.  Does this not sound precariously close to what is happening in the Church in the United States today, a movement of Americanism, called the *"Amchurch,"* the purpose being to create a Church in the United States compatible with, and conforming to, the

---

[26]Read Bob and Penny Lord's *The Rosary, the Life of Jesus and Mary*

culture and the needs of American Catholics?  This is a misnomer itself in that we are not American Catholics, but Catholics who are Americans, a part of the whole--the Universal--the One, Holy, Catholic and Apostolic Church-- the *Roman Catholic Church.*  It didn't work for Luther when he tried to make a German Church for Germans; instead of one Church for Germans he ended up with over "100 Popes," princes in different provinces custom-making their own religion to serve their own purposes.  Is this what some have planned for Americans in the United States?

As with our Pope John Paul II of the 20th Century, Pope Leo XIII desired the return of our separated brothers and sisters to the one true Church; so with this in mind he wrote *Praeclara* in 1894 and *Satis cognitum* in 1896, letters lovingly inviting our Orthodox and Protestant brethren to return home to the Church, which Jesus founded - the Roman Catholic Church.  Now although there was no mention of schisms or differences of the past, it was plain that the Church was not proposing, nor willing to accept a Federation of Churches.[27]  The Pope was not proposing unification, at the price of compromising the teachings of Jesus passed down through the centuries by the Apostles and those who followed.  He was extending a fatherly hand to his children to return to the Church of their ancestors and take their rightful place among the Mystical Body of Christ. The Pope even delved into the validity of Anglican orders; but the committee reporting there was no foundation, he had no choice but to invalidate them.  However he unceasingly prayed for the return of England to Mother Church.

As he was nearing his journey to the Father in Heaven, he set about putting his house in order, only the house was the Church Jesus had entrusted to him.  One of his first

---

[27]as exists among some Protestant denominations today

actions was to form a permanent Biblical commission. Possibly foreseeing the new attacks the enemy of God was preparing, to wound the Church, he issued comprehensive standards of censorship and a new Index.

Like Pope John Paul II, he was loved by people of all races, creeds and nationalities. His gentle, sensitive nature no more on earth, the world would grieve the death of Christ's Vicar on earth.

Our Pope has gone Home; long live the Pope! In keeping with our 2000 year tradition of unbroken succession, as our Pope Leo XIII was breathing his last, the Holy Spirit was choosing his successor. Our precious Pope Leo XIII went to the Father. God, the God of checks and balances saw His Church in crisis, and He raised up powerful Pope Pius X, who would be elevated to Sainthood by Mother Church for his faithfulness to his vocation, first as priest, then as bishop and then as Sweet Christ on Earth.

Read about Pope Saint Pius X in the following chapter.

~ ~ ~ ~ ~ ~ ~ ~ ~ ~ ~ ~ ~ ~ ~ ~ ~ ~ ~ ~ ~ ~ ~ ~ ~ ~ ~ ~ ~

Footnote 4: The Index goes as far back as the Fifth Century, when Pope Innocent I issued a listing of forbidden books, condemned because they were contrary to the teachings of the Church. This became, down through the centuries, a guide not only to protect the faithful from heretical teaching but to provide a guide of sound, suggested reading.

Footnote 5: philosophy mixed with heretical theology, which denies the Divine, and centers devotion on *nature*.

Footnote 6: Humanism denies God, making of man his own god. Vatican Council II stated: "*Unlike former days, the denial of God or of religion, or the abandonment of Them, is no longer an unusual occurrence.*"

Footnote 9: This is not the way Jesus structured His Church; Jesus gave the Keys of the Kingdom to Peter; and calling him Rock, Jesus declared

He would build His Church upon this Rock. As Jesus although God, obeyed His foster father while on earth, so He left us an *earthly father* to the Church, the Pope, to whom we owe obedience.

Footnote 12: *Gallicanism* "*...stated that a general assembly of bishops, acting independently of the Pope, had the highest power to determine doctrines and correct errors. It further alleged that this power did not belong to the Pope, nor to a genuine Ecumenical Council.*"

Footnote 13: *Josephism*, took its name from Emperor Joseph (1765-1790), who, under his mother-Maria Teresa's influence, using certain heresies from *Gallicanism* and *Erastianism*, declared the supremacy of the State in matters of the Faith, with the State's full autonomy over the decision-making of the Catholic Church, including the choosing of priests and prelates of the Church. In addition, adopting parts of another heresy - *Febronism*, he insisted the Pope's authority ruling the Church be limited. Using ambitious bishops, the Emperor made new dioceses, regulated how many Masses could be said, and closed Catholic schools, replacing them with state-controlled institutions. He took over the seminaries, in this way training future priests and bishops in his philosophy, rather than that of the Church. First, he took the control of the monasteries away from the Papacy, and then finally disbanded them, declaring prayer a waste of time and their life thoroughly useless.

Footnote 15; *Pantheism* negates a personal God; rather this heresy teaches that each of us is God, and God is a part of all things - in the birds and the bees, in the trees and beaches, the sea and the mountains. This is a serious heresy, in that we believe that God is the Creator and that He created all, not that He is a part of His creation.

Footnote 16: *Naturalism* denies the Supernatural and centers on nature, alone.

Footnote 17: *Absolute Rationalism* - is the heresy which states: reason is the *"ultimate judge of truth."* It denied revelation and insisted that man only believe that which can be proved by reason. It condemned Supernatural faith and allied itself to deism. *Freethinkers*, deists deny revelation, reject life after death, do not believe in God's providence and involvement in man's life. Closely allied with pantheism, (above) and materialism, it was condemned by the Holy See. Vatican Council II will later declare that there are *"two orders of knowledge"* which are distinct: faith and reason. - Catholic Encyclopedia, Broderick

Footnote 18: Followers of the heresy, *Indifferentism*, refused to worship God. Arising from a willful failure to recognize the duty of man in matters of religion, they turned away from traditional religious practices; they patterned this heresy after *Gnosticism* - the mistaken idea that *all religions* are relatively true.

Footnote 19: *Latitudinarianism*, Seventeenth Century heresy and its adherents refused to follow the doctrines, the rituals and the authority of the hierarchy of the Church, instead stressed *solely* a life of prayer, meditation, and living a godly life. All these aims are good in themselves; but as Doctor of the Church, Saint Teresa of Avila said she did not dare to pray without first reading a holy book, that is a book approved by the Church. This heresy was a throw-back to Luther and the Protestant Reformation, where they solely relied on an individual's interpretation of Holy Scripture - *Sola Scriptura*, rejecting sixteen Centuries of Traditions of the Church.

Footnote 21: *Modern Liberalism* stems from the Eighteenth Century period of Enlightenment and the French Revolution (which by the way was unsuccessful); it advocates relying on self, rather than on the intercession of Jesus to the Father. It uses *rationalistic* historical information rather than Holy Scripture and the authentic teaching of the Magisterium.

# The Church and the World
## suffer Atrocities

### THE BATTLES OF THE NINETEENTH CENTURY
### ACCELERATE IN THE TWENTIETH CENTURY

**Pope Pius X (1903-1914)**

Our new Pope raised his arms joyfully, and greeted the cheering Romanos, who had been awaiting the announcement in St. Peter's Square. The cheering would die down, however, when this new successor to Peter--true to his mission--began addressing the problems in the Church. Like Jesus before him, the more he was true to the Will of the Father, the less popular he would be and the harder his walk would become.

Sadly, there was an undercurrent of dissension seeping through the cracks, invading the Church. The world was on a course of madness: too much *good times*, a general rebellion would lead to the flapper days; prohibition a joke, men and women losing all sense of right and wrong; and sadly--as the world goes, so goes the Church. This sad truism is the direct opposite of God's Divine plan for this earth He created. As it is God Who shaped and formed the world, it is to *the Church*, which He founded, that the responsibility goes to influence the world He created, and not for His *creation* to influence His beloved instrument--the Roman Catholic Church.

We are at the daybreak of the Twentieth Century, the last century for this millennium, and we see our future Saint - Pope Pius X struggling to stem an insidious movement within the Church, *Modernism*, which threatened to destroy the very foundation upon which our Faith stands--the Magisterium, passed down through the centuries from His first Pope and His Apostles to the present time. In so doing, the enemy who never sleeps, planned to bring about his hell-

Left:
*Pope Benedict XV spoke out,
condemning the inhumanity of
man against his fellow man, but it
fell on deaf ears.*

Right:
*Pope Pius X was guided by the
Holy Spirit throughout his
pontificate. He promoted frequent
reception of the Eucharist, even
daily Communion.*

Below:
*Pope Pius XI
When he became Pope,
he took the standard,
"Christ's peace in
Christ's kingdom."*

Above:
*Pope Pius XII, well loved by
Catholic and non-Catholics,
conversed on matters of the Faith,
without exception or compromise.*

bent scheme--the total and complete downfall of the Church left to us by Jesus Christ.  Prophet that he was, Pope Saint Pius X could see Satan holding out the same poisonous apple from the Tree of Knowledge to these, his sons of the new century, duping them, turning the hearts of those who had pledged to serve Mother Church from allegiance to the Truth, to allegiance to themselves.  The father of Pride filled their heads and hearts with new/old lies which had long been exposed and dispelled overwhelmingly by Ecumenical Councils representing Mother Church.

This plague was infecting the priesthood and the bishopric.  Pope Pius X could foresee the fury of hell striking out at the Church, Lucifer leveling his final blow to crush her, using her very own priests and bishops as his weapons. In this way he would be triumphing over that God, Jesus, Who slighted him by becoming Man, choosing to be born of a human, a woman at that, whom he would be obliged to honor and revere as his Queen.  How would Lucifer hurt the Church which had flowed from the Heart of Jesus on the Cross?  Get Jesus' trusted sons, His priests and bishops, those pastors chosen to shepherd their flocks, to lead innocent, trusting sheep through the slaughter gate to their eternal demise!  The Pope could see he had to act decisively and quickly with a strong, sharp sword.

We believe that seeing the end of the story, where this heresy could lead to, Pope St. Pius X dispelled the Heresy of Modernism[1] in two clean, sharp thrusts of the sword, through the decree *Lambentabili* in July 1907 and the encyclical *Pascendi* on the Birthday of Mary, September 8, 1907, and in 1910 ordered an *Oath against Modernism* and a *Profession of Faith* be taken by those same persons mentioned in Canon

---

[1]for more about this heresy and all the heresies that have attacked Mother Church up to today, read Bob and Penny Lord's book: *Scandal of the Cross and Its Triumph, Heresies throughout the History of the Church*

833, today.[2]  It was not contained in the 1917 Code, but a decree of the Sacred Congregation of the Holy Office in **1918** declared that *"the prescriptions are not mentioned in the Code because they are of their nature temporary and transitory; but that, since the virus of Modernism has not ceased to spread, these prescriptions must remain in full force until the Holy See decrees otherwise."*

Seventy years later, they believed that the *"virus"* had run its course, and the observance of the *prescriptions* were discontinued.  In 1967, believing that the *"virus"* had been contained, the Sacred Congregation for the Doctrine of the Faith issued a short form for the Profession of the Faith, more a recitation of what one believes, rather than the taking of an oath.

Those of us who are living in these confusing, troubling times in the Church and in the world, can attest to the fact that the virus is not dead, but has been rapidly spreading like a cancerous growth  under new disguises and new labels. There are priests who *forget* to have the Faithful pray the Nicene Creed at Sunday Mass, insisting, *"If they (the faithful) did not believe, they would not be here."*  But how shall they know what they believe, and how shall they continue believing, if no one leads them in that belief, that oath, that Pledge of Allegiance to Mother Church?  If the faithful do not hear and consequently profess this Creed each Sunday, will this Creed, which was  authored at the Council of Nicaea as far back as 325 A.D., not soon be forgotten?

Now, as the Second Millennium is coming to a close, our present Pope John Paul II and Cardinal Ratzinger of the *Holy Office of the Congregation for the Doctrine of the Faith,*[3]

---

[2]For a full description of this Canon, see the last page of the chapter

[3]Originally called: *"The Sacred Congregation of the Roman and Universal Inquisition,"* it was established by Paul III on July 21, 1542, with the purpose of defending the Church against heresy.

in an attempt to save the souls of not only the faithful who are being led astray by false teachings; but of those who are guilty of leading them into error, have not only redefined this, but the Holy See has required of rectors and presidents of Catholic Universities they sign this profession.

When the new president of Catholic University, in Washington, D.C. was being sworn in, he insisted on taking the Oath, although it was greeted with much opposition from others at the University. He said, as the future president of the largest Catholic University in the United States, he wanted to be the first to obey the Pope and he prayed his example would be followed by others who call themselves and their schools Catholic.

We believe that Pope Pius X hoped, by dispelling the heresy of Modernism, he could prevent it from stemming into a fuller more deadly heresy. Our dear saintly Pope thought he had destroyed Modernism for all time. But what he attempted to deter, refused to be arrested by the Church's official condemnation of Modernism. Instead the dissidents retreated to the serpent's favorite hiding place; they went underground--waiting for the ice to thaw, to break through under a different name, a slick package appealing to man's need to be elite and superior, or as the demon promised Adam and Eve--to be God. Time would show that Modernism never went away; to the contrary, it reared its evil head very strongly after Vatican Council II.

---

Pope Pius X on June 29, 1908 changed the name to: the "*Sacred Congregation of the Holy Office.*"

Pope Paul VI, on December 7, 1965, redefined its authority and structure and gave the Office its present name.

Pope John Paul II, in 1988, giving the *Congregation* authority, declared: "*the proper function of the Congregation for the Doctrine of the Faith is to promote and safeguard the doctrine on faith and morals in the whole Catholic world; therefore it has competence in things that touch this matter in any way.*"

Pope St. Pius X was guided by the Holy Spirit throughout his pontificate. He went out of his way to promote frequent reception of the Eucharist, even daily Communion. At that time, there was a strong Jansenistic feeling of unworthiness to receive Our Lord. Pope Pius X insisted that it was for that reason in particular, that we are unworthy, that we should receive the Eucharist frequently.

He was read a letter that the Little Flower, St. Thérèse of Lisieux, wrote to her cousin Marie Guerin, in which she chided the latter about not receiving Our Lord Jesus in the Eucharist:

*"When the devil has succeeded in keeping a soul away from Holy Communion,* **he has gained all***...and Jesus weeps!.."*

*"...No, it is not possible that a heart 'that finds no rest save in the sight of the tabernacle' should offend Jesus enough to be unfit to receive Him. What offends Jesus, what wounds His heart, is want of trust."*[4]

Pope St. Pius X's reaction was, as noted in the footnote to this letter: *"This letter, with its accurate Eucharistic teaching, a teaching largely forgotten at the time when it was written, was to win the admiration of Pius X. 'Opportunismo! Opportunismo!' he cried out as the opening lines were read; then he exclaimed 'Oh! this is a great joy to me...we must make this process (her Canonization)* **quickly!***'"*

Pope Pius X also promoted First Holy Communion to be received by children. He saw the need for a strong laity, which he tried very much to advocate.

Miracles began occurring during Pope Pius X's life, and continued after his death on August 20, 1914. Well loved by all but a few, his incorrupt body lies in a side altar in St. Peter's Basilica. He was beatified in 1951, and canonized on May 29, 1954.

†††

---

[4]From Collected Letters of St. Thérèse of Lisieux Pg. 94

The calm before the storm; although everyone had confidence that between the Treaty of Paris in 1856 and the Hague Conferences in 1899 and 1907, and certain norms outlined limiting wide-spread war, that war among nations was truly limited, if not ended. Their focus--a lasting peace and equal justice for all, those in authority declared national military codes: non-combatant immunity, the rights of prisoners of war, the sick and the wounded, the general inviolability of private property, and the rights of neutrals. Sounds great, but man, subject to the weakness and sins of their first parents, violated these rights dreadfully on both sides.

Most wars are a farce! When World War I began, it was a patriotic call to arms! The Balkans were a fuming pot of division. The Archduke Francis Ferdinand, the Hapsburg heir apparent, was assassinated at Sarajevo, June 28, 1914, by a destructive force from Bosnia-Herzegovina which touched off World War I. This gave the heads of all countries involved, a motivation to summon their citizens to fight for God and country. In reality, it was nothing but a ruthless beginning of man's most technical means of blowing apart his fellow man.

†††

## Pope Benedict XV (1914-1922)

His being made Pope was a most interesting occurrence. He had only been made Cardinal by Pope Pius X three months before the saintly Pontiff died. But apparently, he was so well thought of by his fellow Cardinals, he was elected by the Cardinals of the universal Church to be the new Pope. However, the gift was not quite what he may have wished for. Far from inheriting a Church and a world enjoying peace, the new Pope, like his brother Vicars before him, would pay dearly, with his last ounce of blood for the Mother he had promised to love and serve--Mother Church. A war just brewing to spill over and spread, World War I erupted in June 1914, just two months after Pope Pius X had installed Bishop della Chiesa, as Cardinal of Bologna.

Now, three months later, he inherited dire times, as he stepped into the velvet slippers of the Papacy. As Bishop Della Chiesa, he had been well thought of by Pope Pius X for the way in which he dispensed his office. At one time, the future Saint Pius X called him *"his right arm against Modernism."* But it was his experience in the diplomatic corps of the Vatican, which his fellow Cardinals believed would be of the greatest value to most expediently serve the Church and the world. As Mother Church had lost all say in matters of the secular world, by decree of past monsters, she could only try to intervene, pleading on behalf of innocent victims, asking for amnesty for captives from occupied villages and prisoners of war.

Pope Benedict XV spoke out, condemning the inhumanity of man against his fellow man, but it fell on deaf ears. He tried to bring about reconciliation and pleaded for mercy on the vanquished, which in this case were the German people after World War I. He was purposely excluded from the *Versailles Treaty* and was allowed no vote in the peace settlements. They knew where he stood and they wanted no part of it. Their mood was one of revenge. They wanted the Germans to pay for what they had done. They wanted them to know beyond the shadow of a doubt what would happen if they ever tried to engage in another war of that kind.

The result was the total purging of a nation--Germany was brought to her knees, reducing the people to such poverty, they were left with either starving or eating their beloved pets. More than the raving of a lunatic, Adolf Hitler caused the annihilation of poor innocent men, women and children, the most inhumane slaughter of mankind up until the holocaust of Abortion.

The German people were without hope or promise; their children were now dying; their husbands and sons had either died in the war or were dying of starvation. They were stripped of all self-worth; they papered their walls with life savings of German Marks which had been devalued, worthless. As we have heard people testify, who lived in Germany at that time, there was no one who showed them a way out; no one came forward with an answer; no one seemed to care but one whom the world would come to call a madman; but to the German people he was a savior, their only hope. Were they justified in following Hitler? I no longer dare judge, lest we are judged someday. What will we say, when we are questioned? Will we insist, we knew no better? No, we know! Just as the German people knew.

But could it have been avoided? Maybe! Maybe if a man of Peace, Pope Benedict XV could have been allowed to be there representing Jesus and His children, pleading for mercy, things might have turned out differently. What we do today, future generations will have to pay for tomorrow.

Pope Benedict XV died in 1922 at age 67, two years after the Turks of Istanbul had erected a statue of him, extolling him as "*the Pope of the great tragedy....the benefactor of all people, irrespective of nationality or religion.*" It was a beautiful tribute to a man of peace, but we believe he never got over the personal defeat he felt at not being able to help his children in Germany after World War I.

†††

## Pope Pius XI (1922-1939)

When he became Pope, he took as his standard, "*Christ's peace in Christ's kingdom.*" He meant his reign to be one of bringing the Church into the world as a sign of hope and justice, actively participating in the everyday works and cares of mankind. Like Pope John Paul II, he recognized the strong part the young were called to play in the Church and the world; he formed youth groups.

174 *Beyond Sodom and Gomorrah*

To combat the rampant worldliness and secularism of the times, and possibly anticipating the devastating Depression and its aftermath, he instituted the *Feast of Christ the King*, on December 11, 1925; he declared 1925, 1929 and 1933 Jubilee years; and he called for Eucharistic Congresses to be held. He continued the campaign for better education of the Faith by the faithful; he further defined what a Christian marriage is called to be, as he formally condemned contraception.

Seeing in the world, a dire need of Role Models, Heroes and Heroines, he **canonized** *John Fisher* and *Thomas More*, both English martyrs dating back to the days of Henry VIII;[5] he canonized *John (Don) Bosco*, pied piper of lost children;[6] and *Thérèse of Lisieux*, Saint of the Little Way (and in 1998 made Doctor of the Church, by Pope John Paul II).[7] The list goes on: St. John Vianney; the little visionary of Lourdes, St. Bernadette Soubirous; and St. Robert Bellarmine. Knowing the pastors, who would feed his lambs, would need all the sound teachings of the Church they could get, he raised to the title, **Doctor of the Church**: *Albert the Great* (Albert Magnus)--teacher of St. Thomas Aquinas (another Doctor of the Church); *Peter Canisius*--Defender of the Faith in the Sixteenth Century; *John of the Cross*,[8] co-founder and co-reformer of the Discalced Carmelites; and *Robert Bellarmine*, Saint of the Counter-Reformation.[9]

---

[5]more about the English Martyrs and Henry VIII in Bob and Penny's book: *Martyrs, They died for Christ.*

[6]more about St. John Bosco and St. John Vianney in *Saints and other Powerful Men in the Church.*

[7]more about St. Thérèse and St. Bernadette in *Saints and other Powerful Women in the Church*

[8]more about St. John of the Cross in *Saints and other Powerful Men in the Church*

[9]more about Robert Bellarmine in *Defenders of the Faith, Saints of the Counter-Reformation* by Bob and Penny Lord

He was best known for his diplomatic encounter with Benito Mussolini--the Lateran Treaty, where it was agreed that the Vatican City would become an independent, neutral state.     But possibly not as well reported are his endless attempts to intercede on behalf of Christians suffering the worst tortures, with millions dying in death camps operated by the Soviet Union.     Seeing the tentacles of communism reaching out to choke all of Christianity into submission to an atheistic god, the Pope, like the English and many others, trusting that Adolf Hitler would live up to his word not to expand into neighboring countries, at first negotiated with Germany (for which he was severely criticized, as this led many, especially the German Catholics to believe Hitler).

But no one speaks of how, upon seeing the advancing cruelty and his oppression toward neighboring countries, the Pope sent more than 34 letters of protest to the Nazi government.     Perceiving the repeated violation of the agreement signed by Hitler, the Pope sent a letter to his dioceses throughout the world, branding Nazism--*anti-Christian* and ordering his priests to read his letter to the faithful from all the pulpits.     That resulted in added persecution of Christians.

Mussolini, once considered a hero of the Italian people because he was so benevolent initiating welfare programs,[10] giving the Italian people something for nothing, soon showed his colors.     After he teamed up with Hitler, he began to share his racist ideology, either expelling Jews from Italy, or leaving them to suffer inhumane treatment by the Nazis.

As well as standing up to Hitler and Mussolini, a Pope who never shirked his duty as Shepherd on earth of Jesus' lambs, nor shrunk from defending the Church, Pope Pius XI, in the early Twentieth Century, sent formal protests to the

---

[10]In the United States our Social Security System was fashioned after a welfare program instituted by Mussolini.

Mexican government, condemning the merciless slaughtering of priests, religious and any laity who were caught attending Catholic services or giving refuge to the religious. Pope Pius XI termed this period in Mexico as "*exceeding the most bloody persecutions of the Romans.*"[11]

Pope Pius XI was totally receptive to dialogue with the Anglican Church and other separated brethren; but although eager to unite the splinters of the Cross, he was not willing to compromise the beliefs of the Church; and so nothing happened. Evangelism--his focus and the education of his flock--primary, and knowing the danger of ignorance, Pope Pius XI was the first Pope to speak to the faithful through the then most modern means of communications, the radio; he installed the *Vatican City Radio Station!*

A sensitive, compassionate Pope, he strove to bring about peace and justice among not only Catholics but all God's children. Seeing the resultant danger of excessive nationalism which had compromised God and His Divine Laws for man and his false promises of glory on earth, Pope Pius XI spent his pontificate speaking out, warning the world of the many diverse enemies of Christ who would swallow up their souls.

We can't single out this dear Pope's Pontificate as being *the* most difficult one in modern times; because it becomes alarmingly clear as we research each of our Popes in this last century, they all had their own unique problems to overcome. The reason we put Pope Pius XI high on the list is that his was a pontificate which took place while the entire continent of Europe was in transition from monarchy or democracy to anarchy, totalitarianism or fascism. It was truly a godless time. The values of countries had completely changed. None of the social or religious ethics that anyone had known were being followed. It was obvious that Satan

---

[11]for more on this read *Martyrs, They died for Christ.*

was ruling the world, and this entire change took place during this pontificate.

Our dear Pope must have shaken his head in disbelief as the years unfolded, each one worse than the other. It never got better; it only got worse. Many truly believed the world was in the throes of destruction, and that these were indeed the last days. His job was extremely difficult, politically and spiritually. But he was truly guided by the Holy Spirit. By his words and his actions, he left an indelible mark on the Church he loved; and for this, he has been called one of the most gifted Popes of the Twentieth Century. He left us these words to meditate on: *"No one can be at the same time a sincere Catholic and a true socialist."*

## Pope Pius XII (1939-1958)

Pope Pius XII took the name of his predecessor, and with the name, inherited the crosses. This is a Pope who, we must say, has been unjustly maligned and dreadfully misunderstood. The sadness that trails closely behind tragedy is fault-finding and accusations. Anger will not contain itself; it cries out to God to be redeemed for its pain! Someone has to pay and often sadly it is not too important where the sword lands as long as retribution has been made, *an eye for an eye.*

Pope Pius XII was elected March 2, 1939 and he spent the next few months tirelessly trying to prevent the outbreak of war. The Pope suggested the four powers meet, Italy and France, to iron out their differences, and Germany and Poland theirs. Hitler knew better than anyone it was all futile, as he had made up his mind to conquer the world. The Pope continued to appeal to the four heads of state, to no avail. Then reaching out to the world, on August 24th he pleaded, *"Nothing is lost by peace; everything is lost by war."* But September came and with it the invasion of Poland by the Nazis. There was no more chance of peace than when he had first started speaking to all parties concerned.

The only one who did not believe that war was inevitable, the Pope kept trying to negotiate peace between the Allies and the Nazis. The Pope had a meeting with Ribbentrop, Hitler's foreign minister; but nothing was resolved, as Ribbentrop refused to discuss the war. He met with the King of Italy, Victor Emanuel III, and corresponded with Mussolini, to no avail. Italy entered the war, and the Pope pleaded for Rome to be considered an open city kept free of troops and attacks by air. It was said that *"Above all others, it was the Pope, who merely by staying in Rome forced the opposing armies to spare the city."*[12] The Pope was determined to remain in Rome and contrary to those who either do not know their history (I pray), or who purposely distort it, the Pope never left Rome.

All the Pope's pleading with the Axis powers[13] fell on deaf ears. They bombed relentlessly and it was fascist bombs which fell on the Vatican, March 1, 1943. As he could not prevent war, the Pope went about giving aid to the victims of war, opening the churches to all; but especially caring for the Jewish people--providing asylum, ransoming Vatican treasures to pay for the release of the Jews--over $4 million dollars. He came out strongly condemning the extermination of the Jewish people and was responsible for hiding and smuggling out of Italy thousands upon thousands of Jewish refugees.

Pope Pius XII's courageous actions inspired other Italians to risk their lives, to hide and provide for the needs of Jewish people who were running from the Nazis; the result being that although 67% of European Jews were killed, *85% of Italian Jews were unharmed!*

---

[12]Ernst von Weizäcker
[13]Italy and Germany and later Japan

There has always been a concerted effort by the media of the world to persecute and malign the Church, and in this case by maligning Pope Pius XII. This began with the purely vicious, slanderous, ridiculously fictitious play, *The Deputy*. This travesty depicted the Pope as being apathetically passive and blatantly detached and indifferent to the cruelties being waged by the Nazis. As if that was not enough, they painted him an intrinsically involved Nazi collaborator. Pope Pius XII was not only *not* indifferent to the plight of the European Jews, he wrote countless encyclicals *condemning* Hitler and the Nazis, and gave directives the encyclicals were to be distributed and read to the Church around the world; he was responsible for penning articles advising the world, in *L'Osservatore Romano* of the tragic plight of the European Jews.

Rather than remain safe and silent, as he has been accused, he spoke out uncompromisingly on Vatican Radio, condemning the Nazis and their racism, and Hitler's philosophy of the *Superior Race*. The Pope publicly risked his life, as he went about denouncing the rampant destruction of innocent people who were guilty solely because they were in Hitler's way, and condemned the total disregard the Nazis showed for borders--sweeping over Europe, taking what they willed and scorching the rest. Rather than a collaborator, Pope Pius XII was considered a dangerous *enemy* of Hitler.

To those who today, through a thoroughly biased media, eliminate the truth, act as judge and jury, print false accusations condemning the innocent, broadcast undocumented scandal to get higher ratings, manipulate the public with carefully orchestrated fabrication to satisfy their goals, and spread hate, I caution you to search your hearts and your consciences! Ask yourselves if you are not as guilty as the propaganda machine, which was as guilty as Hitler in bringing about the inhumane treatment of the Jewish people.

With your malicious attacks on one people--Catholics, you are breeding dangerous prejudice!  You are tearing down the loving understanding and brotherhood, built up over the last 50 years, since the end of that terrible holocaust which claimed so many lives.  Don't tell us to condemn a Pope (Pius XII) who should be proclaimed, and probably will be proclaimed, a Saint.  Do not demand we eliminate all of St. Paul's letters or parts of St. John's Gospel, calling them apostates breeding bigotry.  We who are Christians find it offensive and wounding.  Peace cannot come about and reign if we attack each other.

War is war; brutality is no less real if it is dealt in death camps or in the prison of an unborn baby's mother's womb. Pope Pius XII insisted that if the objectives of social reform and social policy are to be realized, then the social question must concentrate on preserving the *dignity, freedom, and eternal value of the human person* and consequently on the proper functioning  of the three indispensable divisions of social structure: the *family, private property*, and the *State*. The *individual and the family take precedence over the State*. The State cannot dispose of a guiltless individual's body and life,[14] or sacrifice his moral or physical integrity in the interest of the common good, or compel him to act contrary to the dictates of his conscience.  It is the purpose of society to serve the individual and not the contrary.

What has happened to the Catholic Christians of the world?  Read the above paragraph again and again and ask yourself what this holy Pope, descendant of St. Peter, is saying to us, today.  For it is no less crucial we read and obey this word, based on God's Divine Law which supersedes man's law.  Only God Who gives life can take life; and no one, not for any reason or justification can take what is not theirs, but God's.  We are only on loan, on this earth.  Our

---

[14]abortion, euthanasia, assisted suicide

babies, our children, our parents, our spouses, siblings are all on loan. The Provider, Who owns all, determines where and when one of His creation is to die.

The New York Times saluted Pope Pius XII for positioning himself *"squarely against Hitlerism."* They later wrote:

*"No Christmas sermon reaches a larger congregation than the message Pope Pius XII addresses to a war-torn world at this season. This Christmas more than any ever he is a lonely voice crying out of the silence of a continent. The pulpit hence he speaks is more than ever the rock on which the Church was founded, a tiny island lashed and surrounded by a sea of war."*

Time magazine wrote, about Pope Pius XII, during the height of World War II:

*"No matter what critics might say, it is scarcely deniable that the Church apostolic, through the encyclicals and other papal pronouncements, has been fighting totalitarianism more knowingly, devoutly, and authoritatively, and for a longer time, than any other organized power."*[15]

And, my brothers and sisters, *That's the truth!*

†††

Pope Pius XII, well loved by Catholic and non-Catholics, conversed on matters of the Faith, without exception or compromise. In 1950, millions pilgrimaged to Rome for the *Holy Year*, and then in 1954 for the special *Marian Year*. Thousands got to know the real Pope Pius XII, as they sat mesmerized listening to him speak so eloquently of the Faith, at general audiences. But at last this Pope, who was the first Pope to use *Radio* and *Television* to spread the

---

[15]Taken with permission from: The Wanderer Newspaper, St. Paul Minnesota--February 18, 1999

Gospel, had given all he had to give and a tired hero died, at last, peacefully at Castel Gandolfo.

Thank you, dear Pope for your daring and integrity, never compromising love, leaving us and all your fellow Popes to follow, an inheritance worthy of the Church. Pray for us and the world you fought to save, and the Church you so loved and defended.

~ ~ ~ ~ ~ ~ ~ ~ ~ ~ ~ ~ ~ ~ ~ ~ ~ ~ ~ ~ ~ ~ ~ ~ ~ ~ ~

Canon 833 reads--The following persons are obliged to make a profession of faith personally in accord with a formula approved by the Holy See:

(1)In the presence of its president or his delegate, *all persons who take part* with either a deliberative or consultative vote in an *Ecumenical or particular council*, in a *synod of bishops*, or in a *diocesan synod*; the *president* takes it in the presence of the council or synod;

(2)those promoted to the *cardinalatial* dignity (that is Cardinals) in accord with the statutes of the sacred college;

(3)in the presence of one delegated by the Apostolic See, *all persons promoted to the episcopacy* (Bishops) and those who are equivalent to a *diocesan bishop*;

(4)in the presence of the college of consulters, a *diocesan administrator*;

(5)in the presence of the diocesan bishop or his delegate, *vicar generals, episcopal vicars, and vicars judicial*;

(6)in the presence of the local ordinary or his delegate and at the beginning of their term of office, *pastors, the rector of a seminary, and the professors of theology and philosophy in seminaries; those to be promoted to the order of the diaconate;*

(7)in the presence of the grand chancellor or, in his absence, in the presence of the local ordinary, or in the presence of their delegates, *the rector of an ecclesiastical or Catholic University at the beginning of a rector's term of office;* in the presence of the rector, if the rector is a priest, or the local ordinary, or their delegates and at the beginning of their term of office, *teachers in any university* whatsoever *who teach disciplines which deal with faith or morals*;

(8)the *superiors* in clerical religious institutes and societies of apostolic life in accord with the norm of the constitutions.

~ ~ ~ ~ ~ ~ ~ ~ ~ ~ ~ ~ ~ ~ ~ ~ ~ ~ ~ ~ ~ ~ ~ ~ ~ ~ ~

# The Windows Flew Open and The Spirit entered

## AS THE WINDOWS FLEW WIDE OPEN, IN ADDITION TO A NEW PENTECOST, ANOTHER SPIRIT ENTERED THE CHURCH AND INTO THE WORLD

### Pope John XXIII (1958-1963)

When he was elected at the conclave of October 25-28, 1958, Pope John XXIII was thought to be a temporary Pope, one who would not make any waves; after all, he was seventy-seven, at the time. But this Pope was to have a powerful impact on the Church, positively and negatively (through no fault of his or the Ecumenical Council he convened), which would affect her till today; some misunderstanding would broadcast seeds which would sprout plants of dissent and division. This holy Pope opened the windows to the Holy Spirit, but sadly more than the Spirit entered the Church.

One day Penny was confessing to her confessor, "I wonder if it was worth it, the price the Church paid, with statues of Mother Mary, the Angels and the Saints being discarded, devotions being disregarded, altar rails removed, Tabernacles moved from the center of the Church until finally they were out of the Sanctuary altogether, and relegated to another part of the building." Her confessor said, "*It was there, before the commencement of Vatican Council II; we just didn't know it. When the Pope opened the windows, not only did the Holy Spirit enter, He revealed all that had been hidden. We have nothing to fear, but fear itself. The dark is that which threatens us. God the Revealer will always expose the evil that would destroy the souls of His beloved children - you and us.*"

Left:

*Pope John XXIII was elected at the conclave October 25-28, 1958, was thought to be a temporary Pope, one who would not make any waves, after all, he was seventy-seven at the time. But this Pope would have an impact on the Church that would effect her until today.*

Right:
*Pope John XXIII with Our Lady of Loreto*
*A photographer snapped a picture of the statue of Our Lady of Loreto in back of him, and She was smiling.*

Above:
*Interior of the Holy House of Loreto*
*The week before Pope John XXIII convened the Second Vatican Council, he went to Loreto and asked our Lady of Loreto to protect and guide the Council.*

Left:
*Pope Paul VI continued the goal of uniting all Christianity. He wrote the famous encyclical "Humane Vitae" on the evils of contraception and sexual permissiveness.*

What has come to pass and has been blamed on the Pope and the Council he convened, was not the will of Pope John XXIII, nor the intent of Vatican Council II. The week before he convened the Second Vatican Council, he went to Loreto and asked Our Lady of Loreto to protect and guide the Council. It was the Feast Day of St. Francis, October 4, 1962. Little did the smiling, jubilant people, who cheered their beloved Pope, know that within one year they would no longer have him with them, on earth. A photographer snapped a picture of our Pope with the statue of Our Lady of Loreto in back of him, and She was *smiling*! Never before or since, has anyone taken a picture of the cedar statue of Our Lady *smiling*. Was She smiling, knowing She would have Mother Church victorious, no matter what attacks and pains she would suffer because of misunderstandings and division over Vatican Council II? Was She smiling because She knew, with Vatican Council II, there would be an explosion of the Holy Spirit, and the laity would take their rightful place beside the priesthood and the religious, defending Mother Church, and the Church would bloom?

How was Vatican Council II interpreted to mean the removal of all statues from the churches?[1] How did Our Lady's magnificent statues get banished to private homes, if one was blessed to be able to rescue them before they were thrown on the garbage heap? Where did it say in the documents of Vatican Council II that the Rosary was not to be recited in church and it was acceptable for priests to crush rosaries underfoot? What directive in the documents said that the Crucifix was to be replaced, if you were so fortunate, by a plain cross? (I guess it was to make our Protestant brethren comfortable; but the funny, or sad thing, according to how you look at it, is our new converts from

---

[1]Removal of statues, crucifixes and etc. in the Church is a throw-back to the heresy of *Iconoclasm*, condemned in the Eighth Century.

Protestant backgrounds want everything Catholic, including Crucifixes and statues! ) Or how about another scenario-- replacing Our precious Lord and His price on the Cross with ribbons or pipes?

When did the *Sacrifice of the Mass* stop being the ongoing *Sacrifice of the Cross*[2] and become solely a celebration, an Easter without Good Friday, Salvation without the Cross? Certainly, that was not the objective of the Council!

There are those priests, as well as religious and laity who would reduce the priest's role to nothing; and yet, it is spelled out very clearly in *Canons on Holy Orders* given to us by not only the Council of Trent but Vatican Council II.[3] We quote from Vatican Council II:

*"Christ, whom the Father has sanctified and sent into the world, has through His apostles, made their successors, the bishops, partakers of His consecration and His Mission.*

*"They have legitimately handed on to different individuals in the Church various degrees of participation in this Ministry. Thus the divinely established ecclesiastical ministry is exercised on different levels by those who from antiquity have been called bishops, priests and deacons.*

*"Priests, although they do not possess the highest degree of the priesthood (bishop), and although they are dependent on the bishops in the exercise of their power, nevertheless they are united with the bishops in sacerdotal dignity.*

*"By the power of the Sacrament of (Holy) Orders,* **in the image of Christ the eternal High Priest,** *they are*

---

[2]One of the Dogmas proclaimed in The Ecumenical Council of Trent was that the Mass is the *ongoing* Sacrifice of the Cross. (*This is My Body, this is My Blood, Miracle of the Eucharist,* Book II)

[3]For more on the Councils, read *Treasures of the Church, that which makes us Catholics*--by Bob and Penny Lord

consecrated to preach the Gospel and shepherd the faithful and to celebrate divine worship, so that they are true priests of the New Testament."[4] *(bolded by author for emphasis)*

We have met priests who seemed embarrassed, when we remind them lovingly that they are *in persona Christi,* and yet we read not only in the Council of Trent but in Vatican Council II that they are **"in the image of Christ the eternal High Priest."**

At his coronation Mass, Pope John XXIII said he wanted, above all things, to shepherd his people; and that he did--his short five years as pontiff!  He went from parish to parish, as Bishop of Rome, celebrating Mass and hearing confessions for hours on end.  Imagine the delight, when without notice, parishioners saw that the main celebrant was Pope John XXIII.  A man of the people, born into humble circumstances, he was truly humble and loving toward all; possibly there were those who took advantage of this, right within the Vatican.  All we know, studying the Documents of Vatican council II is that somewhere, somehow, modernists surreptitiously took the words of Vatican Council II, interpreted them to bring about their own agenda and mayhem ensued.  People left the Church, feeling betrayed.

But this was not of his doing!  Sensing danger, on February 22, 1959, the Pope established a new papal commission to monitor radio, television and motion pictures.  Had he, through inspiration of the Holy Spirit begun to see the spreading decadence which would overtake the world?

Pope John XXIII, like his other brother Popes, had a deep desire to unify the Greek Orthodox with the Roman Catholic Church.  Likewise he had a great love for the churches in the East who had returned to Mother Church;

---

[4]Lumen Gentium #28

and with this in mind, he approved the use of the vernacular
for *certain Uniat churches*.[5]

In his encyclicals, he beseeched everyone to approach
the Truth, Unity and Peace with love; or as we have written,
*"Preach love not at the sacrifice of truth; nor truth at the
sacrifice of love."*   Without compromising the Faith, true
Christ and father on earth, he reached out to our family in
Christ, calling them *"separated brethren and sons."*

He approved new rubrics for the breviary and the missal
on July 25, 1960 (which have been revised and revised until
at times, they are hardly distinguishable).  But this was not
his intent; he just died too soon; or was it God's Mercy he
not live to see how some would try to distort and abort his
desire for a new Pentecost.   In March, 1962 Pope John
XXIII set about a revision of Canon Law, with the
authorization of a pontifical committee to look into it.

Formerly on May 15, 1961 he had reinforced the
teachings of his predecessors--Pope Leo XIII and Pope Pius
XI, (and now as Pope John Paul II has repeatedly pleaded)--
for wealthier nations to address the needs of poorer ones
and help them.  Pope John Paul II, in his talks in Mexico City
and St. Louis in January, 1999, stressed this, calling on the
two continents (North and South) to be one America, with
one Mother-Mary Most Holy, Our Lady of Guadalupe, as
one family helping each other, united in mind and heart.

Then, the Angel of Death coming closer and closer to
bringing him Home, Pope John XXIII issued the encyclical
*Pacem in terris* in which he forewarned all mankind that the
only way to have lasting world peace, human rights must be
demanded and observed; he went on to say, it would not be
accomplished through the *Marxist humanistic ideology* of the
no God and His Love, only man and his will; nor would it

---

[5]calling Christian Churches of the East, which have converted from
the Eastern Orthodox Church and others, to the Church of Rome,
under the Chair of Peter.

flourish under the motivations and ambitions of communist countries who would use man's misery to subjugate the needy to their godless rule. Like our present Pope--Pope John Paul II, he pressed for the East and West to resolve their differences *peacefully.*

Because, during the Cuban Missile crisis in 1962, Pope John XXIII urged both the United States and Cuba to consider the ramification of their actions on their citizens and the citizens of the world; and to carefully evaluate the situation, before making decisions that could suffer worldwide consequences, Pope John XXIII received not only the respect of Nikita Krushchev, premier of the Soviet Union and John F. Kennedy, President of the United States, he was the recipient of the Peace Prize from the International Balzan Foundation.

*"The deeds men do live long after them."* Although the plan he treasured--to bring all creeds together, by dialoguing with men of all religions, with men of like mind and heart--was one that could have brought about the desire of not only this loving Pope's heart but that of his Lord Jesus before him, that *we may be one,*[6] was to be sabotaged by many within the Church (not the official Church) using it to advocate their own agendas, the memory of what can be lingers on and will never die.

Sensing the dangerous modernization that was creeping into the mainstream Church, the Pope issued a warning to New Testament exegetes (or Biblical scholars) cautioning them to disregard the writings of one Teilhard de Chardin.[7] This cost him popularity among the Modernists, who just waited for another day to strike!

A few months before he died, on the 13th of November, 1962, Pope John XXIII had the name of St. Joseph inserted

---

[6]Jn 17:20-23

[7]For more on Teilhard de Chardin, see last page of chapter

into the Canon of the Mass. Had he begun to see the great need of the Protector of the Church to be brought to the forefront of the Mass, the priesthood and the hearts of the laity?

On December 8, the Feast of the Immaculate Conception, 1962 a tired Pope, already seriously weakened by illness, adjourned the Council for nine months. What he had started, he would not live to see completed. He succumbed to gastric cancer and died on June 3, 1963.

A good and holy Pope died, but the good that he did will live long after him. Be not deceived; read the documents of Vatican Council II. We believe that Pope John XXIII, like Pope John Paul II, sensed the enemy's insidious attempt to split asunder the Church which Jesus founded. Modernists chipping away at the Church and her traditions, weakening the very foundation upon which she was built, Pope John XXIII could see the growing decline of vocations to the religious life. We are fairly certain, the Holy Spirit inspired him to commence an Ecumenical Council which would open wide the windows, so that the Holy Spirit and the Heavenly Army of Angels could gather additional troops to defend the Church, an army of laity following their Pope and his Ambassadors of Christ! Perhaps he knew that weeds would mix with the wheat, but as another John, John the Baptist said of Our Lord Jesus, "*His winnowing fan is in His hand. He will clear His threshing floor and gather His wheat into His barn, but the chaff (weeds) He will burn with unquenchable fire.*"[8]

When the world received the news that the Pope had died, we were all devastated; we loved our Pope! The New York Times wrote in their paper that few Popes had so captivated the imagination of the world; and we say the

---

[8]Mt 3:12

hearts. But that honor was not to remain solely for this Pope, as we all know!

*How do you follow a charismatic Pope like John XXIII?*

### Pope Paul VI (1963-1978)

Our new Pope was given the task to follow John XXIII! Although Pope Pius XII had withheld Archbishop Montini's (future Pope Paul VI) promotion to Cardinal,[9] upon Pius XII's death, one of the first things his successor--Pope John XXIII did was to name him a Cardinal. As a close friend of Pope John XXIII, Cardinal Montini (Paul VI), was known to have played an instrumental part in the preparations for Vatican Council II, which would enable him to carry on the work, after Pope John XXIII's passing.

Greatly influenced by his friend and predecessor, upon filling the chair of Peter, Paul VI promptly advised the Church he would continue the work begun by John XXIII, drafting and implementing Vatican Council II; he would further move forward with John XXIII's plan to revise Canon law; and he would promote justice in civil, social, and international life. This some would use to promote their own brand of *Social Justice* and *Liberation Theology*. Now Social Justice, with Christ as the Leader and Model, is living the Gospel; but this was not the Social Justice which was being advocated by dissidents making their own Church laws and interpretations of the Law; their idea of Social Justice was more like that of Barabbas, with the use of force against force. This has never been the mind and heart of the Church, because Our Founder Jesus Christ did not offer freedom from persecution, only from sin!

Pope Paul VI continued the promotion of uniting all Christianity--with the primary focus--a dream close to his heart and that of John XXIII--the reunification of the

---

[9]This was in spite of the pressure from the people of Milan, where he had been Archbishop. Others say Pope Paul VI refused the title.

Church of the East with the Church of Rome. He opened the second session of the Council, implementing important reforms of procedure, which, in the wrong hands, would have a domino effect; these reforms included the admittance of laymen as auditors,[10] the appointment of four moderators, and the relaxing of confidentiality.

When you open the door a crack, things enter you may not have anticipated, as Saint Teresa of Avila cautioned when speaking of the Mansions.[11]  In September, women--religious and lay--were admitted as auditors to the Council! The third session closed in November with the declaration of the Constitution of the Church.  This had a clarification attached outlining the meaning and duties of the collegiality of the bishops: It explained that this was a doctrine which stated that the bishops form a college which, *acting in harmony* with and not autonomous of (*nor separate from*) the head, the *Pope*, has *supreme authority* in the Church.

This is in direct contradiction to the proposal by some bishops of the world, at this time, as in times of heresies past, that they run their own dioceses independently of Rome, knowing the needs and wishes of the members of their dioceses better than people thousands of miles away.  Many laws and changes have been passed down, which the laity have believed were rulings by the Church; whereas they were instead solely from the local ordinary who had no official jurisdiction in the matter.

To the dismay of clerics, who had placed the Mother of God in *Her place*, along with Her Son crucified on the Cross and Our Lord Present in the Eucharist, *out of the church--out of sight and out of mind*, Pope Paul VI proclaimed the Blessed Virgin Mary *Mother--"Mother of the Church."*  No matter what confusion and hurts evolved, with some leaving

---

[10]For the Canon Law on this, go the last page of the chapter.

[11]For more on Teresa in *Saints and Other Powerful Women in the Church* by Bob and Penny Lord.

this Church they no longer recognized, the faithful never stopped loving and longing for all that spoke to them of that God and His Divine Grace which would never leave them. As the people of Spain proved that although they had been without the Name of Jesus proclaimed and revered, with churches closed, no Sacraments being administered, no Gospel preached, the Church did not die, but was ready like their Savior to be resurrected.[12]

Our Popes, always men of peace, as their Savior before them, Pope Paul VI--like his predecessors, went before the United Nations to plead for justice and peace for all.

Because the Holy Spirit is always in charge of the Church and protects her from error, although the wounds of so many unexplained changes were weakening the walls of the Church, the Corner Stone (Jesus) always with us, Pope Paul VI was able to keep the Church from falling prey to schism.

Part of the changes which caused much controversy were the commissions set to formulate and carry out his implementations of:

1. The revision of the breviary, the changes in the lectionary, the order of the Mass, Sacred Music (changed into the entrance of songs reflecting and borrowed from our Protestant brothers and sisters to the death knell of the old familiar Latin Hymns, which filled our churches for generations).

2. Latin was replaced by the vernacular of the country in which the Mass was being offered (dangerously reminiscent of the Reformation, where each prince was determining what their subjects were to believe, resulting in the formation of hundreds of little churches), causing a fracturing of the universality of the Church. Cardinal Ratzinger later said

---

[12]When the Catholic Queen Isabela freed Spain from the Saracens, she restored Spain to the Church and her Founder.

that forcing this upon the faithful was one of the integral causes of separation and division in the Church.

Pope Paul VI said that he went to Fatima, at the special summoning of the Blessed Mother. We believe that sensing the chaos in the world and the Church, he answered the call of Mother Mary and went to Fatima to seek Her guidance, as She had guided the first Apostles. *Was this why he went?* All we know is that it was the beginning of his loss of favor from the liberal fringe of the Church who thought they had the Pope in their pocket.

After he returned, he announced several encyclicals, one being *Mysterium fidei* which paved the way for liturgical reform and reaffirmed the **traditional** Eucharistic Doctrine. In *Sacerdotalis coelibatus* he declared once again, the Church's teaching on the importance and utmost necessity of Priestly celibacy.

For those who might think the Pope did not hold the traditions of the Church close to his heart, his struggle was between his desire to forge ahead with reforms and the danger such reforms would present to the Church. Protected by the Holy Spirit Who makes all things right and good, after his visit to Our Lady of Fatima, he showed the love he had for that Church made perfect by her Founder Jesus Who was perfect; he upheld the 2000 year Tradition of the Deposit of Faith and the Truth which Jesus solely deposited on the Church, as He gave her full authority.

In 1968, ten years before his death, Pope Paul VI closed the door between him and the liberal faction in the Church by writing his highly prophetic and Spirit-inspired Encyclical on Birth Control, *Humanae Vitae*. It made so many people so angry! We recall some of our dissidents in the United States ranting "*Humanae Vitae was not well accepted by the people, so it's not necessary to obey it.*"[13]  Well, folks, that's not the way it works in our Church.

An Archbishop who spent his last hours with Pope Paul VI, said that "...*after the celebration of the Mass (said by the Archbishop) and receiving the Extreme Unction*[14] *and the ritual prayers for the dying, the Pope became absorbed in prayer. We recited the Our Father, the Hail Mary, the Hail Holy Queen and the Magnificat. Then at the moment of the Anima Christi, when there is the invocation "In hoa mortis meae voca me" (call me in the hour of my death), my soul and those of the persons present quivered with emotion, while he instead stated the phrase with great serenity and force.*"

The Pope continued to pray.  Right up to the last instant in which he could speak and understand he did nothing but repeat "*Pater noster qui es in coelis.*"  This, I would say was the single greatest word he uttered while dying."[15]  "*Our Father Who art in Heaven...*"

He died, as Jesus before him, invoking his Father in Heaven.  His words are like a stamp on our hearts, as we recall words of this Apostle, who like the Jesus he tried to imitate on earth, welcomed Death, commending his spirit, his last words to his Father in Heaven:

"*I bend my head and raise my spirit.  I humble myself and extol You, God, 'whose nature is goodness.'*[16]  *In this last vigil let me worship You, true living God, Who tomorrow will be my Judge, and let me render to You the praise most aspired by You, the Name You prefer: You are the Father.*"

---

[13]For more on Humanae Vitae see chapter *From the Culture of Life to the Culture of Death* in this book

[14]now called *The Anointing of the Sick*

[15]This account of Pope Paul VI was written by Monsignor (Bishop-all Bishops are called Monsignor in Europe) Pasquale Macchi, former Archbishop of Loreto, Italy who had been personal secretary of Pope Paul VI and was present when he died.

[16]J. Leone

On August 6th, 1978 the day after the Feast of Our Lady of the Snows, our Pope--a soldier of contrasts and courage--went *Home*! The Cardinals were summoned and began to deliberate on who the next Pope would be.

Well loved, the next Pope was elected on the third ballot. Everyone was filled with joy. By the name he had chosen they believed he would carry on the work of John XXIII and Paul VI. But their joy was to turn into mourning. For one month and two days after Pope John Paul I was elected, he went *Home* to sit at the Feet of God.

A Cardinal, the first non-Italian since Hadrian VI was selected to next occupy the Chair of Peter. He was well known and respected. Pope Paul VI, after having read his *Love and Responsibility*, used it to compose *Humanae Vitae*. God chose our next Pope--Pope John Paul II from a persecuted and bleeding people.

~ ~ ~ ~ ~ ~ ~ ~ ~ ~ ~ ~ ~ ~ ~ ~ ~ ~ ~ ~ ~ ~ ~ ~ ~ ~ ~ ~ ~ ~

Footnote 7 - Chardin, one of the grandfather gurus of *New Age*, an offshoot of *Modernism*, is considered an *ascended master* [New Agers believe that these are the souls of the most enlightened (an old condemned heresy) individuals who ever lived. They contact certain humans to direct history.] Many *theophists* (those New Agers who believe in Ascended Masters claim that the Ascended Masters will become incarnate again to initiate the Age of Aquarius. They believe that those who die and become Ascended Masters will go through the same kind of incarnation by which Our Lord came into the world, in other words--the New Age equivalent of Jesus). Like others of his kind, Chardin promoted evolution, in its fullest sense, extolling man as being part of the cosmos, and not only a product of heredity through biological means. And this from one who promised to defend the Truths of the Magisterium, a Jesuit. Oh how poor St. Ignatius must suffer for his lost sons.

Footnote 10 - Canon 274 states: "*Only **clerics** can obtain those offices for whose exercise there is required the power of **orders** or the power of **ecclesiastical governance**.*" This entitlement of governing and etc. by the laity has raised much controversy. For more on this, read Canon 274 in The Code of Canon Law.

# Pilgrim Pope-Prophet-Peacemaker

## HOPE OF THE FINAL YEARS

*His banner of love to his children - "Be not afraid!"*

### Pope John Paul II

He was formerly Cardinal Archbishop *Karol Wojtyla* of Crakow.  At the comparatively young age of fifty eight, he was chosen by an overwhelming majority of 103 out of 109 votes.  He walked to the window in the center of St. Peter's Basilica, and waved to his children cheering below.  When he took the name of two former Popes, like his predecessor John Paul I, before him, he promised to carry on the work begun by Pope John XXIII and Pope Paul VI.

His first encyclical, called *Redemptor hominis*, proclaimed that true freedom can only be found and human dignity best preserved in the Church.

Then in his second, *Dives in misericordia*, he encouraged all men to show mercy to one another, where mercy can be seldom found--in a merciless world which only grows more merciless.

Early in his pontificate, he chose key people who would demonstrate the direction his political and doctrinal policies would take.  One of these was Cardinal Joseph Ratzinger whom he appointed to the important post of Prefect of the Sacred Congregation for the Doctrine of the Faith.  This holy man and Defender of the Faith--loved by those who love the Church and hated by those who hate her, in company with our Pope would do much to correct the errors being disseminated throughout the world to the Church at large.  The spirit of modernism taking on all the heresies of the past, this would be a full time job for an army of men; as in the days of Gideon, God would have to be content with a handful--Pope John Paul II, Cardinal Joseph Ratzinger, Mother Teresa angel of the dying, and a cloistered Nun who

Right:
*Pope John Paul II*
*Pilgrim Pope*
*Prophet*
*Peace Maker*

Left:
*Pope John Paul II*
*On his many Pilgrimages*
*throughout the world, he calls*
*himself the Pilgrim Pope.  He*
*has been accredited as being*
*the most powerful force behind*
*the fall of Communism.*

Right:
*Pope John Paul II*
*with*
*Mother Teresa*
*of Calcutta*
*The Angel of*
*the Dying*

would spread the Gospel, the Eternal Word to the whole world; Mother Mary Angelica, Abbess and Foundress of the Poor Clares of Eucharistic Adoration and Our Lady Queen of the Angels Monastery, and Foundress of the Global Eternal Word Television and Radio Network. Contradictions in our time, this *"remnant"* of the Lord would stand by Mother Church and speak the Truth, not counting the cost.

As Prefect of the Sacred Congregation for the Doctrine of the Faith, one of the painful duties Cardinal Joseph Ratzinger had to exercise, early in his appointment, was to take disciplinary action against some formerly prestigious theologians who had gone astray and refused to obey the Magisterium, and the authority of the Holy See, choosing instead to become heretics and dissidents proselytizing, causing division and disobedience: Jacques Pohier, Hans Kung, Edward Schillebeeckx, and Charles Curran.

Never before in the history of the Church has a Pope done so much, travelled so far and wide, been so well-known and loved by so many men and women of good faith and all religions.

Ambassador of peace--Pope John Paul II has won the hearts and souls of the world; all races and creeds calling him their Pope. Like Jesus before him, he has walked among the people, loving God's children. Born into a modest, humble home, like his Savior before him, the poor and the down-trodden embraced him for they, looking into his eyes could see a brother and father who knew and cared.

Now, our Pope has always had a devotion to Mother Mary; his emblem--*Totus Tuo* (all yours) bears witness to this fact. On May 12-15, 1982, he made a pilgrimage to Fatima to the Lady, whom he attributes with saving his life. On May 13th, the anniversary of the first day of the apparitions of

Mother Mary to the children in Fatima,[1] our Pope knelt before the statue of *Our Lady of Fatima*, his ardent desire to render to Her homage, love and thanksgiving. You see, it was one year to the day that on May 13th, 1981 he was felled by an assassin's bullet in St. Peter's Square. Before the audience, as he was greeting the faithful in his Popemobile, and just as the assailant was about to shoot him, the Pope bent down and kissed the statue of Our Lady of Fatima, the bullet missing his heart, instead piercing his abdomen.

Just three weeks before he was shot, we were at an audience with the Pope. As we were leaving St. Peter's Square, Bob looked at the roofs all around St. Peter's and commented, "*Oh how vulnerable he is.*" We had seen him many times in this defenseless position, but never thought he would ever be hurt. I remember one time in 1979, after having returned from Poland, our Pope processed on foot, through the streets of Rome, from the Cathedral of St. John Lateran to the Basilica of St. Mary Major, accompanied by us and 250,000 people. His guards were looking up at the Romans cheering from their windows and waving handkerchiefs from their balconies, hailing their Pope. Not he nor his guards seemed to be aware of the possible danger of walking so unprotected. He carried his Jesus in the monstrance, never lifting his eyes, pressing his Lord lovingly against his forehead.

The world clung breathlessly to their television sets, following the Pope's progress in the hospital. After going through a hard time, a viral infection adding to his pain and compromising his recovery, Pope John Paul II was finally released from the hospital. One of his first acts was to go to the prison where his assailant was incarcerated. This man had tried to assassinate the Pope and what was our Vicar's

---

[1]For more on this apparition and other apparitions of Mother Mary, read Bob and Penny Lord's book: *Many Faces of Mary, a love story.*

retribution--the Pope gave him a private audience in his cell; and true Vicar of Christ that he is, forgave him!

We have seen, during countless pilgrimages, our most sophisticated pilgrims and proud priests melt, when the Pope merely turned their way, his loving, compassionate eyes saying, *I understand and I love you.* We have seen him embrace the crippled and hold sick children in his arms, tears welling up in his eyes. As the years have been rapidly advancing, his body has oftentimes shown the ravages of the bullet wound he suffered and his bout with cancer. But those most critical were the slings and arrows which have pierced his heart, at the hands and tongues of his beloved sons and daughters--his religious, priests and bishops.

On his many pilgrimages around the world, calling himself the *Pilgrim Pope*, he singles out the youth, his special army, whom he calls the *Church today*! At his audiences, although he is generous and tries to pay attention to all who come to see and hear him, he gives the most time to the sick and the handicapped. The poor and disadvantaged, farmers, and urban workers alike, feel special in his presence. He makes it a focus to reach out to minority groups, often speaking in their language or dialect. Like Jesus before him, he looks deeply into your eyes, down to the depths of your soul, and you are changed; you are in love with the Jesus before you in the person of your Pope. No matter how many audiences we have had the privilege of attending, every picture taken of Penny and the Pope, shows her looking wistfully at the Pope.

As every man is his brother; every woman his sister; every child born and unborn his child, is there any wonder, we see him stooped over! Is he not like that other strong Figure Who too was stooped over, under the weight of the Cross, the Cross which was ladened down by the sins of the world?

Pope John Paul II has been accredited as being the single most powerful force behind the fall of Communism, which may account for the assassination attempt on his life in 1981. It was also reported that another attempt was on the planning board just before the fall of Communism. Fearless, loving, honest and true to his vocation from Priest, to Bishop, to Pope--he has travelled throughout the world bringing love, hope and dignity to all he encounters. He has been acclaimed by the world the most influential and most popular man on earth; he will some day be known as one of the *holiest men* on earth.

Even when he is firm and resolute on matters of faith and morals, he has never been anything but empathetic, responsive, and charitable. He stands before us--an example, a role model, an unflinching, uncompromising servant of God in a world which, at this time, is in the hands of the godless. Always true to his mission and true to the Keys entrusted to him, although merciful and compassionate, he has never compromised the Church and its 2000 year tradition, its authentic teachings found in the Magisterium.

One year after he attended a Synod of Bishops, our Pope came out with a teaching, addressing the matter of sin and the need for penance and reconciliation. He began by clarifying and correcting the errors concerning sin and its repercussions, in his apostolic exhortation, *Reconciliatio et paenitentia*. Pope John Paul II, rejected any lessening of mortal sin to an act of "*fundamental opinion*" and stressed that general absolution be confined to limited, specific times and occasions.

Although always pleading for equal justice for the disadvantaged, he warned priests against *violently* participating in their quest for equality, but instead--as *Ambassadors of Christ* to help the needy *spiritually* to keep their souls, while engaging in conflicts with their oppressors. He spoke of *Social Justice* as being a *part* of the Gospel, but not the total Gospel; having first-hand knowledge of what it is to go to bed hungry at night (as a young man in war-torn Poland during the Nazi occupation), he still maintained that the soul must be fed, either in conjunction with the body, or if that is not possible, sometimes ahead of the body.

He came out against a pervading madness, a plague infecting and affecting the Church, coined *"liberation theology"* which portrayed Jesus as a revolutionary and a prophet. He warned against any form of *political, economic and social liberation* which would conflict with the 2000 year tradition teaching that salvation is only through Jesus Christ.

He defended the *Magisterium*, by clearly teaching that its truth alone brings about true liberation. He cautioned the faithful against *"parallel magisteriums"* in which the misguided strive to establish a *select, preferential* love of the poor, by preaching a gospel overly exaggerating the social and the political, at the expense of the *Divine mission of Christ* to free men through freedom from sin. In Mexico, March 1979, in his encyclical: *Redemptor hominis,* he pleaded with his priests to remember they *"are not social directors, political leaders or officials of a temporal power."*

He reemphasized his first encyclical in which he said that humanity cannot be understood fully without Christ at the center of history. Without mentioning the atheistic scourge of Communism, he asked Europe to return to their Christian roots. Although he did not allude to their slavery under the hammer and sickle (Communism), his visit to his beloved Poland brought new hope and life to the *Solidarity* movement, focusing them on employing peaceful means (*Fight evil with good*)[2] to bring about a shining, inconceivably dynamic rallying of Polish society, its industry and

---

[2]theme of the homily which Polish Martyr, Father Jerzy Popieluszko, delivered at his last Mass, for the millions of workers who were part of Solidarity.

agriculture. He and martyr Jerzy Popieluszko[3] are credited for the final demise of communist domination by the Soviet Union.

Pope John Paul II appeared before the United Nations apprising them of their responsibility to the world to call tirelessly for global dialoguing concerning problems, spiritual and secular. He appealed to this organization, which had been formed to police the world, and combat wrongs--to uphold *human rights*, fighting for those who are victims of this scourge and cannot defend themselves, irrespective of the guilty nation's power and influence.

If we believe that every man is our brother, then when labor in a nation is provided through the suppression of human rights, we are obliged to boycott products exported into our country, made by slave labor, victims of injustice, especially children, who are our family because God is the Father of us all. If we do not, we become a party to this wholesale inhumanity, selling out Jesus to save a few pennies on an item we are purchasing.

Addressing a Conference of Bishops in Chicago, he spoke out strongly, emphasizing the need for instruction of the faithful regarding the Church's teachings on faithful monogamy,[4] divorce, contraception, homosexual activity, abortion, euthanasia, assisted suicide and one that he would later add in his exhortation of the Bishops--a seventh magisterial teaching on scientific experimentation on genes and embryos.[5]

He further stressed at that conference and when he spoke before the World Council of Churches in Geneva,

---

[3]More about him and other martyrs who died for the Faith in *Martyrs, They died for Christ* by Bob and Penny Lord

[4]the union of a *man and woman* through the Sacrament of Matrimony.

[5]covered in our chapter: *The History of the Church and the world.*

Switzerland[6] that although we are praying for unity with our separated brethren, priests must be careful to apprise non-Catholics that we must maintain the ruling of the Church that only baptized Catholics (not in a state of sin) may receive Communion. In Geneva, he defined his mission to obey and cooperate with the Church whose mission is as mediator between *God and humanity.* He shared his objections, regarding sharing the Eucharist before visible unity is achieved between the separated brethren and the Church. He outlined the differences between the spirituality resulting from the Reformation, especially that of Zwingli and Calvin, and that of the Church.[7] He strongly reiterated his opposition to any change in Catholic canons making reference to the priesthood. He closed with his deep concern over the types of social change fostered by the World Council of Churches.

Our Pope has appeared before conferences, condemning the pressures being exerted on starving Third World countries to either cooperate with Planned Parenthood's agenda of murder of the unborn and receive aid or resist and die.

He went before the United Nations, pleading that Jerusalem be made an *open city* in that it is the spiritual home of three main religions: Christians, Muslims and Jews. His efforts to bring about peace and harmony, in a Holy Land made bloody by man's selfishness and unwillingness to share having failed, our Pope has refused to pilgrimage there. This only added fuel to the fire, inflaming the ire and indignation of a small number of Jewish-American interests, who are not really representative of the Hebrew Religion and its fine Rabbis, but whose agenda has been attacking our Pope in the United States.

---

[6]a stronghold of Calvinism

[7]more on that in Bob and Penny Lord's book: *Tragedy of the Reformation*

Another theme of his second encyclical *Dives in misericordia* stressed among other things--the need of forgiveness "*especially in this modern age*" rooted in our belief that the God who is "*our Model of Mercy,*" is the same God in Judaism, Christianity and Islam.

Our Pope accepted an invitation from the Chief Rabbi of Rome and joined him in the synagogue in a service of song and prayer, the first in the history of the Papacy. He spoke of the strong bonds the Catholic Church has with the Faith of the Jews of the Old Testament. He sealed his overture of mutual respect by drawing from John XXIII and his *Nostra atate* of Vatican Council II, as a basis of future understanding and relations between Catholics and Jews. He expressed, at that time, the deep sense of anguish and sorrow he felt when visiting Auschwitz, and witnessing the horrific evidence of the most inhumane cruelty suffered by mankind.

An ongoing thread running throughout his Papacy has been for his sons, the Bishops to be in communion with the Holy See, and remain rooted in the teachings of the heart and mind of the Church--the Magisterium. To show disunity is to make Jesus a liar; for He pleaded in John 17:20-23: "*I pray not only for them, but also for those who will believe in Me through their word, so that they may all be one, as You Father are in Me and I in You, that they may also be in Us, that the world may believe that You sent Me.*" If some Bishops and members of the hierarchy are not in communion with the successor of Peter, are they not making Jesus a liar? Or are they proposing, as some have heretically said, "*Jesus never said this; the gospel writers put these words into His mouth to bring across their own agenda....*"

Is that not dangerous? For if these are not the words of Christ, is any of the Bible true? Did Adam and Eve fall? Is there a devil? Is there a God? Was Jesus born? Did Jesus die on the Cross and rise on the third day? Are we redeemed of our sins? As St. Paul said: "...*if Christ has not been raised, your faith is in vain; you are still in your sins. Then those who have fallen asleep in Christ have perished. If for this life only we have hoped in Christ, we are the most pitiable people of all.*"[8]

Always a father, anxious to bring his children home, the Pope, on the 500th anniversary of the birth of Martin Luther, reached out to Lutherans, calling for a joint Catholic-Lutheran undertaking to study *anew* the schism which separated millions of the faithful from their Church in the Sixteenth Century. In keeping with this heartfelt desire, and hoping to open the door to dialogue, the Pope paid a visit to the Lutheran Church in Rome and prayed along with the minister and the congregation. How Jesus must have smiled, seeing two of His children praying together, a significant, unparalleled gesture heretofore unknown in the History of the Papacy and the separated Lutheran brethren.

Reaching out to all children of God and the world, and addressing the extreme materialism which is imprisoning mankind, he said, "*When God is forgotten, the creature itself grows unintelligible.*" Have we not seen evidence of this--the churches no longer full, mothers killing their unborn (and some already born), children killing parents, then other children, and people on the streets--play-acting, imitating what they see on TV and in the movies, unmindful of their actions. With the absence of God and His Will, man is following his own will, with no guide as to the inestimable treasure of God and His creation.

As the shepherd of souls, the Pope dared once again to be unpopular, as he addressed those who had wandered from the Truth in Sydney, Australia, and begged them to come back home to God and reason. Here in Australia he

---

[8]1Cor 15:17-19

cried out against the *in vitro fertilization* which was pioneered there by their doctors.

Fighting for life, as his is too quickly ebbing away, more than at any of his other stops, he pleaded and warned them of the consequences resulting from experimentation in altering or customizing genetic makeup, experiments on embryos--which has brought about the wholesale slaughter of unborn babies (conveniently called fetuses), and the horrible fate of poor souls whose lives are ending because of the use of euthanasia to destroy that which man has *not* created.

He went back to West Germany a second time, the Thursday after Easter, to minister to those Catholics who had lived *"under the treacherous tyranny of national Socialism,"* who felt the guilt of not having done anything to try to stop the madness of Nazism, consoling them they could not have done more under the circumstances, that collective or personal opposition would have only caused the lives of more innocent souls. Then travelling to Cologne, he spoke of a martyr who suffered under the Nazis' yoke of horror and torture, whom he was beatifying that day--Carmelite Edith Stein--calling her *"a daughter of Israel."* Then Pope John Paul II left for Munster, where he stood at the grave of two strong, outspoken opponents to forced euthanasia for the insane and mentally retarded, during the Nazi regime. The Pope alluded to abortion and euthanasia for the terminally comatose today, as nothing but insidious manifestations of the more dramatic threat to human dignity and basic rights under the Nazis.

In Canada, he implored the faithful to cry out against religious persecution (of every faith)--to *"overcome the conspiracy of silence"* which is befogging the horrible abuses being inflicted upon those who follow God; atrocities being conducted--brother against brother, because of religious differences.

Our Pope came to St. Louis, Missouri in January, 1999, and reached out to the people of the United States to be leaders and examples of Morality to the world. He called television, the press, radio and other forms of communication good when used to bring the good--God's Word to the world. He spoke to the Youth! Calling them the Church of today and tomorrow, he handed them the torch to light the way to the Kingdom of God, in this new Millennium. As he reacted to them and they to him, you could see a mutual love and respect, almost reverence. They saw Jesus in him, Jesus summoning them and they were saying Yes! He told them he is counting on them to change the world. And they will do it! They will reclaim the world for Christ the King!

His aim to consecrate our continents to Our Lady of Guadalupe and through her bring about unity and family, when he went to Mexico, January, 1999, he reminded America of her innate heritage of protecting the family, especially those who settled here from all parts of the world, seeking a better life for their children. He addressed Americans, referring to all living in North America and South America as no longer two continents but one nation under God and Our Lady of Guadalupe. He pleaded with them not to listen to those who would lead them to kill their own children through birth control or abortion, or their parents through assisted suicide or euthanasia. He asked us, the citizens of America, to make firm commitments to uphold the rights of every man, woman and child to life, dignity, and the pursuit of happiness, no matter what their stations in life, their abilities or lack of abilities, their weaknesses or strengths.

Our Pope told *America* that *"Jesus is calling able lay Christians to assume roles of leadership in society."* Too long have the enemies of God had control over our fate and that of those who will follow. He said, *"On a continent marked by* competition and aggressiveness, unbridled consumerism and corruption, lay people are called to embody deeply evangelical values such as mercy, forgiveness, honesty, transparency of heart and patience in difficult situations." We, especially in the United States of America, were founded under God; we must put the reigns back in His Hands.

✝✝✝

In writing this book, the words of our Popes, past and present have given us the strength to keep going. If this were to be the last book we were to write, we would want to be that voice crying out, *Be not deceived; stay close to the ageless teachings of Mother Church; she is the Ship which will bring you to safety. Pray for our Church and our Vicar. Pray for our bishops, priests and religious and our brothers and sisters of the laity, all those who need God's healing Hands upon them to either strengthen them, convert them or heal them.*

*In the past, lies the present. In the present, lies the opportunity to change the future, for God is in charge; He is always in charge!*

# From the Culture of Life to the Culture of Death

**Pope John Paul II speaks out against The Culture of Death.**

The "*most popular and powerful man on earth*" dared to speak out against what he termed *The Culture of Death*. It's sad; so many of our politicians are giving into The Culture of Death--out of fear, because they believe they must be "*politically correct*" in order to get elected and remain in office. Fearing no one but his Lord, this man has fearlessly admonished heads of nations to cease imposing this *Culture of Death*, on not only *their* countrymen, but forcing it on the poor starving Third World countries--making it a provision to receive aid. This man, our Pope John Paul II who dares to go against the flow of permissiveness and sin, this man who dares to feed the people of the world with the love and promise of Jesus, draws *millions* in contrast to the thousands, which men promoting the Culture of Death draw. Like Mother Angelica, who fears nothing but the day she stands before the throne of God and He asks her why, when He had given her a certain task and opportunity she did not say Yes, our Pope dares to be unpopular.

But is he unpopular? A very secular magazine called the Pope "*the most popular, most powerful man in the world*" with more followers than any king, ruler or potentate on earth. The Pope went to Mexico, on the throes of the commencement of a revolution, and the poor and rich alike, young and old, gathered in the millions, chanting *Juan Pablo Segundo; Te quiere todo el Mundo*[1] (or as their english-speaking counterparts--*John Paul II, we love you!*). As the people spoke, his tiredness left him, his strength renewed, and he was once more the energetic Pope who had visited their land, the first time, twenty years before.

---

[1]translation: *John Paul II the whole world loves you*

*Our Lady of Joy*
*Our Lady of Sorrow*

*The most powerful man on earth, Pope John Paul II speaks out against the 'Culture of Death'*

*As we have well seen with the increasing murder of unborn babies in the womb, a matching acceleration among murders, suicides, and general violence has ravaged the earth. As love propagates love, and peace propagates peace, so hate propagates hate, and violence propagates violence.*

The Pope placed America under the loving embrace of Our Mother, *Our Lady of Guadalupe,* declaring her the Patroness of America!  In 1846, the First Council of Bishops of the United States proclaimed Our Mother Mary: *Mary in Her Immaculate Conception Principal Patron of the United States.*  Our Lady came to this continent in 1531, on the Feast of the *Immaculate Conception* and identified Herself as *Our Lady of the Immaculate Conception.*  Now here was our Vicar, at the end of the Second Millenium, consecrating our country to Our Lady; only now as a part of an *America* who will overcome the Culture of Death, and under the standard of *Our Lady of Guadalupe,* usher in a new Millenium, a Millenium of Life!  He asked those who have been blessed abundantly to open their hearts to those less fortunate, as part of a family with Our Lady as our Mother - guiding us, leading us to victory, as She steps on the head of the enemy.  As brothers and sisters in Christ, he pleaded with the haves to help the havenots, without any strings attached, especially those costing people their dignity and more importantly their souls.

The other reason the Pope came to Mexico, like the Lady he loved, was to avert mass annihilation.  And like Our Lady of Guadalupe he united his Mexican children, mending wounds, avoiding a very present danger of revolution.  He spoke of the *Culture of Life,* imploring the faithful of Mexico to stay firm to the teachings of the Church, that life begins in the womb and only God can terminate that which He alone has created.  How did that forestall a revolution?  Well, as we have seen, with the increasing murder of unborn babies in the womb, a matching acceleration among murders, suicides and general violence has ravaged the earth.  As love propagates love, and peace propagates peace, so hate propagates hate, and violence propagates violence.

We hear the outrage of women crying out for "*Their Right to Choose.*"  God gave us all *The Right to Choose*; but the *Right to Choose* was to choose God and not the enemy of God, to choose life and not death. What God has created, man has no right to destroy; only God who gives life can take life, our Lord in His Will, in His Timetable. How will God react to the death of the holy innocents, today?

**The Bible speaks of Plagues covering the earth.**

*"By these three plagues ... a third of the human race was killed.*[2]

*"The rest of the human race, who were not killed by these plagues, did not repent of the works of their hands, to give up the worship of demons and idols made of gold, silver, bronze, stone and wood, which cannot see or hear of walk. Nor did they repent of their murders, their magic potions, their unchastity, or their robberies."*[3]

Are we not back in the Old Testament Days of worshiping *"the golden calf?"* At the end of the Twentieth Century, will we go down in history as a people who will vote for anyone, no matter his or her morals? Have we really become the amoral people some commentators say we are, voting according to our pocketbooks*?*

We have only to see how the world is spinning out of control, with the Creator having been relieved of control. The madman and his accomplices,[4] posing as benefactors, have taken over and have drugged us into believing the only way out of the struggles of this world is Death, not Life.

A plague is covering the earth, no longer confined to active homosexuals, but its tentacles have spread, attacking heterosexuals--single men and women, husband and wives, children. When *Aids* was first discovered, we saw actors and actresses begin to discreetly kiss on the screen; no more

---

[2]Rv 9:18

[3]Rv 9:20

[4]men and women who have lost their souls to Lucifer and do his bidding and that of his fallen angels

passionate love scenes. Terror ran through the hearts of all walks of life. People feared getting transfusions and they gave blood to hospitals to be stored. The innocent fell victim to this horrible pestilence, babies being born infected, children with hemophilia contracting Aids from contaminated needles. What started as an isolated disease became in short order a growing plague. In the old days, citizens who came from villages infested with plagues, were not allowed to enter other cities. You cannot bring fruit or any kind of plant into California, because if infested, pests could ruin crops. With this blight there were no walls high enough to keep its deadly curse from spreading to the far corners of the world.

What did our Twentieth Century mentality and morality do about it? Failing to accept this as a warning, they ignored the signs calling for repentance and conversion. Our Popes, throughout the history of the Church and consequently the world, have consistently warned that when man takes God out of his life, man needing someone to worship and follow, will seek and worship the anti-god, the devil.

What was the solution? The media started to promote *safe-sex!* A woman would come on the screen; and with sugary sweetness, compassion dripping out of every word, she would promote the practice of safe-sex to impressionable minds of young viewers; and their fear-ridden parents went along! Thinking only of that which is temporary and perishable, they completely discounted what, in their blindness, they could not see--their child's immortal soul and that of their own. Gripped by fear for their child's *mortal body*, they have forsaken God's Commandments, the laws of the Old and the New Testaments, and the teachings of the Church dating back to her very inception, jeopardizing not only her *mortal life* on earth but her *immortal life* in Heaven.

They not only became a party to their child's impending sin on the horizon, but became even more accountable, committing a crime worthy of God's wrath--leading astray their own flesh and blood, and by means of birth control killing one or more of the grandchildren whom they would never see, birth control being another form of abortion. Failing their responsibility to guard a precious soul entrusted to them as parents, by their actions (or inactions) giving that child their consent to sin and through that sin, kill, I wonder what they will feel when they stand before the throne of God and He parades before them, the many babies who were aborted through their yes, and that of their child, to the arch temptor, the enemy of God.

Young girls, barely out of elementary school were getting pregnant. The solution? Mothers rushed their daughters to abortion clinics. Schools addressed the crisis by handing out contraceptives to children, quite often without the knowledge or consent of the parents. *Sex-Education* became a required subject, with material bordering more on pornography than science, children learning things that most parents did not know. Rather than prevent, it titillated and excited the children to investigate.

### In 1929, Pope Pius XI spoke out on Sex Education:

*"In this extremely delicate matter, if, all things considered, some private instruction is found necessary and opportune, for those (i.e. parents) who hold from God the commission to teach and who have the grace of state, every precaution must be taken....***Such is our misery and inclination to sin, that often in the very things considered to be remedies against sin, we find occasions for and inducements to sin itself.*** Hence it is of the highest importance that a good father, while discussing with his son a matter so delicate, should be well on his guard and not descend to details...otherwise it may happen that* **instead of extinguishing this fire, he unwittingly stirs or kindles it in the simple and tender heart of the child."**
*(Rappresentanti in Terra, No. 67)*

With all the preventative instruction and forms of artificial protection, i.e. safe-sex, did the pregnancies decrease? Not if you visit a campus of any school--primary, secondary, college or university. It has grown to such mammoth proportions, there are even Day Care Centers available, in the schools the mothers are attending, for these little souls born out of wedlock. And then there are the grandparents who, wanting their grandchildren to know some kind of normalcy, take care of the little ones while the young mother goes out, and more often than not gets pregnant again. So much for Sex-Education!

The secular media, with its suggestive programming, incited children and adults to offend God and fall into the web of sin, killing not only their bodies (many dying from venereal diseases or botched abortions), but their immortal souls. Unrepentant accessories to murder (for indeed it is murder), sex returned to the TV screen. Intimate love scenes which would not have passed a censor, and before the *enlightened* 80's and 90's would have been classified X, once again appeared on the TV screen, bolder and uglier. This type of program, in years past, could only be rented in cheap and tawdry store fronts catering to perverts--decadence and depravity operating underground behind dark corners, it being against the law; now in our *"get with it; you're living in the nineties"* time, they were invading our homes and destroying our families. The language became more and more offensive, suggestive, and deadly, too often under the guise of harmless comedy.

Not only *fictitious* programs showing the most bloodthirsty murders and all-out violence, but the irresponsible news media, in an attempt to get better ratings showed *actual murders* and assisted suicide (another form of murder), as it was happening. And we wonder and scratch our heads, crying out *"How could little children kill?"* Look to the lineup today and you will see the majority of TV shows are either extremely violent or openly decadent. And this is our children's school room away from school, in our own living rooms! Eight or so hours in school, they are open to all forms of temptation; the home should be a haven, a safe place! We see commercials coming against child-abuse and we see a little girl or boy pitifully crying, some showing the evidence of the abuse they have suffered. But there are no commercials showing the children lost because their souls have been sorely wounded. When do we take a stand!

*What can we do?* One day Penny spoke to a young girl working in a store she frequents and remarked she was beautiful, and had a treasure, someone will want to steal. The girl replied, *Oh I am not about to marry, now; I want a career.* Now, we usually do not go around speaking to young people about chastity, but Penny went on, *It is your beautiful, spotless soul, your chastity someone will try to steal. Do not allow anyone to soil God's gift to you.*

Her answer was that she could not understand why people didn't use *protection*, as her Psychology professor had told her class that there is a strain of Aids which does not show up in testing and is not detectable until it is too late. Penny insisted, *There is only one way to protect yourself - abstinence.* Was Penny politically correct? I believe she would rather be *spiritually correct*. Penny buys in that store, and every time she sees her, the girl has to be reminded. Not another word has been said, but a seed was planted!

*No one speaks of chastity!* We believe if more young people knew there were others who felt as they do, who wanted to remain virgins, there would be less unwed mothers, less abortions, less suicides. But as in the days of Pilate, when he asked the crowd whom they chose--Our Precious Savior or a murdering insurrectionist, you can bet there were those, who in their hearts chose Jesus; but the very vocal few intimidated and coerced them into going along, and the worst crime ever committed was perpetrated, the death of Our Lord on the Cross. It is no less an evil now, and we are asked to once again choose. The Baby Jesus stands before us, representing all the babies who silently plead for their lives. We were not there to choose Jesus, but we can now; for as Jesus said, *"Whatsoever you do to the least of My children, you do unto Me."*

**Pope Leo XIII in 1878 issues a warning in his encyclical!**

On April 21, 1878 Pope Leo XIII issued an encyclical called: *"On the Evils of Society"*--in the *Nineteenth Century!*

*"For, from the very beginning of Our pontificate, the sad sight has presented itself to Us of the evils by which the human race is oppressed on every side: the widespread subversion of the primary truths on which, as on its foundations, human society is based; the obstinacy of mind that will not brook any authority however lawful; the endless sources of disagreement, whence arrive civil strife, and ruthless war and bloodshed; the contempt of law which molds characters and is the shield of righteousness; the insatiable cravings of things perishable, with complete forgetfulness of things eternal, leading up to the desperate madness whereby so many wretched beings, in all directions, scruple not* (have no problem) *to lay violent hands upon themselves; the reckless mismanagement, waste, and misappropriation of the public funds;* **the shamelessness of those who, full of treachery, make semblance of being champions of country, of freedom, and every kind of right**; *in fine* (in conclusion), *the deadly kind of plague which infects in its inmost recesses, allowing it no respite and foreboding ever fresh disturbances and* **final disaster.**"

Could this have not been written in these, the final years of the Second Millennium? Does this not describe our world, the world we have allowed to happen and the world we leave to our children, and grandchildren, and great-grandchildren? *But we can change the world!* If you feel hopeless and helpless, as if you're the only one who cares, remember Jesus only had twelve; one betrayed Him; one denied Him three times; and all but one deserted Him, as He walked to the Cross.

*"Now, the source of these evils lies chiefly, We are convinced, in this, that the holy and venerable authority of the Church...has been despised and set aside. The enemies of public order, being fully aware of this, have thought nothing better suited to destroy the foundations of society than to make unflagging attack upon the Church of God, to bring her discredit and odium* (hatred) *by spreading infamous calumnies and accusing her of being opposed to genuine progress. They labor to weaken her influence and power...and* **to overthrow the authority of the Bishop of Rome.**

*"From these causes have originated* **laws** (Roe vs. Wade) **that shake the structure of the Catholic Church**...*also, has arisen...***unchecked freedom to teach and spread abroad all mischievous principles,** *while the Church's claim to train and educate youth is in every way outraged and baffled.*

*"We have recalled to your minds,...this deadly mass of ills...because we believe that you will most plainly see how serious are the matters claiming our attention...and with what energy We should work and, protect, so far as in Us lies, the Church of Christ and the honor of the Apostolic See.*

*"And if any one of sound mind compare the age in which We live, so* **hostile to religion and the Church of Christ,** *with those happy times when the Church was revered as a mother by the nations, beyond all question he will see that our epoch is* ***rushing wildly along the straight road to destruction.***

*"...civilization which* **conflicts** *with the doctrines and laws of holy Church is nothing but a worthless imitation,*

*"...***spreading false principles,** and freely indulging the **sensual gratification of lustful desires**...*Delusive, perverse, and misleading as are these principles, they cannot have any inherent power to perfect the human race and fill it with blessing, for* **'sin maketh nations miserable.'** *Such principles,*

*as a matter of course, must hurry nations* **corrupted** *in mind and heart,* **into every kind of infamy, weaken all right order,** *and thus, sooner or later, bring the* **standing and peace of the State to the very brink of ruin."**

If what the world is preaching is so wonderful, the answer to all our problems, then why is there such an increase in divorce, adultery, murder, teen-age pregnancy, suicide and death from drug overdoses?  Ask yourself if this new *feel good* freedom is working!

*"Our predecessors, to provide for the people's good, encountered struggles of every kind, endured to the utmost burdensome toils, and never hesitated to expose themselves to most dangerous trials.  With eyes fixed on Heaven, they neither bowed down their head before the threats of the wicked, nor allowed themselves to be led by flattery or bribes into worthy compliance.  This apostolic chair it was that gathered and held together the crumbling remains of the old order of things...in short* **this was a common center from which was sought instruction in faith and religion..."**[5]

### Pope Paul VI speaks out!

Pope Paul VI not only helped draft the documents of Vatican Council II (as Cardinal Montini), when Pope John XXIII died, he was left with the responsibility of implementing them.  When Pope Paul VI seemed to be conveniently instituting ideas agreeable with the new movement within the Church, he was praised and followed, obediently and without question.

Pope Paul VI's popularity began to dim and then plunge, when he inconveniently wrote *Humanae Vitae*.  A priest once said that the more Jesus spoke the Will of the Father, the more unpopular He became--to the point that the Jews who had been listening to His every word, who had

---

[5]Pope Pius XI -- thanks to ewtn.com/library

seen Him perform countless miracles, turned their backs on Him and walked away, when He declared,

*"I am the living Bread come down from Heaven; whoever eats this Bread will live forever; and the Bread I will give is My flesh for the life of the world."*[6]

The encyclical on the regulation of birth control-- *Humanae Vitae*, was to lead Pope Paul VI to suffering his last ten years, rejected and persecuted, with priests and religious openly dissenting (a privilege he had given them, which our present Pope John Paul II has wisely rescinded[7]). Did he know the uproar he would start with this bold step, speaking the Mind of Our Father in Heaven, and still dared to go against the trend back to Modernism? Had he seen his Church speeding out of control, no longer *influencing* the world; but instead *following* the world with its rationalism and naturalism which would have God following the dictates of man, and man following the dictates of the devil.

I believe, our dear Pope looked up at Jesus on the Cross and said, *Lord, I will follow you to the Cross, if You will lead Me.* At that moment, *Humanae Vitae* was born in the heart of the Pope to later be given to the universal Church, to *"Venerable Patriarchs, Archbishops and Bishops, and other local ordinaries in peace and communion with the Apostolic See, to Priests, the Faithful and to all men of good will..."*

This encyclical has reminded us of our first Marriage Encounter weekend in 1975, when the priest called us holy and said our Sacrament is the only Sacrament coming directly from God, with the priest acting as the witness. He said, we must revere one another. I can remember saying over and over, *We are holy; we are called to Sainthood; we are to revere one another.* I have never known a day I have not loved my spouse, but suddenly God had stepped into the

---

[6]Jn 6:51
[7]revoked

center of our lives and it was different; all I wanted in life was to revere my husband and to care for this beautiful soul the Lord had deigned to share with me! It was different; our marriage became centered on Jesus and how He saw us.

That weekend, those words ringing in our ears and beating in our hearts, the letter of St. Paul to the Ephesians came alive, *"...husbands should love their wives as their own bodies. He who loves his wife loves himself. For no one hates his own flesh but rather nourishes and cherishes it, even as Christ does His Church."*[8] *"In any case, each one should love his wife as himself, and the wife should respect her husband."*[9] *"and live in love, as Christ loved us and handed Himself over for us as a sacrificial offering to God for a fragrant aroma."*[10]

Now in *Humanae Vitae*, Christ was speaking to us again, of the journey to holiness and the great privilege that man and wife have in communion with Our Creator, the *two* (husband and wife) *plus One* (God) *becoming One*--husband and wife, having been given the gift of procreation, becoming one with God in His Plan to fill the earth with good things.

*"The most serious duty of transmitting human life, for which married persons are the free and responsible collaborators of God the Creator, has always been a source of great joy to them, even if accompanied by not a few difficulties and by distress."*[11]

Pope Paul VI spoke to married couples asking them to remember that their Christian vocation, which began the day they were baptized, is:

*"...reinforced by the Sacrament of Matrimony...the Lord entrusts the task of making visible to men the holiness and sweetness of the law which unites the mutual love of husband*

---

[8]Eph 5:28-29
[9]Eph 5:33
[10]Eph 5:2
[11]Pope Paul VI

and wife with their cooperation, with the love of God the Author of human life."

He spoke of difficult hardships inherent to married life, *"'the gate is narrow and the way is hard, that leads to life.' But the hope of that life must illuminate their way, as with courage they strive to live with wisdom, justice and piety in this present time, knowing that the figure of this world passes away."*

†††

At the Cairo conference they tried to coerce Third World countries into the forced use of contraceptives and abortion to stem the tide of inevitable famine, making aid the hook--to bring about *forced depopulation*, or annihilation, or sterilization. *Horrors of the Nazi age, revisited?*

Food shortage? And yet, farmers are being paid to not grow crops! In National Geographic we read:

Farmers are being paid by the government to flood thousands of acres of fields, once used to farm crops, and to turn them into *"wetlands."* Their justification: *"With the* **grain surplus** *and the present economic turmoil in agriculture, farmers are willing to do this."*[12]

So what do we do about it, kill unborn children, limit the number of children? We know a farmer who had no more than an 8th grade education and almost all his *ten* children graduated from college, with master degrees and doctorates in either engineering, psychology or teaching.

*"A change is also seen both in the manner of considering the person of a woman and her place in society, and in the value to be attributed to conjugal love in marriage, and also in the appreciation to be made of the meaning of the conjugal acts in relation to that love."*[13]

We are in prophetic times, times where men and women are no longer distinguishable, women with short hair and

---

[12]National Geographics, VOL. 195, NO.4, April, 1999--p.144
[13]*Humanae Vitae*

men with long, both sexes wearing earrings (and some in the most bizarre places), men and women wearing tailored men's suits with masculine shoes to match. *Men no longer pull out women's chairs or open doors for them, give them their seats on buses; they no longer ask them out on dates; men are staying home and caring for the children while the woman goes out and earns a living.* Not only are women being denigrated,[14] but men as well, losing all the respect St. Paul speaks of when he writes:

*"Wives should be subordinate to their husbands as to the Lord. For the husband is the head of his wife as Jesus is Head of the Church...Husbands love your wives, even as Christ loved the Church and handed Himself over for her, to sanctify her.*[15]

*"Finally and above all, man has made stupendous progress in the domination and rational organization of the forces of nature, such that he tends to extend this domination to his own total being: to the body, to psychical life,*[16] *to social life and even to the laws which regulate the transmission of life."*[17]

The Pope is referring to regulating how many children will be born--by the use of the artificial means of birth control and by determining beforehand how many will live long enough to emerge out of their mother's womb--through the horror of all horrors-abortion, murdering billions of babies (that we know of) throughout the world.

That not depopulating fast enough (sound like Nazi Germany and the Soviet Union?), assisted suicide has fought to become legal and has succeeded in one of the states of the United States of America, *"a nation founded under God,"* a nation which promises that *"all men are created equal with an inalienable right to life, liberty and the pursuit of happiness."*

---

[14]put down or belittled

[15]Eph 5:22-25

[16]a person who is supposedly sensitive to forces beyond the physical world.

[17]*Humanae Vitae*

The enemy of God leading us to hell; inch by inch, this state, not content with having made assisted suicide legal, their Medicaid program has removed from the approved list, 67 prescriptions which alleviate pain, help to prolong the life of the elderly and the handicapped, possibly to bring about a remission or cure; but instead has encouraged doctors to suggest medicines covered under the plan which the patient can use to take his life. *Is that not murder!!!*

They have to adopt these *death-camp* methods, refusing much-needed financial aid to those on Medicare, as people are not taking advantage of this ghoulish law designed to rid the world of the elderly and unwanted. As women are no longer taking advantage of the hospitals which provide abortion, women instead choosing Catholic hospitals which will *not* commit abortion, now, the butchers and butcheresses are trying to take away the non-profit status of Catholic hospitals in an attempt to make them buckle under.

*Euthanasia* and *Epivalothanasia* (or Imposed death) are not far behind forced sterilization through abortion, on the Hemlock Society's agenda of legalizing death. Before we began writing this book, we had never heard of *Epivalothanasia*, so let us take some definitions from that holy apostolate *Human Life International*:

*Epivalothanasia* is the greek word for "*imposed death.*"

Imposed death on an infant is called *abortion* (and punishable as far back as the Old Testament).

*Imposed death* on an adult has been erroneously coined, as well as maniputively called *euthanasia or assisted suicide*, which has been deceptively hailed as a *mercy death* -- to delude the unaware and coerce the masses into voting on genocide! You know, what drives us crazy is, the world is appalled and shocked at the brutal, inhumane slaughter, the genocide taking place in countries like Kosovo, and rightly so, and yet we do not see what is happening in our own country, in the world, before our very eyes. As Jesus said, we notice and condemn the speck in our brother's eye and ignore and condone the beam in our own. Life is life; death is death; the genocide of innocent babies being blown apart in their mothers' wombs is no less horrible, no less reprehensible and criminal than the genocide going on in the world.

All the above, no matter what names you give them, are just an expedient means of economic murder or murder for profit, with the victims of *infanticide* being used for experimentation and the premature death of *adults* to lower health care costs of insurance companies. Does this sound cruel and inhumane, heartless? Do you check out how each candidate you vote for, votes on these issues?

As for mercy killing of senior citizens, yesterday *you* were one, today *I* am one. The years fly! There is a story that has been told that goes like this:

"When Nazi Germany began its reign of terror, and first annexed Austria, I was sad for the Austrians; but I used the excuse I didn't understand the complexity of it all and I did nothing; *after all it wasn't me.* Then they took the Sudetenland, the western border of Czechoslovakia claiming it belonged to Germany, because of the 3.5 million Germans living there and I looked away; it made sense; *after all it wasn't me.* Then although they had agreed to leave the rest of Czechoslovakia to the Czech people, shortly after, they took all of Czechoslovakia. Again I didn't get involved; *after all it wasn't me.* They walked through Poland, and one month later, between Germany and their new ally the Soviet Union, Poland was no longer free. I felt really bad *but it wasn't me.* No one was safe-the low countries of the Netherlands fell, the Nordic countries of Norway and Sweden fell. Hitler and his storm troopers walked through Belgium and France, occupied Italy who was supposed to be an ally; the world was being enslaved; *but it wasn't me.* I heard about the thousands upon thousands of Jews being rounded up and killed in concentration camps and although it was appalling, *it wasn't me*. Then one day, they came pounding at my door and *it was me!*"

Is Pope Paul VI in *Humanae Vitae* not speaking out for those who cannot speak for themselves--those unborn confidently waiting to be born, trusting in the safety of their mother's womb? Is he not speaking for those who are *judged* unfit to live, whose quality of life has been determined so poor, they are better off dead? What happened to a people who believed that only God Who gives life can take away life, in His Will, in His manner, and in His timetable? How far will they go? In one *enlightened* country,[18] they do not even ask the patient if he or she desires to live or die, nor do they seek the permission of a member of the family; the doctor makes the decision, which is God's right alone!

"*...by extending to this field the application of the so-called "principle of totality," could it not be admitted that the intention of a less abundant but more rationalized fecundity*[19] *might transform a materially* **sterilizing** intervention into a **licit**[20] *and* **wise control of birth**?"[21]

There are, today, millions in Third World countries who are being extorted and pushed into *forced sterilization*, by those wolves in sheep's clothing threatening--*Do it or watch your children who are alive die from starvation*. And the amazing, very puzzling, very upsetting contradiction that I am having a problem with is not hearing all the liberals who cry out for the rights of the underdog, the downtrodden, thereby winning their votes, say nothing about these forms of prejudiced, imposed death on the helpless. Where are their voices, now, which scream *Social Justice*?

---

[18]the Netherlands

[19]fecundity means: germination, conception, insemination, propagation, reproduction

[20]licit--legal, lawful, authorized

[21]*Humanae Vitae*--

Pope Paul VI wrote further, quoting his predecessor **Pope John XXIII**:

*"Human life is sacred; from its very inception it reveals the creating Hand of God."* He continued: *"...in conformity with these landmarks in the human and Christian vision of marriage, we must once again declare that the direct interruption of the generative process already begun, and, above all, directly willed and procured abortion, even if for therapeutic reasons, are to be absolutely* **excluded** *as licit means of regulating birth. Finally to be excluded, as the teaching authority of the Church has frequently declared, is direct sterilization, whether perpetual or temporary, whether of the man or woman."*[22]

Speaking of the responsibility of a married couple, he clearly stated that conjugal acts made *"intentionally infecund,"*[23] cannot ever be considered as a *"lesser evil"* to, for example, performing the taking of an unborn life by means of abortion. Pope Paul VI spoke of the resulting effects of such actions:

*"the consequences of methods of artificial birth control, how wide and easy the road would thus be opened up towards conjugal infidelity and the general lowering of morality."*

Needless to say this was surely a prophecy; we only have to open our eyes and look around us.

As Pope John Paul II has also reiterated in the Catechism of the Catholic Church,

*"It is also feared that man, growing used to the employment of anti-conceptive practices, may finally lose respect for the woman and, no longer caring for her physical*

---

[22]This would refer to *tubal ligation* (or the tying of a woman's tubes) or a hysterectomy (except as a life-saving measure), or the vasectomy of a man to prevent the procreation process of bringing about God's Plan, which began with Adam and Eve, to go forth and multiply. *Tubal ligation* is illegal, except where the woman's life is endangered.

[23]that is to use birth control of any kind

*and psychological equilibrium, may come to the point of considering her as a mere instrument of selfish enjoyment, and no longer as his respected and beloved companion."*

As we read Humanae Vitae, which caused such controversy, we see prophecy fulfilled before our very eyes:

*"Let it be considered that a dangerous weapon would thus be placed in the hands of those public authorities who take no heed of moral exigencies.[24] Who could blame a government for applying to the solution of the problems of the community those means acknowledged to be licit for married couples in the solution of a family problem? Who will stop rulers from favoring, even imposing upon their peoples, if they were to consider it necessary , the method of contraception which they judge to be most efficacious?[25] In such a way men, wishing to be individual, family or social difficulties encountered in the observance of the Divine Law, would reach the point of placing, at the mercy of intervention by public authorities, the most personal and most reserved sector of conjugal intimacy."[26]*

Our dear Pope Paul VI prophesied:

*"It can be foreseen that this teaching will perhaps not be easily received by all: Too numerous are those voices-- amplified by the modern means of **propaganda**--which are contrary to the voice of the Church. To tell the truth, the Church is not surprised to be made, like her Divine Founder, 'a sign of contradiction,' yet she does not because of this cease to proclaim with humble firmness the entire moral law, both natural and evangelical. Of such laws the Church was not the author, nor consequently can she be the arbiter; she is only their depository and their interpreter, without ever being able to declare to be licit that which is not so by reason of its intimate and unchangeable opposition to the true good of man.*

---

[24]requirements
[25]effective, efficient, handy
[26]*Humanae Vitae*

*"On this occasion, we wish to draw the attention of educators, and of all who perform duties of responsibility in regard to the common good of human society, to the need of creating an atmosphere favorable to* **education** *in* **chastity**, *that is, to the triumph of healthy liberty over license by means of respect for the moral order."*[27]

How are we to deal with the daily temptations of daily life? Pope Paul VI wrote:

*"Everything in the* **modern media** *of social communications which leads to sense excitation and unbridled customs, as well as every form of pornography and licentious performances, must arouse the frank and unanimous reaction of all those who are solicitous for the* **progress of civilization** *and the defense of the common good of the human spirit. Vainly would one seek to* **justify** *such depravation with the pretext of artistic or scientific exigencies,*[28] *or to deduce an argument from the freedom allowed in this sector by the* **public authorities**."

Our Pope spoke out to the heads of nations, when he writes in his encyclical *Humanae Vitae*:

*"To Rulers, who are those principally responsible for the common good, and who can do so much to safeguard moral customs, we say: Do not allow the morality of your peoples to be degraded; do not permit that by legal means practices contrary to the natural and Divine law be introduced into that fundamental cell, the* **family**. *Quite other is the way in which public authorities can and must contribute to the solution of the demographic problem: namely, the way of a provident policy for the family, of a wise education of peoples in respect of moral law and the liberty of citizens."*

The Pope spoke of his awareness of the problems facing the heads of nations, especially in developing countries, but

---

[27]Pope Paul VI's encyclical-*Humanae Vitae*
[28]or license

rather than promoting or enforcing mandates which in fact are a means of sterilizing their peoples, they should address the needs of the peoples which could be resolved by more equal distribution of the country's opportunities, wealth, and resources, *"ensure the raising of living standards."* What Planned Parenthood and all those who demand birth control and sterilization do, rather than acting for the good of all women, instead, *"do violence to man's* (and woman's) *essential dignity, and is based only on an utterly materialistic conception of man* (or woman) *himself and of his life."*[29]

He spoke to those who had fallen prey to the sins of the world and had strayed, imploring them to turn to the Eucharist for strength to live according to God's Divine Law, and to not be discouraged but to place themselves in the shadow of God's Mercy, through the gift of that other great Sacrament, Penance.

He spoke to his *beloved priests,*

*"You know, too, that it is of the utmost importance, for peace of consciences and for the unity of the Christian people, that in the field of morals as well as in that of Dogma, all should attend to the* **Magisterium** *of the Church, and* **all should speak the same language.** *Hence, with all our heart we renew to you the heartfelt plea of the great Apostle Paul: 'I appeal to you, that there be* **no dissensions** *among you, but you be* **united** *in the same mind and the same judgment.'"*

The Culture of Death first began with more young people dying from drug over-doses each year, than died in the entire Vietnamese War. Our own son was a victim of this experimentation initiated in our finest universities by a professor testing the effects of drugs, or so they say! Not enough death or decrease of *over-population,* our society began promoting *safe-sex* as an answer to the permissive life-

---

[29]*Humanae Vitae*

style being promoted, and so babies were killed before they had a chance to grow in their mother's womb.

That not enough for Lucifer (he has always been envious of the gift of Life - Creation reserved solely by God for God), he began convincing women to have abortions, even late-term abortions with babies being killed as their little arms reached out and their chubby little legs kicked, pleading, *Look Mommy I can dance, if you will only give me a chance!*

Oh, my God, what have we done? How can we just have stood by and done nothing? Has it become like the violence we see on our television screen, where non-fiction becomes fiction? Have they conditioned us to death, horrible death? Have countless Americans--babies and senior citizens died because we have become hardened or conditioned, their lives *numbers*, not reality? What does God have to do to let us understand? Will He allow us to stand by and look the other way, while murderers are protected by legal maneuvering and the innocent punished--some for speaking out, others for praying? Did you know that praying in the streets has become unlawful assembly, but demonstrating, forming a picket line, is perfectly legal. What happened to equal justice for all?

Today--unborn babies, tomorrow--assisted suicide, then--euthanasia, then checking how the baby is faring in the womb and destroying those who are not the perfect baby of a perfect race (ala Hitler)! What would the world have been like without Mozart or Beethoven, or better yet Saint Leopold (all of 4'6") or Blessed Margaret of Castello (born blind, hunch back, and terribly deformed) and so many others who have brought such riches to the world?

Sparing nothing, willing to be a contradiction, to the point of persecution, Pope Paul VI dared to prophesy: **If we have Artificial Birth Control, it will lead to Abortion, which in turn will lead to Euthanasia.**

With every abortion, the voice of a future priest, religious, prophet or evangelist may be stilled and then *"...how can they call on Him Whom they have not believed? And how can they believe in Him of Whom they have not heard? And how can they hear without someone to preach?"*[30]

Too long, have the enemies of God had control over our fate and that of those who will follow. *Enough death! Choose Life!* We looked into the eyes of our new great-grandson and thought, Oh what a wonderful place the world is because you are in it. Little more than seven pounds, he had stolen our hearts and we would never be the same.

August 15, 1993, World Youth Day in Denver, Pope John Paul II told the cheering youth, totaling in the millions:

*"When the Founding Fathers of this great nation enshrined certain inalienable rights in the Constitution...they did so, because they recognized the existence of a "law"--a series of rights and duties--engraved by the Creator on each person's heart and conscience."*

*"The family is especially under attack. And the sacred character of human life is denied...Death battles against Life: a "culture of death" seeks to impose itself on our desire to live, and to love to the full.*

*"Christ needs you to enlighten the world and to show it the "path of life...You have shown that you understand that Christ's gift of life is not for you alone. 'I have great confidence in you, I have great pride in you; I am filled with encouragement, I am overflowing with joy."*

**America open your hearts to the truth of Christ's promise.**
*Choose Life over death, and vanquish the enemy of God!*

---

[30]Rom 10:14

# History of the World and the Church

History's major function, as set down through the centuries by philosophers and theologians, has been *first:* to try to unveil God's Will in man's life; *second:* to somehow through studying the past, gain understanding into the meaning and the direction of man's life, and *third:* and probably most neglected--to learn and profit from the historic past, in order for man to best live in the present and most influence the future. History, when most honestly reported, paves the way for the future to be influenced by the present and the present to learn from the past.

Through history's faithful recounting of the strengths and weaknesses of those who have gone before, man has heroes or anti-heroes to follow or ignore and, through this, avoid the mistakes and pitfalls facing him in his generation, thus breaking the devastating cycle of man's history of horrors past and tragedy repeated.

## Another word for history could be prophecy

As another word for history could be prophecy, so another word for historian could be prophet. To know the past is to sadly predict the future; for history is sure to repeat itself, unless we break the chains which bind us to the world's empty promises. St. Augustine said that another word for the world is the devil. If we follow the ways of the world to the exclusion of God in our lives, we are doomed to follow the path of the devil which leads to the endless darkness of the abyss. With his eyes on Jesus, Peter was able to walk on water; it was only when he looked down that he began to sink and drown. As with Peter, our first Pope, it is never too late; Jesus is waiting to catch us in His loving Arms.

Jesus said, we cannot love two masters, we will love the one and hate the other. The world and its prince will tell you that you can have it all. He has always been a liar. To follow the world and its demands will ultimately lead to compromising God and His rightful place in our lives.

One of Satan's primary goals is to convince us we have plenty of time. John the Baptist had a mission and lived every day as if it were his last. Jesus knew why He was born and as He grew in wisdom,[1] more and more recognizing His Father's Will in His life, He did not spare Himself, to the point of carrying His Fiat on the Cross, to Calvary. Jesus walked with His eyes on the Father, God's Word on His Lips and the Father's Will in His Heart. He lived His time on earth with *urgency*, spending every waking moment forgiving men's sins, healing their minds, bodies and souls and bringing them the Good News, there is a God and this God loves us.

When ever I think of God the Father, my mind and heart fly to Michelangelo's fresco on the ceiling of the Sistine Chapel, where the Father is stretching out His Hand to bring life to His first creation, Adam. God has been reaching out to His children from the moment He breathed life into our first parents, Adam and Eve, till today. God sent messengers, in the form of Angels, in the Old Testament. He sent the prophets to warn His children, to call them to repentance; and our fathers, the chosen people killed them. Surely, He thought, they will not kill My only Begotten Son, but we did, again! And He never gave up on us!

Along with those of the Old testament, God called *new prophets* in the New Testament, first John the Baptist prophesied and then His only begotten Son Jesus. And after them, He continued to summon prophets, from all walks of life, from one corner of the earth to the other; and having summoned them, He commissioned them to spread His Truth, through the Church which flowed from the Heart of Jesus on the Cross. We have been recounting the lives of the Saints in many of our books and programs. In this book,

---

[1]Lk 2:52

we will cover the prophecies of those Saints, which we judge are critical to the present time and its impending danger.

**To search the past is to learn about the future.**

If we are not careful, one day we will find ourselves awaking, as if, like Rip Van Winkle, from a deep sleep; the world has changed and we no longer recognize our families, our friends, our Church, our country. It is as if the earth is spinning out of control. We try to cry out, but we look about us, and it appears that those around us are not aware something is seriously wrong. We think, Can't they hear our hearts beating wildly, like drums in the jungle, issuing warnings the enemy is about to strike?

Suddenly we recognize what the Father of Time has been doing. He has been wildly ticking away seconds into minutes, minutes into hours, hours into weeks, weeks into months, months into years. It is as if we have been on a speeding train, accelerating more and more, until we finally become aware it is going too fast. Now we want to shout, *Stop, we have things yet undone.* We see signs that the station we are fast approaching is that final moment when it is time to stand before the throne of God.

The years have flown by; the tomorrows have become todays and the todays become yesterdays; the Angel of Death is standing on the threshold of our life, holding out his hand, and we cry out, *Where did the time go? It was only yesterday we were someone's children; we turned around and we were someone's parents; the years flew by as if days, and our children had made us grandparents, and then in a blink of an eye our grandchildren had made us great-grandparents!*

When the fog lifts, the dawn will cut through the mist, the sun will peek out from behind the mountains, and a rainbow will stretch across the sky bringing the promise of a new day. The mist clouding our vision will be lifted. Then, we will see the reason we were born; we will glimpse God's glorious dream for us; and the world will be changed, men's hearts will be melted, each man will be his brother's keeper; there will be no more starvation, no more violence, no more division; only the unity that Communion with the Lord can bring about. For you see, a prophecy is a vision, is a dream, is a promise--a *vision* of what life can be when we walk in the Way of the Lord--a *dream* of His plan for us, when the world was created--a *promise* of what lies ahead in this world and the next for those who love Him and obey His commands.

Then, as with the different prophets from different walks of life, who came before us, we will have the urgency to share this joy, heretofore unknown to the world, and the world will never be the same. Was this not what the prophets had in common, a burning desire to preach the Good News of what happiness awaits those who adore the Lord and keep His covenant?

And how shall you know these prophecies are from God? They will agree with the Word of God and the teachings of the Church He founded - the Roman Catholic Church. You will find in this book and all the books we have written, only those prophets, mystics and visionaries who have passed the test of time, have been accepted by Mother Church, have not written anything contrary to the Magisterium, have been recognized by the Church and raised to the Communion of Blesseds and Saints in Heaven.

**God has been talking to His children down through the ages**

God gave hope to the Jewish people by heralding the coming of the Messiah, Our Lord Jesus Christ. Through His prophets, God revealed that the Messiah, the Anointed One would come from their race; and although they would reject Him, the Father declared *why* His Son would come and *what* His mission would be. So that they would believe Jesus was His Son and that He, their God, had sent Him for their salvation, the Father foreshadowed in the Old Testament, the miracles Jesus would perform. And they rejected Him, refusing to see Him for Who He was. Incarcerated in a jail of their own making, they allowed their stubborn disbelief to cloud their vision; they refused to see God's Mercy, sending His only Son to release them from a different kind of captivity than that which they knew under the Romans.

God was once again opening the Red Sea, only the Red Sea was the Blood His Son would shed on the Cross, opening the way to Salvation, an exodus from the captivity brought about by their first parents' original sin. And once again, God was rejected.

Not even witnessing the Sacrifice of His only Begotten Son on the Cross, did His poor children recognize God and what He was doing. Blinded, they were unable to follow His Light. Deafened by elusive promises of the world, they were powerless to hear His Voice. When Jesus gave over His Spirit to His Father, they did not grasp the meaning of Jesus' words, *It is finished*; and so when the curtains of the Temple split, the Gates of Heaven opened and with them the promise of eternal life with the Father; having rejected God's Grace, God's supreme sacrifice, they walked away, waiting for the Messiah yet to come. But before we judge the Jewish people, they were only following their trusted priests, those chosen by God to lead them Home to Him. The condemnation was, and will be, on those of whom Jesus spoke, those who lead the smallest of His children astray,[2] and those of whom the prophet Ezekiel spoke in Ezek 34:

*"Woe to those shepherds of Israel who have been pasturing themselves. Should not shepherds, rather, pasture sheep...the sheep you have not pastured. You did not strengthen the weak nor heal the sick nor bind up the injured. You did not bring back the strayed nor seek the lost, but you lorded it over them harshly and brutally. So*

---

[2]Mt 18:6

*they were scattered for lack of a shepherd, and became food for all the wild beasts. My sheep were scattered and wandered over all the mountains and high hills; My sheep were scattered over the whole earth, with no one to look after them or to search for them.   ...because of this, shepherds, hear the word of the Lord: ...I swear I am coming against those shepherds.  I will claim My sheep from them and put a stop to their shepherding my sheep so that they can no longer pasture themselves.*"[3]

Who will warn My people, the Lord cries out!  Whom shall I send?  Do we answer, Here I am Lord, I have come to do Your Will?  Do we dare speak?  Do we dare be Catholic?  And what is the price for our silence, how many dead will be left in the wake of our silence?

I remember seeing a movie once, with people walking in a daze.  They appeared to be peaceful, but as the plot thickened you realized they had been programmed how to think, how to act, no feelings, no involvement--all robots living in their own solitary world, oblivious to what was happening around them.  People were disappearing; but no one seemed to notice; no one seemed to care.  Later you find out that at age thirty-five, they were to be used as nourishment for the following generation, being killed and recycled to feed those who, because of statistics, had a greater life expectancy left and were subsequently considered more useful.  No one seemed to mind; I wonder how they felt when it was *their* time to be sacrificed for the greater good?

Does this sound like grotesque science fiction; I thought so; how ridiculous a concept; it sickened me.  Now, we have not written this to do either, but to ask you to reflect on what is happening in our civilized world today; possibly we need to tell the producers to update the scenario.  When you walk

---

[3]Ez 34:1-11

into the cosmetic department of a department store and you see not one but two signs reading, "*Contains human ingredients,*" I say it is a time to wake up, and speak up!

What the young in the movie did not consider was that the time would come when they would not be apathetic bystanders but involved subjects being led to be reprocessed. Today, unborn babies are being sacrificed in their mothers' wombs for science. Patients on life support systems, who have willed their bodies to be used as body parts after their death, are being sacrificed, taken off even liquids, given sedatives so they will not move, having organs harvested while they are still alive. You don't believe it; neither did the German people believe the atrocities committed against helpless men, women and children. This was their defense, when their grandchildren questioned them, "*What did you think was burning, the stench that filled the air? Did you not know it was God's children?*" And what will we reply, when they ask us "*What did you do to stop the barbaric slaughter of the Holy Innocents of the Twentieth Century?*" Will we, like the German people, hang our heads and cry? I hope so! I hope someone will mourn the systematic killing of Americans in this land of the free and brave, this land our forefathers died for.

People are having a hard time believing in the latter days; I must admit we were among their number. We would protest, *we are a positive people believing in the Mercy of God. God would not allow this to happen.* But now, as I read the headlines, each day, I must ask how much will God take before He comes down on us? With one breath, we are killing babies by the millions; with the other, scientists are cloning. It doesn't make sense, until you remember Hitler and the master race he strived to create! We are not only making ourselves into self-styled gods, killing God's precious creations, we are again playing God, getting into God's business of creation, as science dares to clone first sheep and then humans.  Where will it stop!  *When will we finally go beyond Sodom and Gomorrah, or have we already?*

Prophecies, exposing the Antichrist, were preached by the Early Church Fathers right from the beginning, announcing all that the apostles had passed down to them. At the cost of their lives they went about preparing the Mystical Body of Christ for the persecution that was awaiting them.  By their dedication, they did more to fortify them to withstand the temptations they would face, than by their words.  They pleaded with the brethren to not trade in Jesus for false gods and false teachings; they implored them to not go along with the crowd and choose the Barabbas of their day over Jesus; they warned them to not trade in their immortal souls in exchange for temporary life on earth; they encouraged them to remember how St. Peter wept his whole life for having denied Jesus, in his attempt to flee from persecution.

The Fathers cautioned, the Antichrist would tickle their ears, sweet-talking them into accommodating the enemy by apostatizing, insisting they could do no good dead.  They reminded the brothers and sisters of Jesus' Words, *"Do not fear he who can kill the body, but he who can kill the body and the soul."*[4]

Although the Early Church Fathers faced imprisonment, torture and death, for sowing the seeds of truth which had come down to them from the Apostles, they could do naught but speak out!  Arming them with the double-edged sword St. Paul spoke of,[5] they went about instructing the brothers and sisters, using the sound doctrines of the Church.  Warning them of the rising of the Antichrist, they tirelessly preached, strengthening the Early

---

[4]Mt 10:28
[5]Heb 4:12

Church, fortifying them for the inevitable martyrdom they would face.

Are we not in the days St. Paul spoke of, where man is following the passions of the flesh, disdainfully trading in God and eternal life with Him, for the passing pleasures of this world?  Paul said that when man rejects the Divine, renounces Christ as the Son of God, disdainfully spurns the authority of the Church, refuses to follow Jesus, instead choosing the powers of sin, mimicking those who cried out, *We have no king but Caesar,* then the God of Justice will lash out, with a fury, meting out the punishment sinful, defiant man has been begging for.  Our God is a jealous God; and you shall have no gods before Him, says Holy Scripture.

God has not been past giving sinful man what he wants; He did it when the Israelites wanted a king.  When God has had enough of man rejecting His Son Who is the Truth, the Way and the Life, for the darkness of sin, God will grant man his heart's desire.  It is man who chooses sin; the devil is powerless without man's consent, as is the Antichrist or the antichrists who are preceding him.  Sinful man closes his eyes to sin and consequently to the signs coming from the Antichrist that it is he who is taking over the world.  How God must grieve, when He sees how easily He is passed over by His creation for the temporary promises and comforts of the enemy of God.

Mother Church has gone through 2000 years of persecution.  In the beginning, she was injured by those who did not believe in her and Jesus, as she had to stand helplessly by and see her children, the early Christians, die martyrs' deaths in the Circus Maximus and the Coliseum, ripped apart not only by the fury of the lions, but the hate of the Roman spectators who cheered the beasts on.  But, she survived!  Jesus was true to His promise; a perfect Church, strengthened by the blood of the Martyrs, became legitimate and was able to rise from the catacombs, into the daylight.

But now, a new torture and violence awaits her, more painful and devastating than anything she has suffered--an arrow of discontent and division piercing her heart, inflicted by her beloved priests, bishops and religious. They have rejected the Magisterium of the Church, their own prideful ideas replacing the truth passed down by Jesus and the Apostles.[6] Because they have been looked upon as respected voices of Jesus and His Church, all they espouse spreads throughout the Body of Christ, lies becoming truths and truths becoming lies. The persecution has taken on a new form, a more deadly form, for the enemy is unrecognizable; and as in the past, when exposed, it might be too late--the deluded maintaining loyalty and allegiance to heretics whom they believe are the Church.

Our beautiful Church, the Hope Diamond of the world, has been walking the Way of the Cross, shouldering the Cross her Founder carried, suffering scourging after scourging, mocked by those from without and those within the Church. Every time the nails on her body are pounded deeper and deeper, she cries out, but there are few who will brave walking by her side. Mother Mary, Mother of Jesus and Mother of the Church, are you crying out, *What has my Son done to you that you are persecuting Him and His Church?* As the Church, like Jesus before her, stumbles and falls under the weight of her children's sins, is there no one who will step forward to help her carry the Cross? As before, a lone woman steps forward, another Veronica, only now a cloistered Nun called Mother Angelica, who walks past the menacing, unspoken threats of those who are dragging Mother Church to Calvary, to console her, to walk beside her, to let her and her enemies know that she is not alone.

---

[6]To learn more about the Heresies which attacked the Church for the last 2000 years, read Bob and Penny Lord's book: *Scandal of the Cross and Its Triumph, heresies throughout the History of the Church.*

Where have the women gone?  At least with Jesus, the women walked with Him, remained at the foot of the Cross with His Mother; but in these days, many of Jesus' brides have deserted His Church, crying out with the pagans, Crucify her!  Although wounded mortally, her hands and feet pierced, she is raised high on the Cross for the world to see.  To the foolish, she appears dead, but like her Savior she will rise again; for Jesus made a promise that hell would not prevail against her, His Church.

Has God not summoned us at this time and place, to give Jesus permission to use our voices and our hearts to evangelize to the whole world?  Jesus has no less called us by name, than He did His first disciples, the day we were baptized, conferring upon us the mission to bring His prophetic words to the whole world.  On the day we were initiated into the Church, Jesus filled us with a heart yearning to know Him, to Love Him and to serve Him.  The day of our Confirmation, the final initiation (into the Church), the Bishop slapped us on the cheek,[7] and called us *Soldiers of Christ,* reminding us we must be prepared to suffer if need be, for the Church Jesus founded.

When we become aware how Jesus sees us, how He fashioned us to be, what His Divine Plan is for us, we find ourselves restless, wondering what we have done with our lives.  As the Word of God is ageless, for all people, for all times, is the Lord not speaking to those who are even more accountable, those who have the gifts of the Holy Spirit, for that matter all the Sacraments, to strengthen them against the onslaughts of the enemy who conquers by pride and division?

Because of the Incarnation, God becoming Man, joining us to the Divine, making us part of His family, sharing God the Father with us, we are no longer the same; we belong to

---

[7]at the time Bob and Penny were confirmed; this is rarely done today

the Royal Family, the Holy Family and the castle we will live in for eternity is with the Blessed Trinity and Mother Mary, the Angels and the Saints.  With this heritage, we have been given, to have and to hold, through the generosity of God's Grace, and the Sacraments we have received in His Church,

Are we not all called to be Defenders of the Faith!

***What a glorious moment to be alive!***

# Apostasy and the Antichrist

When we look at the entire Twentieth Century, we can see the Antichrist or a series of antichrists weaving a net to ensnare the human race into destroying itself. If any one of them were to identify himself, and propose the annihilation of the human race to sane men and women, you can bet there would not be many takers. The antichrists, as with the devil, with whom they are in league, have systematically given man's downfall different names over the centuries, with the same goal in mind - the end of all that God so lovingly created, the human race.

We talk of the devil with disdain, and he is worthy of contempt, but we must respect what he can do. As God gave him his gifts, we must not look down on his power. To belittle the power of the devil is to belittle God's Power; for the devil can only do what God permits him to do. So, you might ask, why has God and why will God allow Satan, through the Antichrist, to strike down His children? In the Old Testament, we read how God used the enemies of the Israelites to punish them, when they turned away from Him. Punish them yes, but loving Father it was not *His* Will they be annihilated, but *their* choice. As when we stand before the Throne of God, it is *we* who choose between Heaven, Hell or Purgatory,[1] so it is *we* who choose to hope or despair.

As we have been researching the writings of different prophets of the Old Testament, those in the New Testament, and those who followed, seeking a key to what the Lord is trying to tell us, we have found ourselves discovering pieces of the puzzle coming together, forming an image of the final days.

Throughout the Old and New Testament, it has been prophesied that the Antichrist will come in the form of a

---

[1]for more on this, read Bob and Penny Lord's book: *Visions of Heaven, Hell and Purgatory.*

man. First through deception,[2] and then tyranny, he will rule the world, he will deceive not only the masses but leaders of nations, and shepherds of the Church. He will encompass and embrace all that is evil; he will be the antithesis of Our Lord and Savior Who, like God the Father, is all good, all love, perfect love. The Antichrist, like his mentor - Satan, is evil and as evil is consumed with the will to delude, to conquer, to enslave, to entice even those who should know better; and in so doing, by ensnaring the elect - the shepherds, he entraps the sheep who, trusting blindly, follow their pastors' voices. It does not give us reassurance or hope because, for centuries before and after Christ, the #1 enemy of God, he who is sin personified, Satan has been roaming the earth seeking the ruin of souls.

We are endeavoring to show you, through different prophets how this, the end of the Second Millennium, has been prophesied to be possibly the ushering in of the latter days. We say *possibly* because Jesus in Holy Scripture tells us that no one knows the place or the time but His Father in Heaven.[3] The Old Testament contained veiled prophecies of Christ's coming, as man was not able to assimilate the fullness of God's Word, yet to be brought to God's people by His only Begotten Son. Through Jesus Christ, and the New Testament brought to us by the Apostles, those veils were lifted and revealed all that had been hidden.

†††

There are certain points which most every one is agreed upon, because they come from Scripture as well as from private revelation from solid sources. One of them is that the Antichrist will come as a result of a great apostasy. He will be spewed up from the bowels of hell and vomit on mankind through that apostasy.

---

[2]fraud, perjury, lying, trickery
[3]Mt 24:26

The Great Apostasy has been given many denotations. Apostasy is interpreted in the secular dictionary as the abandoning of what one has believed in. The Church defines "Apostasy as a total repudiation of the Christian Faith by one who has been baptized."[4] An apostate denies all the teachings, the Dogmas of the Catholic Church, after having full knowledge of the meaning of these teachings; although it seems like a contradiction in terms how anyone who has full knowledge of our Faith and Our Lord Jesus Christ could walk away and reject it.

The Catechism of the Catholic Church speaks about Apostasy in two sections:

*"In fact, 'in this one and only Church of God from its very beginnings there arose certain rifts, which the Apostle strongly censures as damnable.    But in subsequent centuries much more serious dissensions appeared and large communities became separated from full communion with the Catholic Church - for which, often enough, men of both sides were to blame.'[5] The ruptures that wound the unit of Christ's Body - here we must distinguish heresy, apostasy, and schism[6] - do not occur without human sin."[7]*

In another part of the Catechism it spells out the above:

*"**Incredulity** is the neglect of revealed truth or the willful refusal to assent to it.    '**Heresy** is the obstinate post-baptismal denial of some truth which must be believed with divine and catholic faith, or it is likewise an obstinate doubt concerning the same; **Apostasy** is the total repudiation of the Christian faith; **Schism** is the refusal of*

---

[4]*cf* Code of Canon Law 751
[5]*Unitatis redintegratio* 3
[6]*Unitatis redintegratio* 3-1
[7]Catechism of the Catholic Church # 817

*submission to the Roman Pontiff or of communion with
the members of the Church subject to him.*"[8,9]

In 1917, Our Lady appeared to three children in a little
farming village in Portugal, Fatima. The place was the Cova
da Iria. As part of the apparitions which spanned the
months of May through October, always on the 13th of the
month, Our Lady gave certain messages to the oldest of the
children, Lucia, 3 secrets which were not to be told to
anyone unless and until she was given permission from
Heaven. One of the secrets was given to the world just prior
to the Second World War. It was a prophecy of that war and
just a small indicator of the devastation that would be rained
down on sinful men.

The third secret was written down on paper, and given
to the Pope, to be opened and read to the world in 1960.
Pope John XXIII, who had only been in his pontificate for a
year and a half when he read the message, is said to have
wept and put it back in the safe place where it had been for
these many years. We believe that each Pope has looked at
that message from Our Lady through Sr. Lucia at some time
in their pontificate. The message has never been read to the
people.

For many years, it was believed by many people that the
secret which had been given to the Pope concerned the end
of the world, which would most likely occur after a major
nuclear holocaust. But it's been over eighty years since that
message was sent to the Pope, and he has not given us any
indicator as to what the secret could be.

As of late, probably in the last twenty years or so, a new
theory has surfaced as to what the apocalyptical message
from our Lady might have been. In prayer, a great many
people have been given to believe that the third Secret of

---

[8]Code of Canon Law 751
[9]Catechism of the Catholic Church # 2089

Fatima is the great Apostasy, which will bring with it the appearance of the Antichrist, signaling the beginning of the end of the world.

†††

**The Coming of the Antichrist**

The coming of the Antichrist is part and parcel of the great Apostasy. Most respected theologians admit that we are now living in the age of the great Apostasy, so it is only natural that the Antichrist will follow, and ultimately we will experience the Second Coming of Our Lord Jesus Christ.

But the coming of the Antichrist has been predicted from the very beginning. St. Paul believed that Nero was the Antichrist, and that the Second Coming of Christ would be in his lifetime.

***Who is the Antichrist?*** The name itself defines the person to whom it refers - *anti* means *against*, therefore Antichrist is one who is against Christ; or one who is opposed to the work of God, especially that accomplished through Jesus the Messiah. In Holy Scripture, in the Old Testament the Antichrist is called *"the abomination of desolation."*[10] In the New Testament, St. Paul refers to the Antichrist as *"the man of sin,"* and *"the son of perdition."*[11] Then St. John in the Book of Revelation calls him *"the beast that ascended out of the abyss* (or hell)."[12]

*"About the coming of the Lord, brothers, and our being gathered to Him: please do not be too easily thrown into confusion or alarmed by any manifestation of the Spirit or any statement or any letter claiming to come from us, suggesting that the Day of the Lord has already arrived. Never let anyone deceive you in any way.*

---

[10]Dn 9:27
[11]2Thes 2:3
[12]Rv 11:7

*"It cannot happen until the Great Apostasy has taken place and there has appeared the man of sin, the lost one, the enemy, who raises himself above every so called god or object of worship to enthrone himself in God's sanctuary and flaunts the claim that he is God. Surely you remember my telling you about this when I was with you? And you know, too, what is still holding him back from appearing before his appointed time. The mystery of wickedness is already at work, but let him who is restraining it once be removed, and the wicked one will appear openly. The Lord will destroy him with the breath of His Mouth and will annihilate him with His glorious appearance at His Coming.*

*"But the coming of the man of sin will be marked by Satan being at work in all* **kinds of counterfeit miracles and signs and wonders,** *and every wicked deception aimed at those who are on the way to destruction because they would not accept the love of the truth and so be saved. And therefore God sends on them a power that deludes people so that they believe what is false, and so that those who do not believe the truth and take their pleasure in wickedness may all be condemned."[13]*

In John's letter on the Antichrist, he distinguishes between *the* Antichrist and many antichrists. Evidently, the distinction he was making was between genuinely evil people who would torture the Church throughout Salvation History, and *the Antichrist*, who will come just before the end of the world.[14]

---

[13]2Thes 2:1-12

[14]Applicable only to the one enemy who will appear before the Last Judgment and draw many away before being defeated by Christ.-- Catholic Encyclopedia--Broderick 1970

*"Many deceivers have gone out into the world, those who do not acknowledge Jesus Christ as coming in the flesh; such is the deceitful one and the Antichrist."[15]*

*"Children, it is the last hour; and just as you have heard that the Antichrist was coming, so now many antichrists have appeared. Thus we know that this is the last hour."[16]*

*"Who is the liar? Whoever denies that Jesus is the Christ. Whoever denies the Father and the Son, this is the Antichrist."[17]*

The Church has had many theories on the Antichrist. All are correct.

One is that the Antichrist is any one person, group or philosophy in opposition to the Person of Christ, the teachings of Christ and the Church of Christ.

Another equally accepted and more popular is that the Antichrist is a specific person, who will come upon the scene towards the end of the world to try to take as many believers away from the true Church of Christ.

It is said that the Antichrist will appear to be another Christ, another god, complete with prophecies, miracles, signs and wonders.

The Catechism of the Catholic Church takes Scripture Passages and puts them together in the following prophetic teachings:

*"Before Christ's Second Coming the Church must pass through a final trial that will shake the faith of many believers. The persecution that accompanies her pilgrimage on earth will unveil the 'mystery of iniquity' in the form of a religious deception offering men an apparent solution to their problems at the price of Apostasy from the truth. The supreme religious deception is that of the Antichrist, a pseudo-messianism by which man glorifies*

---

[15]2Jn 1:7
[16]1Jn 2:18
[17]1Jn 2:22

*himself in place of God and of his Messiah come in the flesh.*

*"The Antichrist's deception already begins to take shape in the world every time the claim is made to realize within history that messianic hope which can only be realized beyond history through the eschatalogical[18] judgment. The Church has rejected even modified forms of this falsification of the Kingdom to come under the name of millenarianism,[19] especially the 'intrinsically perverse' political form of a secular messianism.[20]*

*The Church will enter the glory of the Kingdom only through this final Passover, when she will follow her Lord in His death and Resurrection. The Kingdom will be fulfilled, then, not by a historic triumph of the Church through a progressive ascendancy, but only by God's victory over the final unleashing of evil, which will cause His Bride to come down from Heaven. God's triumph over the revolt of evil will take the form of the Last Judgment after the final cosmic upheaval of this passing world."[21]*

Down through the centuries, Saints and holy people have prophesied about the coming of the Antichrist. In each age, Satan has used at least one if not more, extremely evil instruments (people) to do his dirty work and fight against Jesus and His Church in an attempt to destroy it. Very often these cohorts of Satan have been labeled the Antichrist, especially during their lifetime, (i.e., Nero, Ghengis Khan, Napoleon, Hitler, Stalin, and the latest butchers of the

---

[18]dealing with Doctrines and Dogmas concerning the Second Coming, the Resurrection, the Last Judgment, and Heaven and hell.

[19]movement which interpreted incorrectly the Book of Revelation, using a literal translation, especially regarding "the thousand years"

[20]Pope Pius XI, in *Divini Redemptoris*, condemning the *'false mysticism'* of this *'counterfeit of the redemption of the lowly.'*

[21]Catechism of the Catholic Church # 675-676-677

Balkans) only to be relegated to the minor role of an antichrist, one of many, after they died, and the Second Coming was not imminent.

Most all of these candidates for the claim were wicked enough to gain the coveted title, but they did not possess the other quality which is most important, and that is the charismatic nature, the ability to get people to believe that they were another Christ. They were not able to draw people to them in the same way that Jesus could. And so we, the people of God, breathed a great sigh of relief at their passing, and waited for the next barrage from Satan, saying to ourselves, "Could the next one be the one?"

Meanwhile, there have been no end of prophecies about the coming of the Antichrist, and the great Apostasy, which goes hand-in-hand with it.

## The Antichrist of the Twentieth Century -- Lord Maitreya

We want to share with you a full-page ad which appeared in more than twenty major newspapers around the world on Sunday, April 25, 1982 at a cost of over $500,000.

~ ~ ~ ~ ~ ~ ~ ~ ~ ~ ~ ~ ~ ~ ~ ~ ~ ~ ~ ~ ~ ~ ~ ~ ~ ~

"THE WORLD HAS HAD ENOUGH...
OF HUNGER, INJUSTICE, WAR.

"IN ANSWER TO OUR CALL FOR HELP;
AS WORLD TEACHER FOR ALL HUMANITY

### "THE CHRIST IS NOW HERE.

"HOW WILL WE RECOGNIZE HIM?

"Look for a modern man concerned with modern problems--political, economic, and social. Since July 1977, the Christ has been emerging as a spokesman for a group or community in a well-known modern country. He is not a religious leader, but an educator in the broadest sense of the word--pointing the way out of our present crisis. We will recognize Him by His[22] extraordinary spiritual potency, the universality of His viewpoint, and His love for all humanity. He comes not to judge but to aid and inspire.

## "WHO IS THE CHRIST?

"Throughout history, humanity's evolution has been guided by a group of enlightened men, the Masters of Wisdom. They have remained largely in the remote desert and mountain places of earth, working mainly through their disciples who live openly in the world. This message of the Christ's reappearance has been given primarily by such a disciple trained for his task for over 20 years. At the center of this 'Spiritual Hierarchy' stands the World Teacher, LORD MAITREYA, known by Christians as the CHRIST. And as the Christians await the Second Coming, so the Jews await the MESSIAH, the Buddhists the FIFTH BUDDHA, the Moslems the IMAM MAHDI, and the Hindus await KRISHNA. These are all names for one individual. His presence in the world guarantees there will be no third World War.

## "WHAT IS HE SAYING?

"'My task will be to show you how to live together peacefully as brothers. This is simpler than you imagine, My friends, for it requires only the acceptance of sharing.

"'How can you be content with the modes within which you now live: when millions starve and die in squalor; when the rich parade their wealth before the poor; when each man is his neighbor's enemy; when no man trusts his brother?

"'Allow me to show you the way forward into a simpler life where no man lacks; where no two days are alike; where the Joy of Brotherhood manifests through all men.

---

[22]Caps for him and his part of the ad, placed by the cult who made up the ad, not meant by the authors to suggest that the man mentioned is truly God.

"'Take your brother's need as the measure for your action and solve the problems of the world.'"

## "WHEN WILL YOU SEE HIM?

"He has not yet declared His true status and His location is known to only a very few disciples. One of these has announced that soon the Christ will acknowledge His identity and within the next two months will speak to humanity through a worldwide television and radio broadcast. His message will be heard inwardly, telepathically, by all people in their own language. From that time, with His help, we will build a new world."

**"WITHOUT SHARING THERE CAN BE NO JUSTICE; WITHOUT JUSTICE THERE CAN BE NO PEACE; WITHOUT PEACE THERE CAN BE NO FUTURE."**

~ ~ ~ ~ ~ ~ ~ ~ ~ ~ ~ ~ ~ ~ ~ ~ ~ ~ ~ ~ ~ ~ ~ ~ ~ ~ ~

The head of the organization which put this ad campaign together was a Benjamin Creme, a Scottish New Age guru who has been lecturing all over the world trying to bring about the New Age agenda of Lord Maitreya. It's been seventeen years since Creme created this ad campaign and began circulating his story of Lord Maitreya. He's still passing around pretty much the same story about him, with a few key updates.

In a sense, you might say that there has not been a great deal of progress with Lord Maitreya taking over and saving the world. And that would be correct, to a degree.

For instance, the worldwide TV and radio interview which was predicted in 1982 still has not come to pass, but in 1999, Benjamin Creme's Internet outlet, Share International, insists it's just around the corner.

But Benjamin Creme's most recent series of press releases, show very frightening similarities between his Lord Maitreya and the prophetic descriptions of the Antichrist in

Scripture and through various Saints and Holy People down through the centuries.

Creme does insist that some of the 1982 predictions have come to pass,

that Lord Maitreya has appeared before thousands of witnesses on many occasions and healed 40 to 50 people of varying diseases and illnesses, and that they immediately recognized him as the Christ;

that he predicted the fall of Communism;

the release of Nelson Mandela from prison

the resignation of Margaret Thatcher as prime minister of England well before she left office.

He is known to be very charismatic, socially conscious.

Although Benjamin Creme insists that Jesus was not the Messiah, that Lord Maitreya is the Messiah, he emphasizes that Lord Maitreya fulfills prophecy regarding Jesus Christ.

As you read the signs, does it come to mind that this Lord Maitreya fulfills prophecy regarding the Antichrist? This is what is said of the Antichrist:

*"But the coming of the man of sin will be marked by Satan being at work in all kinds of counterfeit miracles and signs and wonders, and every wicked deception aimed at those who are on the way to destruction because they would not accept the love of the truth and so be saved. And therefore God sends on them a power that deludes people so that they believe what is false, and so that those who do not believe the truth and take their pleasure in wickedness may all be condemned."*[23]

Some of the Early Church Fathers had powerful statements to make on the coming of the Antichrist. St. John Damascene writes very convincingly and matter-of-factly about when and why the Antichrist must come.

---

[23]2Thes 2:1-12

St. John Damascene rationalizes that the Antichrist must come at the end of the world, because it has to be after the Gospel has been preached to all the Gentiles.

He further makes the point that after that's been done, the Jews will still not have accepted Jesus as Messiah, using the Scripture passage, "*I have come in the name of the Father, and you receive Me not; if another shall come in his own name, him you will receive.*"[24]

His prophecy in the Second Century was that the Jews would not accept Jesus, but they would accept the Antichrist.

Regarding Lord Maitreya, in her book on New Age, Constance Cumby reported, that he fits the description of the Antichrist, in what would seem the fulfillment of the prophecy of St. John Damascene:

"*Hiding behind an aura of undeserved respectability, the New Age Movement has managed to actively recruit many unsuspecting* **Jews and Christians** *to work for their own destruction.*

"*They were unsuspecting that they were supporting a movement that parallels Nazism in every grotesque detail, including a teaching that a* **'blood taint'** *rested on those of Jewish extraction and another being that of a planned new 'super race.'*

"*This (her) book sets forth a small portion of my research findings. What will be difficult to fully convey is the sense of mounting horror I found while piecing this multitude of data together. It appears to culminate in a scheme* **both fulfilling the prophetic requirements for the Antichrist as set forth in the Bible, and also matching Nazism down to use of swastikas.**"[25]

---

[24]Jn 5:43
[25]Hidden Dangers of the Rainbow, Pgs 17-18

Benjamin Creme's guru, or role model, is a woman called Alice Bailey, who expounded on the importance and values of the New Age Movement, from the late 1940's. Part of her philosophy, which we think is important for you to know and be aware of, is as follows:

"...*the new 'messiah' will not be Jewish as the Jews have forfeited that privilege and that they must pass through the fires of purification in order to learn humility. (See* <u>the Rays and the Initiations</u> *by Alice Bailey. This particular passage regarding the New 'Messiah' was written in 1949 when the entire world knew what had happened to Europe's Jewish population.) These teachings are also strongly opposed to 'Zionism' and a possession of a homeland by the Jewish people. These teachings also state that what happened to the Jewish people in World War II was a result of their 'bad national karma'.*"[26]

She also made a statement in 1957 regarding the use of nuclear weapons, aimed directly at the Vatican in Rome.

"*The atomic bomb does not belong to the...nations who perfected it....It belongs to the United Nations for use (or let us rather hope, simply for threatened use) when aggressive action...rears its ugly head. It does not essentially matter whether that aggression is the gesture of any particular nation or group of nations or whether it is generated by the political groups of any powerful religious organization,* **such as the Church of Rome, who as yet are unable to leave politics alone...**"[27]

The above quotations from Benjamin Creme and Alice Bailey, make it crystal clear that the New Age Movement, which fabricated their own version of Lord Maitreya as messiah, is obviously anti-Jesus, anti-Christian, anti-Semitic, and yet is receiving a great deal of support from Christians

---

[26]Hidden Dangers of the Rainbow, Pg 115
[27]Alice Bailey, The Externalization of the Hierarchy, Pg 548, taken from Unicorn in the Sanctuary, by Randy England, Pg 93

and Jews. If that's not a fulfillment of John 5:43 and St. John of Damascene's prophecy, nothing is.

Saints John Damascene, Augustine, John Chrysostom, Cyril of Jerusalem, all the Early Church Fathers, took the Scriptures as handed down to them, and Tradition, and wrote prophecies regarding the End Times and the Antichrist. There has never been a doubt by the Early Fathers that the Antichrist was an individual person who would come to the earth, work wonders and miracles, bring people back from the dead, win over the confidence of the masses, eventually be proclaimed the Christ, and eventually be killed by Jesus. But all that would take place in between his beginning and his end, has been prophesied by Saints, whose revelations agree with Scripture and Tradition. The Catechism of the Catholic Church teaches us:

*"...the Apostolic preaching, which is expressed in a special way in the inspired books, was to be preserved in a continuous line of succession until the end of time.*

*"This living transmission, accomplished in the Holy Spirit, is called Tradition, since it is distinct from Sacred Scripture, though closely connected to it. Through Tradition, 'the Church in her very doctrine, life and worship perpetuates and transmits to every generation all that she herself is, all that she believes.'"*[28]

Now, as the loving Father in the *Old Testament* enlightened the Israelites of the coming of the *Christ*, but they did not heed Him; are we ignoring Jesus, and the signposts in the *New Testament* warning us Christians of the coming of the *Antichrist*? As revelations in the Old Testament prophesied the coming of the Messiah - the *Hope* of the world, so the New Testament prophesies the *Antichrist* - the *destruction* of the world. Our Lord, always balancing the odds, refusing to allow His children to be unwittingly led

---

[28]Catechism of the Catholic Church #78-79 Page 27

262        *Beyond Sodom and Gomorrah*

astray, uses the New Testament to uncover the origin of the Antichrist - where he will come from, it outlines his objectives - his plans to take over the world, and warns us of the false miracles that will take place to delude and lead the innocent to perdition and eternity in the abyss.

For generations, Satan has sent emissaries of hate and violence, forerunners of the real Antichrist, to deceive the faithful, so that when the people of God are confronted by the real Antichrist, using the concept of the boy who cried wolf to throw them off guard, they will discount the seriousness facing the world, leaving this dangerous monster heretofore unknown in the world, free to enslave God's children.

We are a *Good News* people; known for the positives we teach--the Treasury which makes up our Church--the Eucharist, Mother Mary, the Angels and the Saints; but if we do not speak up, as Jesus said entering Jerusalem on Palm Sunday, "*should we be silent, the very stones would cry out.*"[29] We are living on the edge, in the most deluded of times, with educated people not only being led to slaughter, but leading their brothers and sisters to their spiritual deaths. Wake up, world. We still have a chance. As St. Augustine said, "*Tolle Lege*" - Take and read!

**Let us recap what the Lord is telling us in this chapter.**

We cannot ignore the prophecies of the last days which were passed down first orally by the first disciples, and then in the written Word. The Early Church Fathers further authenticated these warnings, giving them an indisputable credibility, as they spoke of these prophecies coming from the first followers of Jesus, the disciples, many of whom they knew first hand. Just as Satan desires more than anything else that we believe he is a joke and does not exist, so he would, through the bait held up to good men, that of fame

---

[29]Lk 19:40

and recognition, lure them to lead others into the den of the enemy.

Often, it is asked why the Lord Who is Omnipotent allows His children to be left as lambs in the midst of wolves. This is no different than any war, except the stakes are higher - the conquering of men's souls, the enslavement of God's creation to the wiles and designs of the Antichrist. The flowers of the Church have always been nourished by the blood of the Martyrs. God reaches out to us, enlightens us; as with the Angels, He reveals to us life eternal with Him. He gives us a choice. We are not unprepared; the Lord has given us an intellect, a free will to choose Him and eternal life, or His enemy and endless misery in the pits of hell. They say, there are no atheists on the battle field. I wonder how many there will be on Judgment Day, when they face their Savior and He shows them His wounds suffered out of love for them? What can the Antichrist offer us that equals the Supreme Sacrifice Jesus made for us?

†††

*How shall we know the Antichrist?* I believe we are seeing the forerunners of the Antichrist, with the *amorality* of the world, the lies being preached as truths, sins being laughed into oblivion, the taking of a life no longer a scandal, confusion and chaos replacing honesty and peace.

In the final days, the Antichrist will incorporate the horror of the first centuries and the deception of the following centuries to attack the people of God with a fury, as yet unleashed. For close to 400 years, the faithful did not know they were no longer Catholic, but instead Arian. Today, we walk amidst our brothers and sisters, and we think, Do they not know what is going on? When did right become wrong, and wrong become right?

†††

It doesn't have to be this way.  Sr. Faustina wrote about the power of Intercession in her Diary:

"One day Jesus told me that He would cause chastisement to fall upon the most beautiful city in the country (probably Warsaw).  This chastisement would be that with which God had punished Sodom and Gomorrah.  I saw the great wrath of God and a shudder pierced my heart.  I prayed in silence.  After a moment, Jesus said to me, **'My child, unite yourself closely to me during the Sacrifice and offer My Blood and Wounds to My Father in expiation for the sins of this city.  Repeat this without interruption throughout the entire Holy Mass.  Do this for seven days.'**

"On the seventh day I saw Jesus in a bright cloud and began to beg Him to look upon the city and upon our whole country.  Jesus looked (down) graciously.  When I saw the kindness of Jesus, I began to beg His blessing.  Immediately Jesus said *'For your sake I bless the entire country.'*  And He made a big sign of the cross over our country.  Seeing the goodness of God, a great joy filled my soul."

BLESSED SR. FAUSTINA'S DIARY # 39

†††

We ask you, brothers and sister, no we beg you to take to heart the warning given us by St. Paul:

*"Put on the armor of God,*
*that you may be able to stand against the wiles of the devil.*
*For our wrestling is not against flesh and blood,*
*but against the Principalities and the Powers,*
*against the world rulers of this present darkness,*
*against the spiritual forces of wickedness on high."*[30]

---

[30]Eph 6:11-12

# Y2K - Three Days of Darkness?
### *Is your soul* Y2K *compliant?*

The massive headlines in the media, in newspapers, on television, in magazines and the Internet are geared to create fear. The great spin word being used to frighten everyone is **Y2K**. In laymen's terms, this means Year 2000. The countdown has begun. In Paris, at the Eiffel Tower, there is a huge digital display, showing second by second, how we are speeding headlong into the next millennium. In every post office in the United States, the situation is the same; blaring out at us, as we wait on line to buy stamps, the digital display bringing us closer and closer to...*the end?*

Are you ready for the Year 2000 physically, spiritually and psychologically? It has become the major topic for speculation these days in the computer world, and in the world which has made the computer its god. The world is hurtling towards the year 2000. The media is prophesying that when the clock strikes midnight on December 31, 1999, none of the programs which are controlled by computers will be able to roll into the year 2000; they will cease to operate. The president of the United States came out in early 1999 to assure the people that the Social Security system was working feverishly to insure the government will be ready to issue checks to its recipients, even though this appears to create a tremendous burden on those who would need to line up their computer networks with the Social Security department to guarantee that the operation would run smoothly in the new millennium.

Under normal conditions, you would expect doomsday prophecies to come from certain circles. But we're finding that catastrophic prophesies are coming from the most *unlikely* sources. We hear from transportation companies that their systems will be paralyzed. The Department of Forestry for the State of California stated that the utility

Left:
*Blessed Anna Maria Taigi prophesied: "There shall come over all the earth an intense darkness lasting three days and three nights. Nothing will be visible and the air will be laden with pestilence, which will claim principally but not exclusively the enemies of religion..."*

Below:
*Our Lady of Beauriang "Do you love my Son, then sacrifice yourself..."*

Above:
*Blessed Sister Faustina Early in the twentieth century, the Lord gave us a simple servant, Helen Kowalska, born in the small village of Glogowiec, Poland, on August 25, 1905, the day before the National Feast of Our Lady of Czestochowa.*

companies in California will not be **Y2K** compliant until sometime in 2003 or 2004. They anticipate power outages, as nuclear, coal and hydroelectric plants shut down when the clock strikes twelve on New Year's Eve. Oil companies have reported they will dock all their ships throughout the world on New Year's Eve 1999. The public will be warned not to be in buildings where they are dependent on elevators to get them from one floor to the other. Hotels will have to keep everyone in the lobbies. Cooking will have to be done on wood-burning stoves, Coleman burners or little charcoal-burning hibachis (outdoors please).

There are warnings that banks will lose records of accounts - savings and checking, as well as outstanding loans. Bills: gas, electric, telephone, department stores, credit cards, will be wiped out. Balances in the bank on December 31, may be gone by January 1st. By the same token, all interest that depositors have accumulated in their CD's, savings accounts and etc., may be wiped out as well. The Treasury Department is anticipating that there will be a run on banks to take money out before there is none, and have stated they will print extra paper money to accommodate the anticipated run on the banks. Financial chaos is predicted. Is the golden calf[1] turning into a useless alloy?

We want you to envision the following scenario: the massive, glistening ball at Times Square, a new ball by the way, made of handcrafted crystal by Waterford Glass in Ireland, slowly slides down the big pole as the great countdown begins, heralding in the new year, the new millennium. Ten, nine, eight, seven, six, five, (the frenzy builds as it gets closer to the bottom) four, three, two, one, only to go completely black as it hits the stroke of midnight, as will the entire sea of electric lights on the great *white way*

---

[1]Ex 32:8

of Broadway in the *big apple*, as well as all over our country, *as well as all over the world?* Total and complete darkness.

And when the lights go out all over the world, people are being cautioned to stay close to their homes and businesses, to protect what they have from those who would steal it from them. We're told there will be rioters attacking stores and homes; there will be business owners and homeowners defending themselves in every way possible, with whatever means are available. The destruction will go on and on and on. And Happy New Year 2000 will not be happy at all.

Should the days turn into weeks into months, and the supply of food diminishes, because there are no stores open, because delivery trucks cannot deliver any supplies to them, the hungry, like the virgins in Holy Scripture will ask for help from those who are prepared, and as they will be denied, people will go wherever they can and get whatever they can to feed themselves and their families. There will be a run on farms and dairies and canneries all over the country. Those who prepared for **Y2K** by storing food and water, buying camping equipment, wood-burning stoves and etc., will be converged upon by those who did not. At first, when the crisis begins, those who will not share what they have will be looked down upon and possibly even cursed. But as the situation becomes graver and graver, due to the lack of means of sustenance and no end in sight, the have-nots will turn on the haves, and take what is not theirs at any cost using survival by any and all means as a justification.

The possibilities are endless. And all because we've given over our lives to a new set of gods, the gods of computers, trusting completely in the created rather than in the Creator. We have compromised our ideals and values, trusting that the people who invented the computers, and programmed them for the last fifty years, had enough foresight to program them into the next millennium. But we were wrong. They didn't; and we may have to pay the price. We, not just you and us, but the entire world put our very existence into the hands of people we knew virtually nothing about. We put our trust in the corporation, and they betrayed us. We turned our backs on God, made computers our god, and now, we may have to bear the consequences.

**Last Day Prophecies**

For the last 2,000 years, prophets have been warning about the last days. We never knew *when* they would come. Many people have speculated greatly as to *how* the last days would come about. In the minds of those of us who were born prior to the Second World War, we were sure the world would be destroyed by an atomic holocaust, followed by a nuclear winter, which would exterminate all living things. In the cold war years after 1949, many fictional accounts in books, films and television programs speculated on how the end would come, and many even went beyond the great atomic explosion to show how the scientists envisioned what the aftermath of a nuclear war would be like. We were all bracing ourselves for that great explosion in the sky which would devastate the world.

But Jesus told us not to dwell on the time and the place.

*"But of that day and hour no one knows, no, not the Angels of Heaven, but the Father alone."*

But Jesus is also cautioning us, to be prepared spiritually for the conceivably approaching, serious last days.

*"And as in the days of Noah, so shall also the coming of the Son of Man be. For as in the days before the flood, they were eating and drinking, marrying and giving in marriage, even till that day in which Noah entered into the Ark,*

*"And they knew not until the flood came and took them all away; so also shall the coming of the Son of Man be.*

*"Then two shall be in the field; one shall be taken, and one shall be left. Two women shall be grinding at the mill; one shall be taken and one shall be left.*

*"Watch, therefore, because you know not what hour your Lord will come."*[2]

## Three Days of Darkness

There have been many prophecies, especially in this last century, regarding Three Days of Darkness. This does not signify the end of the world, but a calamitous event. There have been so many dates predicted in the Twentieth Century for the Three Days of Darkness, which never came about, that it became somewhat of a joke. The suggestion was made to those who walked around with signs that they just pencil in the dates, and erase them when the Three Days of Darkness did not occur on the day predicted, much like the prophecies of William Miller, founder of the Seventh Day Adventists. He predicted Jesus was coming on March 21, 1843; when there was no appearance by Our Lord on that date, he recalculated it to March 21, 1844. When that didn't happen, he chose the date of October 22, 1844, which also did not pan out. It was very embarrassing for Mr. Miller and the Seventh Day Adventists, until someone came up with the concept that Jesus had actually come; we just didn't see Him. Strangely enough, many people actually believed this new explanation.[3]

**Three Days of Darkness** is something altogether different however. It's pretty well accepted that it is coming; we just don't know when, and everyone who has attempted to predict a time has been wrong. But that is only a subterfuge by the enemy. He wants us to believe that it's a hoax because it has never taken place when people said it would. That's not so. It will happen. But if you recall, in

---

[2]Mt 24:42
[3]*cf Cults: Battle of the Angels* pg 136

Matthew 24:22, Jesus told us we would not know when the end is coming. We don't even know when Three Days of Darkness is coming, but could this Y2K be running a parallel course with Three Days of Darkness?

There are Scripture Passages which affirm the coming of Darkness, and of Three Days of Darkness in particular. Ecclesiastes speaks of *days of darkness* in our lives:

*"However many years a man may live, let him, as he enjoys them all, remember that the days of darkness will be many."*[4]

†††

Jesus lived each day as if it were His last, in anticipation of His entry into Heaven. Recall His words, *"Do not worry about tomorrow; tomorrow will take care of itself. Sufficient for a day is its own evil."*[5]

†††

In Ecclesiastes, we read:

*"Remember your Creator in the days of your youth, before the evil days come.*

*"And the years approach of which you will say, I have no pleasure in them.*

*"Before the sun is darkened, and the light, and the moon, and the stars, while the clouds return after the rain."*[6]

Then in Exodus, we hear Moses speaking of three days of darkness:

*"Then the Lord said to Moses, 'Stretch out your hand toward the sky, that over the land of Egypt there may be such intense darkness that one can feel it.' So Moses stretched out his hand toward the sky, and there was dense darkness throughout the land of Egypt for three days. Men could not see one another, nor could they move from*

---

[4]Eccl 11:8
[5]Mt 6:34
[6]Eccl 12:1-3

*where they were, for three days. But all Israelites had light where they dwelt."*[7]

Curiously enough, some of the conjecture as to what will happen in the aftermath of **Y2K** seem very similar to the description of Three Days of Darkness in Moses' prophecy, and that could be frightening and yet promising for those who place their lives in God's Hands. Bringing you this Scripture, we're not trying to predict dates or project what could happen, but instead we want you to be aware of the *possible* connection of the two.

It has been foretold that Three Days of Darkness will be a period of devastation. All the lights in the world will go out. No one will be able to see during the daytime or nighttime hours. It will literally be three days of darkness, a heavy cloud of black covering the earth. Some predictions state that no one can go outside their home, and that the outside windows and doors must be sealed tightly. Whereas in Exodus, Moses said the Israelites would be able to see, in the predictions of Three Days of Darkness, we're told that only those who use *blessed candles* will be able to have light. Those in the secular world who are warning people of the possible devastating effects of **Y2K** have also recommended the use of candles, only not *blessed candles* as Scripture and the prophets forewarned us to use. Although they appear to see, they are in the dark, as the eyes of their souls have not been opened to the Light, yet.

In addition to Holy Scripture, there are more recent prophecies of Three Days of Darkness, as well as a correlation to the possible effects of **Y2K**.

*St. Hildegard* (1179 - Germany)[8] - *"A powerful wind will rise in the North carrying heavy fog and the densest dust (darkness?) by Divine command and it will fill their*

---

[7]Ex 10:21-23
[8]The Prophets and our Times pg 139

*throats and eyes so they will cease their savagery and be stricken with a great fear."*

God has sent us many warnings, many signs, and what have we done?

There are many spirits and fallen angels roaming the earth. We pray against them when we pray the prayer to St. Michael. But they can do nothing of themselves. They get mankind to do their dirty work for them.

In Germany, in the year 1824, a mystic-*Venerable Anne Catherine Emmerich*, made last-days predictions:

*"I see the Apostles, not those of the past, but the apostles of the last times, and it seems to me, the Pope is among them."*

*"I was likewise told, ....that he (Satan) will be unchained for a time fifty or sixty years before the year of Christ 2000.*

Those of us who have lived through these times which these prophets speak of, can attest to the fact that Satan has been loosed on our land.

*"The Jews shall return to Palestine and become Christians towards the end of the world."*

Well, the Jews have returned to Palestine, only renamed it Israel; and the exodus to the promised land of Christianity has begun. We viewed a documentary on the Shroud, where a *rabbi* from Israel was stating that without a doubt, all the evidence proves that the Man on the Shroud was *Jesus!*

In the early Nineteenth Century, *Blessed Anna Maria Taigi*[9] a mystic in Italy, prophesied:

*"There shall come over all the earth an intense darkness lasting three days and three nights. Nothing will be visible and the air will be laden with pestilence, which will claim principally but not exclusively the enemies of religion.*

---

[9]*Visionaries, Mystics and Stigmatists*-by Bob and Penny Lord Pg 286

*"During this darkness artificial light will be impossible. Only* **blessed candles** *can be lighted and will afford illumination. He who out of curiosity opens his window to look out or leaves his house will fall dead on the spot. During these three days the people should remain in their homes, pray the Rosary and beg God for mercy."*

In the year 1837 *St. Gaspar del Bufalo*[10] of Spain predicted:

*"...the destruction of impenitent persecutors of the Church during the three days of darkness. He who outlives the darkness and fear of the three days - it will seem to him as if he were alone on earth because of the fact that the world will be covered everywhere with carcasses."*

We cannot help recognize the depth and breadth of these prophecies of Three Days of Darkness that we find *first* in the Scriptural passages in Exodus and Ecclesiastes that so clearly tie in with prophecies which took place anywhere from the *Twelfth* Century to the *Nineteenth* Century-prophecies from different times, and from dramatically distant parts of Europe. Now, given the limitations of communications and transportation of those days, it does not seem likely that one group could have easily heard it from another, and yet they all say the same thing.

We can't say for sure that the Y2K fright is a manifestation of Three Days of Darkness. It very possibly could be. We do know that Three Days of Darkness will come; it's scriptural; it will happen. We don't know that any or all the doomsday prophecies of Y2K will actually take place. It's really hard to believe that a situation is coming, heading towards us, as quickly as each second ticks, that we cannot do anything about, that we can't make better. Or can we?

---

[10]The Prophets and our Times pg 193

Y2K reminds us of the prophecies about comets and asteroids coming to devastate the earth. The movies and television programs of late, have been on prophecies regarding comets colliding with the earth. The Word of the Lord says:

*"The Day of the Lord cometh, because it is nigh at hand. A day of darkness and of gloominess, a day of clouds and whirlwinds: a numerous and strong people as the morning spread upon the mountains: the like to it hath not been from the beginning, nor shall it be after it even to the years of generation and generation. Before the face thereof a devouring fire and behind it a burning flame (tail of the comet?): the land is like a garden of pleasure before it and behind it a desolate wilderness, neither is there any one that can escape it. The appearance of them (comets?) is as the appearance of horses, and they shall run like horsemen. They shall leap like the noise of chariots upon the tops of mountains, like the noise of a flame of fire devouring the stubble."*[11] (400 B.C.)

Scientists say that some of the results of a comet of this magnitude coming so close to earth would be:

Mountains will split as at the time of the Crucifixion.

The hydrogen from the comet's tail coming in contact with the earth's oxygen, a great fire will flare up, using all the oxygen available. People are cautioned to not venture outdoors or they will die of asphyxiation, their lungs burning from the fire in the air. The smoke will cause everything to turn dark. People will be able to see neither from their doorways nor from their windows, and are advised to keep doors and windows sealed tightly.

But they also predict, violent hurricanes will follow and drench the earth, extinguishing the fire; then in a short while, an oxygen supply so plentiful, will return that everyone will

---

[11]Jl 2:1b-11

be able to breathe again, within ....what ...*three days?* This may be where some of modern-day prophecies, linking the comet with Three Days of Darkness, come from.

We could go on and on. There have been so many prophecies down through the centuries, from different times and different places, it's hardly possible they could have been copied from one another. They all appear to point to this time, these last days at the end of the Second Millennium. The terrifying truth is that they all seem to come together and, taken on their individual face values, could be accurate. These prophecies, other than those which come directly from Scripture, come mostly from Saints or Blesseds. It is hard to deny that times are looking a little grim. And while we have no one to blame but ourselves, because we didn't change the world, instead let it change us, God is not finished with us, yet. God does love us and will make things work for His Glory, if we only cooperate with His Grace which He bestows upon us at Mass and when we adore Him in the Blessed Sacrament.

Doomsday prophecies of yesterday and today parallel so closely the prophecies of the Three Days of Darkness, it can be frightening. And yes, the projected calamity of Y2K, the Year 2000, could very well be part of the disaster forecasted. But it may not happen! It doesn't *have* to happen, at least not as dire as it's been projected.

Our Lady of Beauraing, in 1932, said "*Do you love my Son, then sacrifice yourself...*"

And then in Banneux, Our Lady said, "*Believe in me and I will believe in you.*"

We told you that *Our Lady of Hope came to Pontmain, France* and said,

"*But pray, my children....your prayers will soon be answered.*" and then "*My Son allows Himself to be touched. He will change His Mind.*" What we didn't say was that what resulted from that visit by Our Lady was the end of the Franco-Prussian War within ten days.

The secret, which is not meant to be a secret, is in *Prayer.* **The answer, the weapon, the ammunition is prayer.** And what is the greatest prayer we have in our Church? - the Sacrifice of the Mass, in which we are given the Miracle of the Eucharist, Jesus coming down to earth to protect us, defend us and cover us with His Precious Blood, and the Furnace of His Sacred Heart.

**Don Bosco** speaks of a fierce battle and ultimate victory:

*"Suddenly, the pope falls, seriously wounded. He is instantly helped up, but, struck a second time, dies. A shout of victory rises from the enemy, and wild rejoicing sweeps their ships!"*

The above is part of a dream experienced by St. John Bosco on May 30, 1862. He saw a large ship, with the Pope at the helm. Also, in his words,

"In the midst of this endless sea, two solid columns, a short distance apart, soar high into the sky. On the one side, a statue of Our Lady, the Blessed Virgin, stands high above the sea. At her feet is a large inscription, which reads **'Auxilium Christianorum'**, (Help of Christians). On the other side, and much higher, is a Giant Host, at the base of which is written **'Salus Credentium'** (Salvation of Believers). The two columns stand tall and strong, warding off the thrashing of raging winds."

St. John Bosco describes smaller ships surrounding the large ship and the columns. Many of them attack the flagship, while others defend it. No sooner is the Pope killed than he is replaced by another Pope. The battle continues. The new Pope tries to steer his ship between the two columns, but is having an extremely difficult time of it because of the constant pummeling by the furious hurricane.

Finally, he succeeds in bringing his ship between the columns. He ties it up at each column. The wind cries out a bloodcurdling shriek, heard round the world, and dies. The enemy ships scatter in great fear, their battle lost, while the defending ships sing out praises to Our Lord Jesus, as they, too, tie up at the posts. A peaceful calm blankets the sea.

Ward off Year 2000, with the two-edged sword of God's Word: "...*if my people, upon whom My Name has been pronounced, humble themselves and pray, and seek My Presence and turn from their evil ways, I will hear them from Heaven and pardon their sins and revive their land.*"[12]

When was the last time you went to adore Our Lord in the Blessed Sacrament? Is this the Presence Our Lord is making reference to? Do we acknowledge before all men that Our Lord has given us all we have that is good, and Holy is His Name? Have we gone to confession and reconciled with Our Lord and with those who have offended us and whom we have offended? Is God the center of our lives? We need not be afraid of the dark, if Jesus is the Light of our lives.

There is a rainbow which is waiting to break through the clouds, a promise from the Lord that He has not given up on us. But that does not mean that these prophecies should be ignored. We are living in a time of chastisement, a chastisement man is manufacturing himself, almost daring God to act, challenging Him with sins compounding sins! Will the God of Justice make His Presence known? You can bet on it! These prophecies spell it out for us. But the answer is not, to go out and hang ourselves from a tree. As Judas, before us, we have the opportunity to repent and ask Jesus' forgiveness, to turn our lives back to Him, and to the Church which poured from His side.

The Y2K scare may never materialize, at least not in the proportions in which it has been predicted. New Year's Eve 2000 may come and go, much the same as others have for

---

[12]Jer 35:15

most our lives. So, at this time, allow us to pass on, a tradition which has been part of our family for the over 40 years that we have been married. New Year's Eve has always been a time for family! We do not go out to night clubs. We all gather at our house and celebrate the passing of the *old year*, thanking God for the gifts and blessings which have been heaped upon us and our loved ones, and praising Him in advance for the gifts and blessings we look forward to receiving in the *new year*. Those years, those painful years, when we did not understand God's gifts nor appreciate them, judging the old year was not particularly memorable, we'd bang it out with pots and pans with all our might and thank the Lord that it was over.

But it was a time for family! Our home was open to relatives and friends; we enjoyed spending the last hours of the old year and the first of the new, with them. Our children brought over their friends. When we had our little Junior Legion of Mary, we would invite all our little people to be with us. Monsignor Tom O'Connell and his associate pastor would always stop in. And so, as our gift to you for the year 2000, we would like to suggest you do the same.

Let us not focus our attention on the year 2000, to the exclusion of today. Jesus lived each day, with an urgency, as if it were His Last Day. Center your eyes and heart on Jesus and the values He left us. Live *today* with what is really important in the forefront. Do not leave till *tomorrow* what should be done *today*. *Do it this day, this week, this month, this year.* Surround yourselves with your loved ones; they are your treasure. Reconcile with those with whom you have differences. It is not too late to say you are sorry and to accept those words from someone else.

*Be sure your soul is Y2K compliant.*
May God continue to bless you! We love you!
***Blessed and Happy New Year!***

# Who can You trust?

In this time of madness, these last days of the Second Millennium, when all indications point to Satan ruling the earth, man has sold his soul to the *company store*--the large corporation, with its enticements of great wealth and guaranteed security (which can be loosely translated into as little as a pickup truck, a burger and fries and a six-pack). Only the *company store*, like the enemy of God, betrayed those who worshiped it, very often to the exclusion of family and God. And how did the corporation do it? They came up with a new *catch-phrase* as a method of shirking their responsibilities, a new creative way to get rid of their loyal employees. They wouldn't think of firing their loyal employees, or laying them off; they *down-sized* them. People who gave most of their lives to their job, found themselves victims, cheated out of their promised pension, forced to leave their jobs, in some cases--just months before they would begin collecting their coveted retirement benefits. And the justification for all this was responsibility to the stockholders, the hungered-for *bottom line*.

Imagine a person in his fifties or sixties, still in his prime, forced to seek employment in a work environment which labels anyone over 35 an old-timer, a senior citizen, ready for the scrap heap! He's reduced to working *part time* for McDonalds or Wal-Marts (and thank God for those companies who are able to see the value in our seniors, and will hire good workers who have been discarded by mainline corporations in favor of younger, cheaper help). Now with no pension, these victims realized they had been worshiping false gods to whom they had given their entire lives and they had clay feet, their balance sheet and after-taxes profits more important than loyalty. *Too late*, these poor souls came to realize they were on their own, all they had planned on for their old age would not be forthcoming. *They were forced to learn the hard way that there is only one God!*

**The Image of the Divine Mercy**
*"Jesus, I trust in You."*

We can remember a time, when the full extent of the average American's dream was to have a car in every garage and a chicken in every pot. It seems so long ago, it is barely a nostalgic memory. Today, we trade in our car at least every third year for the latest model--our spouses and teenagers each driving a car of their own. And what did this take to accomplish; what lies did the *slimy one*[1] use to trick us? What was the price exacted? Who did we have to bow down and worship? To whom did we pledge our loyalty? When were our souls placed on the auction block like so many sheep, going to the highest bidder? Now, one sheep will not lead another to slaughter; they have to place a *"judas goat"* in the corral who will lead them to the slaughter gate and death. Who are the *judas goats* in our society?

God gave us an intellect, a mind to choose between good and evil, and a will to follow the Shepherd or the devil. The Shepherd bought our souls on the Cross. Now the devil is trying to steal us away from Him and eternal joy with Him in His Heavenly Home. Are there *judas goats*, disguised as sheep, leading us to our death inch by inch? We, unlike sheep, have a choice. The enemy of God will make the highest bid, offering us the world and all its treasures, and he'll betray us. *But he makes it sound so good!*

Are there not those whom the devil uses, who boldly flaunt their sins in front of us, and we look the other way, making excuses for outrageous behavior? After all, *he is giving us so much*; *it's none of our business what he does behind closed doors; it doesn't concern us*--as long as he keeps on giving. Don't you see what has been happening? Not only have our bodies and our brains been deep-fried, our souls are being fried as well! We have been systematically set up! With sin no longer being preached from the altar, no good role models coming from any direction, we excuse

---

[1]the devil

everything away, accepting evil as good and good as evil. We are in the days of the emperor's clothes, refusing to see, and too frightened to acknowledge, the emperor is naked!

What can we do? There is no great mystery to unravel; only great courage and resolve, a gentle revolution, a giant reform, a conversion of men's hearts, a reformation of men's will and an adoption of God's Will. We can begin by saying *NO!* to self, and *YES!* to God. We must be willing to let go of some of the perks we've been given by the *evil one* to keep us lulled into apathy. We have to clear our minds from all the fat that's been deposited there, and exercise our souls to get in shape for the battle ahead.

There is still time! The Lord has always given us time to repent and come *Home* to Him. But we don't know how much time; we don't know when the Bridegroom is coming to the wedding feast.[2] And God has not been past giving us what we want; even if we choose hell. Throughout Old Testament History, we see God using our enemies to chastise us when we will not heed His Word. He sent His Angels, we ignored them; then the Prophets, we killed them; finally His Only Begotten Son; and we not only did not listen to Him, we crucified Him. We believe the time is now! We only have to read between the lines of the propaganda fed to us by the newspapers, watch the *culture of death*[3] being promoted on secular television, to know the time is now!

In the 1998 political campaigns, the battle cry by those who won the election was that they would guarantee women their right to abortions, and gay sex partners would be given the status of married couples under the law. Now they're getting us prepared for the next election by lauding and applauding those who stood up for the rights to murder children in our country! And do you know that if Catholics,

---

[2]Mt 25:1-13
[3]Pope John Paul II

not Christians, not Protestant brothers and sisters, but only Catholics would vote against these agendas and these politicians, they would not see the light of day.

Are we too busy with matters of consequence, like refinancing our home, so we can buy a boat or a Mercedes, or the latest sports utility vehicle which in the end will cost us double or triple in interest charges, *but won't have to pay it off for another fifteen or thirty years?* When the Lord comes, will He find us busily engaged in running off to the newest bank to take advantage of *their* lowered interest rates so that we can be strangled in our own debt?

Through our own life experience and that of others, the Lord has put in our path over the years, we know how our values change when we lose a loved one. We know that there are some of you who believe that you have lost *The Loved One*, our Lord Jesus, by falling into some of the traps we've listed above. Don't be taken in by the evil one. God, because He is Love, never stops loving us, not even when we are sinning against Him. He never stopped loving our first parents, Adam and Eve, planning the Salvation of their offspring, as they were sinning against Him.

Today, as never before, we are all called to be the new *Jonahs*[4] of the Old Testament, and new *St. John the Baptists*[5] of the New Testament pleading with this fallen generation to repent. They will tell you that for generations, people have thought the end of the world was coming in their time. But, even they must admit, man never had the means to destroy himself the way he has at this present time.

Our Ministry has always been known as the Good News Ministry, and we do have Good News for you. We are not helpless and hopeless. In the light of all the darkness threatening the skies of our lives, there is a rainbow, a

---

[4]Jon 3:1-10
[5]Mt 3:1-12

double rainbow representing the Lord and His Mother, a rainbow of promise and hope! Mother Mary is holding up Her Son's Arms and, as with Moses, as long as She is so doing, God will not mete out His Justice. But hear this and take it to your hearts, Our God of Mercy will not allow the inhumanity that has pervaded our country and our world, swarming over and infecting everyone with whom it comes in contact, to continue. There is little time; but there is time! *We can make a difference. We must make a difference!*

If we will only turn back to the Lord Our God, the final price exacted will not be disastrous. God is ready to embrace us, to take us back, to forgive us. But He will allow us to refuse Him, to reject His Mercy, to turn our backs on Him, to go to hell if we insist. But one thing we can hold onto, and I guess it is the most painful thing to remember--it is so one-sided, is God's never-ending love, forgiveness, and sacrifice for us, which began on the Cross.

Is that why the enemy of God has misled pastors into ripping the crucified Lord from their altars and replacing Him with fancy bars of gold and silver? Are we emulating Judas when he sold Jesus out for thirty pieces of silver? Are we willing to let the enemies of the Cross strip the memory of the extent of pain and suffering Our Lord Jesus was willing to endure to prove how much He loves us? Does the enemy want us to rely on sinful man for our salvation and, knowing how man will fail, despair?

Well, as never before the people of God are well armed, like Blessed Miguel Pro with a Crucifix in one hand and a Rosary in the other, and the double-edged sword of the Word as our shield, we will fight for our Church and for this country founded under God, our United States of America. *We are reclaiming our beloved country back for God!* Pray and teach your families to pray! **Who can you trust? You can trust God!**

*General George Washington - Founding Father and*
*First President of the United States of America*
*Here he is depicted praying for our country during the winter at Valley*
*Forge, PA. As one of the Founding Fathers of our country, he helped*
*write the First Amendment to the Constitution, with the sole intention of*
*preventing the government from forming a State Church, which would*
*deprive the people of the United States of Freedom of Religion.*

# Rage and Righteousness

**To pray or not to pray; that is the question.**

The title of this chapter is *Rage and Righteousness.* Maybe a better title would be *Outrage!* When we awakened this morning, and turned on the radio, instead of being upset by the weather report, we were saddened by a new challenge to us and our nation, to pray or not to pray, to stand by and do nothing or, like the Founding Fathers of our Constitution, fight for Religious Freedom.

A college basketball team and their coach made the *unconstitutional* act of praying before and after each game *(although this act was wholly constitutional for 210 years until 1962).* When someone spied a photo of them praying, in the newspaper, they threatened to sue the school and the coach, charging they had violated the Constitution regarding separation between Church and State. These young people and their coach were *not* violating the Constitution, for that Amendment (the First Amendment to the Constitution[1]) was written with the sole intention by the early Founding Fathers of preventing the *government* from creating a *State Church,* which would deprive the people of the United States of the Freedom of Religion (that of choosing how and where they would worship).

†††

This was interpreted as follows:

"(First Amendment) embraces all who believe in the existence of God...This provision does not extend to atheists, because they do not believe in God or religion; and therefore...their sentiments and professions, whatever they may be, cannot be called religious sentiments and professions." COMMONWEALTH V KNEELAND 1838

---

[1]For the full text of First Amendment, see last page of chapter

In earlier decisions of the First Amendment, neither atheism nor secular humanism qualified as "religions" for obvious reasons.[2]

Now the Court contradicts the 1838 decision by stating in 1961, "Also included under the protection of the religion clauses of the First Amendment would be religions which do not teach a belief in the existence of God, including Buddhism, Taoism, Ethical Culture, Secular Humanism, and others." TORCASO V. WATKINS 1961

And if that's not enough, in 1989 our friends from the ACLU won a victory against Freedom of Religion with the following decision: "These Words [from the First Amendment]...are recognized as guaranteeing religious liberty and equality to 'the infidel, the atheist.'" ALLEGHENY V. ACLU 1989

The Supreme Court has, without foundation, used this right *against* the citizens of this nation, founded under God, usurping the original intent of the Founders of the Constitution.

In its decision,[3] "...*the Court ruled in favor of a* **single atheist** *not involved in the classes but who was* **personally** *offended by religion* (in general?) *and therefore did not want* **any** *students taught religious principles.*

"*This decision foreshadowed what was soon to become routine: a single individual, unable to advance his or her goals through legitimate political and legislative means, convincing a willing Court to violate the rights of the overwhelming majority of its citizens in order to accommodate the wishes of that individual.*

"*A concurring Justice observed, through this ruling, the Court was now assuming 'the role of a super board of*

---

[2]For original definition of Religion in Webster's Dictionary, see last page of chapter

[3]McCollum v. Board of Education, 1948

*education for every school district in the nation*[4] *an ominous prediction of what has now become the norm.*"[5]

We would just like to give you some quotations from the Founding Fathers of our country, signers of the Constitution, regarding prayer and religion:

"Religion and morality...(are) necessary to good government, good order, and good laws." WILLIAM PATTERSON, SIGNER OF THE CONSTITUTION AND US SUPREME COURT JUSTICE

"True religion affords to government its surest support." GEORGE WASHINGTON, FIRST PRESIDENT OF THE UNITED STATES

"Religion and virtue are the only foundations...of republicanism and of all free governments." JOHN ADAMS, SECOND PRESIDENT OF THE UNITED STATES

"God grant that in America true religion and civil liberty may be inseparable and that the unjust attempts to destroy the one may in the issue, tend to the support and establishment of both." BENJAMIN RUSH, SIGNER OF THE DECLARATION OF INDEPENDENCE[6]

††††

Enough is enough! It is a sad day when the young, in this case Afro-American students and their coach are penalized and threatened for doing a righteous act. Let anyone in this nation commit a crime, no matter how heinous and their rights are to be carefully respected; one false move and there is a mistrial and the guilty go scot-free. Many convicted murderers are being set free, long before their sentence has been satisfied, because there is no room in the jails.

We hear cries of outrage, demanding help for disadvantaged minorities, and as a courageous Baptist Minister said, "*Here are a group of Afro-American students,*

---

[4]McCollum v. Board of Education, 1948

[5]Original Intent, Page 155

[6]All of the references to the Constitution and decisions on it comes from *Original Intent by David Barton, WallBuilder Press - Aledo, TX*

*clean-cut athletes, looking to God for a better way and we censor them!"* My question is, Do we really care or are we just using citizens against other fellow citizens?

**When you take God out of the schools, *who* takes His place?**

*Separation of Church and State!* Where did this come from, and what was the *original intent* of the Founding Fathers on this matter, a phrase mis-used which would drastically affect and undermine a nation founded under God?

One of the Founding Fathers, "Jefferson believed that God, not government, was the Author and Source of our rights and that the government, therefore was prevented from interference with those rights. Very simply...it was *not* to limit religious activities in public; rather they were to limit the power of government to prohibit or interfere with those expressions."

Earlier courts long understood Jefferson's intent. In fact, when Jefferson's letter was invoked by the Court (only once prior to the Everson case--the Reynolds v. United States case in 1878), *unlike today's Courts* which publish only his eight-word separation phrase, that Court published Jefferson's full letter, and then concluded:

"Coming as this does from an acknowledged leader of the advocates of this measure, it [Jefferson's letter] may be accepted almost as an authoritative declaration of the scope and effect of the Amendment thus secured. **Congress** was deprived of all **legislative power** over mere [religious] opinion, but was left free to **reach actions which were in violation of social duties or subversive of good order.**"[7] (emphasis added)

That Court therefore, and others, identified actions which--if perpetrated in the name of religion--the government **did** have legitimate reason to intrude. Those

---

[7] *Original Intent* by David Barton

activities included human sacrifice, polygamy, bigamy, concubinage, incest, infanticide, patricide, advocation and promotion of immorality and etc.

"Such acts, even if perpetrated in the name of religion, would be stopped by the government since, as the Court explained, they were 'subversive of good order.' However, the government was **never** to interfere with **traditional** religious practices outlined in 'the Books of the Law and the Gospel'--whether **public prayer**,[8] the use of Scriptures, etc."

Jefferson also said that the "power to prescribe any religious exercise...**'must rest with the states.'**"[9]

Our *federal* courts who inventively misapply Jefferson's *separation statement*, thoroughly disregard this declaration, as they overrule hosts of State laws sanctioning and supporting religious organizations and their programs; and this in direct abuse of Jefferson's *original intent*, twisting and warping his words to push their own agendas.

To bring closure to this instrument of destruction, the (now made) notorious "*separation dogma*" which we will show has proved to be so disastrous, affecting our very way of life, it is interesting to note: During months of contention, controversy, and differences, *not one* of the ninety Founding Fathers, who framed the First Amendment, brought up "separation of church and state."

Why is this so important? Now, unlike Bob, I went to secular schools. But I remember how we opened each day, pledging allegiance to the Flag of the United States, our hands over our hearts, with those who objected for one reason or another: whether because of religious beliefs,[10] or because they would not mention the Name of God no less pray for His intercession,[11] having the right to abstain. *When*

---

[8]emphasized by authors
[9]Original Intent by David Barton
[10]for example: Jehovah Witnesses
[11]children of atheists, etc.

*did that all change?*    One lone atheist, who has since disappeared from the face of the earth, a former Catholic--Madeline Murray O'Hare--was able to take God out of our schools and eventually out of mainstream America.  And is this the express wish of the nation?

If so, then why do millions come to see and pray with His Holiness the Pope, when he visits our land--assumedly no longer under God?  Could it be because our Courts are cleverly filled with those opposing God in our society?  And have we done nothing about it, often voting these judges in or voting for a President who will tip the scales by placing them in positions of power?  And if you remember the Scripture about the empty house, who will rule our country and our lives; if not God?

*"When an unclean spirit goes out of a person it roams through arid regions searching for rest but finds none. Then it says, 'I will return to my home from which I came.' But upon returning, it finds it empty, swept clean, and put in order.  Then it goes and brings back with itself seven other spirits more evil than itself, and they move in and dwell there, and the last condition of that person is worse than the first.*  **Thus it will be with this evil generation.**"[12]

†††

What has been the consequences of our actions or lack of actions?  You may recall in the Penitential Rite[13] we say

*"I confess to Almighty God,*
*and to you my brothers and sisters,*
*that I have sinned through my own fault*
                    *-we strike our breast-*
*in my thoughts and in my words,*
**in what I have done**

---

[12]Mt 12:43-45
[13]Confiteor

*and what I have failed to do*;
*and I ask Blessed Mary, ever Virgin,*
*all the Angels and Saints,*
*and you, my brothers and sisters,*
*to pray for me to the Lord our God."*

What have we done, and what have we failed to do?

## God and Prayer thrown out, violence and hatred enter the schools!

They successfully took God out of our schools and we thought that the worst scenario was that without God and prayer balancing the secularism of the world, our young would be inundated with *materialism* and *humanism* to the exclusion of the *Supernatural!* Then with so few parents going to church, we would become a nation truly without God, God not only *not* in the center of our lives, but not even in the *outer perimeter* of our lives, a God long forgotten. That's all true, but it's only the tip of the iceberg.

We hate to turn on the radio in the morning, especially this last year, for we are sure to hear of some disaster, some killing, some ambush--with no place free from attack, no members of our society given a reprieve from being maimed, kidnapped, tortured or murdered. We no longer trust sending our children out to go to the store to pick up some groceries. We wait with them, right up to the moment they get on the bus. No more walking to school with friends; no more playing in the park, no matter what age, without a parent nearby. Do I sound hysterical? I wish I did! Oh what have they done with our country and our children who are not allowed to be children, forced to grow up too quickly? And what have we done or failed to do? As we have mentioned in other parts of this book: *"Someone will have to pay for this."*[14]

---

[14]*Saint Teresa Benedicta della Croce* (Edith Stein)

In this the year of the Father, we are experiencing a furious battle between God the Father and Satan the father of all evil. For the last sixteen months, we have not been able to turn on secular television without viewing horrifying scenes of young people bleeding, their broken bodies being drained of life, before our very eyes. And we can barely write, we are so overcome with grief! We have said that when we have been to funerals, in certain parishes, we found ourselves mourning not only for the death of a loved one, but for our beloved Catholic Church in the United States. Now, reading and listening to the news each day, we feel we are at a funeral for our country.

### Littleton, Colorado--April 20, 1999--Hitler's Birthday

According to available information, a plot which had been on the drawing board for at least a year, was hatched from hell with Satan using two teen-aged boys as his tools. They entered Columbine High School, where they were students, and began a bloodbath of murder and mayhem, killing fifteen people (12 students, 1 teacher and 2 assailants) and injuring another thirteen. They caused such havoc in that school and that middle-class suburban community that we don't know when or if the young people will ever be the same. The young assailants took their own lives in the melee. But from the time of the attack, countless pipe bombs, booby traps, larger bombs were found all over the school grounds. It was like one huge land mine. It has been called the greatest American Massacre in history.

### Richmond, Virginia--June 15, 1998

A male history teacher and a female guidance counselor were shot in the hallway of a high School in Richmond, Virginia during final exams.

### Springfield, Oregon--May 21, 1998

A fifteen-year old student opened fire in the school cafeteria, killing two students.

## St. Charles, Missouri--May 21, 1998

Three sixth grade boys worked up a "hit list" of students they intended to kill on the last day of school.

## Onalaksa, Washington--May 21, 1998

A fifteen year old boy boarded a school bus with a gun in his hand, forced his girl friend off the bus. He took her to his home where he killed himself in her presence.

## Fayetteville, Tennessee--May 19, 1998

An 18 year old honor-student killed a young man, who was dating his ex-girl friend, in the parking lot of the school.

## Pomona, California--April 28, 1998

Two teen aged boys were murdered playing basketball in the elementary school gym. A third classmate was wounded.

## Edinboro, Pennsylvania--April 24, 1998

A 48 year old science teacher was shot and killed by a 14 year old student at a graduation dance at the school.

## Jonesboro, Arkansas--March 24, 1998

Two students, ages 11 and 13, hid in combat fatigues in the woods across from the school parking lot and set off a false fire alarm. As they exited the school, the boys opened fire, killing four girls and one teacher, wounding ten others.

A comment about this atrocity--President Clinton sent a videotaped message in which he said "*Like all of you, I do not understand what dark force could have driven young people to do this terrible thing.*"

Dear Mr. President: don't you remember Mother Teresa's words when she spoke at the National Prayer Breakfast on February 3, 1994? She said:

"*...if we accept that a mother can kill even her own child, how can we tell other people not to kill one another?*

"*Any country that accepts abortion is not teaching its people to love, but to use any violence to get what they want.*

*"Many people are concerned about all the violence in...the United States....But often these same people are not concerned with the millions who are being killed by the deliberate decision of their own mothers."*

You were there Mr. President, with your wife, and Vice President Gore and his wife.[15] Didn't you listen? The following week, she addressed the Supreme Court:

*"The so-called right to abortion has pitted mothers against their children and women against men.*

*"It (right to abortion) has sown violence and discord at the heart of the most intimate human relationship.*

*"It has portrayed the greatest of gifts - a child - as a competitor, an intrusion and an inconvenience."*

Also, Our Holy Father, Pope John Paul II, in a speech at the Denver Airport on August 12, 1993, at which the President and his wife were present, said:

*"Too many obstacles are visited upon them (young people) by natural calamities, famines, epidemics, by economic and political crises, by the atrocities of war...*

*"...In developed countries, a serious moral crisis is already affecting the lives of many young people, leaving them adrift, often without hope, and conditioned to look only for instant gratification."*

*"...I present this invitation: Let us pause and reason together. To educate without a value system based on truth is to abandon young people to moral confusion, personal insecurity and easy manipulation. No country, not even the most powerful, can endure if it deprives its own children of this essential good."*

And then at the end of World Youth Day, on August 15, 1993, Feast of the Assumption of Our Lady, our Pope made this powerful statement:

---

[15]Everyone present, every senator and congressman gave Mother Teresa a standing ovation, with the exception of four people, Bill and Hillary Clinton and Al and Tipper Gore.

*"In our century, as at no other time in history, the 'culture of death' has assumed a social and institutional form of legality to justify the most horrible crimes against humanity: genocide, 'final solutions,' 'ethnic cleansings' and the massive 'taking of lives of human beings even before they are born, or before they reach the natural point of death.'"*

*"The family especially is under attack. And the sacred character of human life is denied. Naturally, the weakest members of society are the most at risk: the unborn, children, the sick, the handicapped, the old, the poor and unemployed, the immigrant and refugee..."*

In his last visit to St. Louis, Missouri in January, 1999, Pope John Paul II pleaded with the powers of the United States to be moral leaders as well as military and political leaders. Did our Holy Father not realize his words were falling on deaf ears?

## West Paducah, Kentucky--December 1, 1997

A fourteen year old student opened fire on a group of students, holding a prayer service in a hallway at the high school there. He killed three and wounded five of the students.

## Pearl, Mississippi--October 1, 1997

A sixteen year old student killed his mother, then proceeded to the local high school where he shot nine students. Two of the victims died, including the assailant's girl friend.

## Bethel, Alaska--February 19, 1997

A 16 year old student opened fire on a group in the common area of his high school, killing the principal and a student. In the attack, two other students were wounded.

†††

God is all good! To remain God, He can only do good and create what is good. If our young and old are not allowed to pray together, to be a sign to one another and others of God's place in our lives, who will the young turn to? Everyone chooses a god. Take away God Who is the only Eternal Omnipotent God and they, out of need, will worship false gods. And we have seen the proof of that philosophy. With no or little respect and knowledge of God, the most brutal hostility is spreading throughout our nation! *We need God!*

When the Saracens invaded Christian countries like Spain, the faithful did not hear the Name of Christ for close to 700 years. When the Catholic Queen Isabella reclaimed Spain, God once again reigned, leading the nation to prominence around the world. Without God, Spain lost all her possessions. Once a major nation, she was reduced to the status of a minor entity. Is this what will happen to the United States? Major companies are moving their operations out of the United States, because they cannot compete with countries which our government is granting special privileges (favored nation status), countries that do not have the strict observances of human rights that we have, very often using slave labor and child labor. The consequences, tens of thousands, and now hundreds of thousands of Americans are being *down-sized*. Now if it is your neighbor, he is being *down-sized*; if it is a member of your family, he is being *fired!*

What message are we sending to our young? They have to wonder, *Who are we and where are our hearts? What kind of a government would grant such privileges? And what kind of a people would vote candidates into office who would be party to a government which forbids each family to have no more than one child?* Are we not in the days of worshiping the golden calf? And how long do you think Our Lady is going to be able to hold back God's wrath? God's justice has already begun being manifested; I wonder how many, who have been worshiping the golden calf, have discovered it isn't gold at all, but *fool's gold!*[16]

†††

*God is upset and we get upset! -*

*We get upset* -- and very frustrated with people in power (in the secular world), whose agenda is to wipe the Name of Jesus and all He stands for, from the face of the earth!
*...and we have to be dragged down with them!*

*We get upset!* -- and confused by the actions of those within our Catholic Church who hold positions of power, and abuse that power to belittle the traditions and weaken the structure on which the Church has stood for centuries. Rather than pasturing the flock, they appear more like wolves in sheep's clothing.
*...and we have to be dragged down with them!*

*We get upset!* -- because we can't find a candidate for public office, whose platform includes anything affirming family values. It seems that the only campaign platforms, which deliver votes, are those which promote wholesale abortion, homosexual and lesbian agendas, same-sex marriages, assisted suicide, Euthanasia, condom-distribution to grade school children and on and on.
*...and we have to be dragged down with them!*

*We get upset!* -- when our government stands by and watches our children being butchered in the schools, and still won't put prayer back in school.

**How many more children have to die
before prayer is put back into public schools?**

†††

Well, my brothers and sisters, this great economy has begun wobbling under the impact of the loss of companies and consequently jobs being lost or leaving the country. This

---

[16]iron pyrites (native iron sulfide) or copper pyrites (native copper-iron sulfide) resembling gold in color.

avalanche, which has been trickling down, will soon be cascading, covering all stations in life. All the pie-in-the-sky internet stocks are crumbling because they show absolutely no profit.

And then who will we blame? The God Whom we just stood by and let be crucified once again? Will He say, *I do not know you*, when we cry out for help? And at the rate we are going, with God being pushed farther and farther out of our daily lives, will we even think to turn to Him for mercy?

What has happened to that young country, which was formed because of a desire for freedom, freedom from tyranny, from religious persecution, where all men are created equal? What have we done with our franchise to choose? What are we leaving our children and grandchildren and great-grandchildren? I wonder what our ancestors would have done, had they known this land, where they sought freedom of religion, would not allow their future generations to pray in public? Will we become like those in Nazi Germany, during Hitler's reign, where we will be required to hail a false god? Will we worship *man*? It is always the enemy of God who advocates the adoration of *man* and the humanistic glorification of man and his accomplishments, rather than God's Divine illumination and direction of the course of events in our lives.

We are being told, irrevocably, that those young basketball players and their coach were not allowed to make any reference to God, by word or action, (like praying silently in public). George Washington *prayed* before going into battle, supplicating God for His Mercy on our original thirteen states, and victory came about! I wonder what the results might have been, had he relied on the poor ammunition and training in his camp to be victorious against the British and their well-prepared troops!

The bad news is that this is happening in our time and in our country, all a sign of the dire circumstances in which we are living.   The Good News is that it has raised up a controversy; the *moral majority* has raised their voices, the people of the United States whom Pope John Paul II exhorted to be leaders in the world, leaders of moral goodness, have raised their voices.   The high school basketball coach continues to give all credit for his team's victories to God and he has advised everyone, including the school board that he will not cease praying for the success of these fine young men, who are trying to do something positive with their lives.   And these young men have said they will not stop praying before and after each game. Maybe, this courage will rub off on the rest of us and change will come about.

†††

When we wrote our book: *Scandal of the Cross and Its Triumph*, about the Heresies that have attacked the Church for the last 2000 years, we placed an excerpt in our introduction.  Read these words and take them to heart, for without God in our lives, there can be no lasting peace.

"....*we will have peace, and then we will have justice for all, and then everyman, no matter what race or creed, will be brother and sister to other brothers and sisters.  We will become family, united as Jesus commanded in John 17:20.  The lion will lay down with the lamb.  And then, the world will know our Loving Father in Heaven.*

"*There will no longer be a need for demonstrations, except in thanksgiving.  There will no longer be people sleeping in the streets, nor parents helplessly watching their children dying of starvation.  No, since everyman is our brother or sister, every child is our child by virtue of the unity that comes about when we are changed by the Lord.*

"*This is the plan.  This is what the Lord has wanted and wants for us, now.  We were all born to live in the Kingdom. But like our celestial cousins, the Angels, we were given Free*

*Will. We have to make the decision! Our ancestors, Adam and Eve, originally made the decision in our name. Eve ate the fruit; the rest is history. That one act of selfishness and pride, committed thousands and thousands of years ago, changed the course of history, forever. There's a truly important point to be made here. Do we really think about the consequences of the things we do before we do them? Do we consider how our actions will affect others, like a ripple in the stream?*

"No man is an island, entire of itself;

Every man is a piece of the continent,

a part of the main;

Any man's death diminishes me,

Because I am involved in mankind;

And therefore never send to know for whom the bell

tolls;

It tolls for thee."

*John Donne*

*"Our actions are never just for ourselves. They are not even necessarily for our immediate circle of family and friends. We have to know, we are all involved in mankind."*[17]

††

Humans have become expendable, with women around the world being told how many children they can have and being counselled how they can do away with inconvenient children, the murder of trusting tiny prisoners in their wombs, through the death-camp techniques of birth control and abortion. Do I sound too harsh? In Webster's Dictionary, we read *"Murder is the unlawful and malicious or premeditating killing of one human being by another."* Since we are a people created by God, we must put *His* Divine Law above *man's* fleeting, ever-changing law, and so we are

---

[17]*Scandal of the Cross, Heresies throughout the History of the Church* by Bob and Penny Lord

obliged to follow the Ten Commandments; in this case, *Thou shalt not kill.*

The mothers who have committed this travesty against their own flesh and blood, we have to believe, did not know what they were doing, no more than those who stood by and watched Jesus be condemned to death. They, like those at the time of Jesus, did not know what was going on and were manipulated by those who did, those who will be accountable till the end of the world.[18]

Man has need to worship a higher being. Saint John Vianney, the Curé of Ars, said that without a priest the people will worship animals. As God is being methodically thrown out of our lives, along with our men of God-our priests, man has begun to worship animals, caring more for God's four-legged creatures than the two-legged creation He made in His image.

What is the answer? Pray and sacrifice! And then evangelize; spread the Truth Who is Jesus. Like His cousin, St. John the Baptist, announce His Coming, His Second Coming, for then and only then...*will the lion lie down with the lamb.*

~ ~ ~ ~ ~ ~ ~ ~ ~ ~ ~ ~ ~ ~ ~ ~ ~ ~ ~ ~ ~ ~ ~ ~ ~ ~ ~

Footnote 1 - First Amendment to the Constitution June 15, 1790

CONGRESS SHALL MAKE NO LAW RESPECTING AN ESTABLISHMENT OF RELIGION OR PROHIBITING THE FREE EXERCISE THEREOF; OR ABRIDGING THE FREEDOM OF SPEECH, OR OF THE PRESS, OR THE RIGHT OF THE PEOPLE PEACEABLY TO ASSEMBLE AND TO PETITION THE GOVERNMENT FOR A REDRESS OF GRIEVANCES.

Footnote # 2 - Definition of Religion - Original Webster's Dictionary:

"INCLUDES A BELIEF IN THE BEING AND PERFECTIONS OF GOD, IN THE REVELATION OF HIS WILL TO MAN, AND IN MAN'S OBLIGATION TO OBEY HIS COMMANDS, IN A STATE OF REWARD AND PUNISHMENT, AND IN MAN'S ACCOUNTABLENESS TO GOD; AND ALSO TRUE GODLINESS OR PIETY OF LIFE WITH THE PRACTICE OF ALL MORAL DUTIES...THE PRACTICE OF MORAL VALUES WITHOUT A BELIEF IN A DIVINE LAWGIVER AND WITHOUT REFERENCE TO HIS WILL OR COMMANDS, IS NOT RELIGION."

---

[18] *cf* Jn 19:11

Left:
**The Prophet Jonah**
**The Lord told Jonah to**
**walk through Nineveh**
**and preach a**
**chastisement against it.**
**At first, Jonah fled from**
**the Lord and wound up**
**in the belly of a whale**
**for three days. Then he**
**set out to fulfill the**
**Lord's command. He**
**walked through the city**
**and proclaimed, "Forty**
**days more and Nineveh**
**will be destroyed."**

Above:
*"Then the wolf shall be a guest of the lamb, and the lion shall lie down*
*with the kid; the calf and the young lion shall browse together with a*
*little child to guide them."*

# We can Change the World!
# We must Change the World!

Most beloved family, we have traveled a rough road together and we are nearing the end of this book and this Century. If we truly believe in Holy Scripture, that the Lord has used prophets down through the ages to speak to us, we have reason to be frightened. There is every indication, we may very well be speeding *headlong* toward the last days. Our concern should be not necessarily for ourselves (if we have been traveling the straight and narrow path which leads us to the Kingdom), but for our children and grandchildren, and great-grandchildren, the future generations who deserve to live in a world free from plagues, nuclear holocausts and cataclysmic disasters of one kind or another. We need to pray for our Church, our country, and our world, and then do something about it!

**"Take back our country; we must take back our world!"**

The church was filled with mourners, people of all faiths, all backgrounds, including not only members and friends of the students who had been killed, but people from this small peaceful village, where peace once reigned and was taken for granted. The townspeople cried, "This doesn't happen in our village!" As we heard those cries, we remembered crying out much the same thing when we lost our son to an overdose of drugs. But it does happen, and there are no border guards to keep it from striking anywhere, where God is not the Supreme Head.

During the writing of this book, a massacre at Columbine High School in Littleton, Colorado took place, Tuesday, April 20, 1999, where fifteen lives were lost and thirteen others wounded, not to count the countless others who will be scarred by this holocaust. It was pointed out that this having been the anniversary of the birthday of Adolf

Hitler, the youthful terrorists planned their bloodbath for that day, in some twisted sense of honor to him.

Like most Americans, and probably a good deal of the population of the world, we sat shocked in front of our television sets as the story of this *American disgrace* unfolded. It reminded us of the Assassination of President Kennedy on Friday, November 22, 1963. We stayed glued to the television sets the entire weekend, right up to the funeral.

In Littleton, on Saturday night, at the funeral of one of the girls murdered in the High School, a minister preached to the young people, dazed and weeping uncontrollably for their classmate whose only crime was she loved Jesus, and she passed that love on to every one she met; she was everyone's favorite. When the killers approached her, they asked, "Do you believe in God? and when she replied, "**I believe in God!**" they shot her! A godless act against God and His little messenger on earth.

"**I believe in God!**" One pastor said that *Prayer had returned to the schools!* As we watched the scenes over and over again, almost praying it was not real, but another one of television's gory programs, we could hear the students crying out, "*God! Oh my God!*" as they ran for cover, their hands on their heads (instructions from the police who were afraid the gunmen would change their clothes and mix with the other students).

One minister told the students and the parents, "*You must take back your schools!*" He repeated it many times, "*You must take back your schools!*" This entire tragedy has had a great impact on us and our family. Our book, not yet finished, we were given an inspiration to go one step further and cry out to you, "*We must take back our country; we must take back our world!*" And how shall we do that?

A man of God had the courage to say, "*Prayer has returned to the schools!*" No one tried to stop those children from reaching out to the only real Help - God! And we believe, with all our hearts, that there will be a new beginning in Littleton, Colorado--God has entered the school and they are not about to let Him be shoved out!

*This horrible negative, the killing of innocent children and teacher, is destined, like the killing of the Innocent One on the Cross, to become a positive*; as Salvation came about on the Cross and Jesus rose from the dead, so these beautiful souls whose life was snuffed out prematurely will not have died in vain! Through the death of these martyrs, who had been earmarked to die (by possessed gunmen from their own school), prayer has returned to Littleton, Colorado and that will snowball until Prayer and God is resurrected in our schools, in our land, returned to a nation called to holiness by Pope John Paul II! Our Pope called upon us as a *Continent of Hope* to be a *Nation of Life with Dignity for all.*

**Who is to blame for what happened last week in Colorado?**

...or for that matter, the *ten other* high school shootings which have taken place within the last sixteen months in the United States?[1]

We have to answer that with a question:

*Who* took God out of our schools?

*Who ordered* the ban on voluntary prayer by students in schools? (Will the next thing, as in Nazi Germany, be in homes?)

*Who ordered* teachers and coaches in schools to not allow, nor support or encourage prayer by students in school, under penalty of imprisonment or loss of jobs or both?

*Who ordered*, that the religious rights of the many be suppressed, for the agenda of even one atheist? The question you have a right to ask is, Why does one atheist have more rights than thousands of believers?

Do we have a system of checks and balances as our Constitution calls for, or is our country ruled by the Supreme

---

[1]Resource - ABCNEWS.com

Court, which is just an extension of the president who appointed the Justices *for life*?

There is a godlessness taking over this once Godly land. A godless people have infiltrated our country, our government, our courts. The words of our sacred Constitution, to accommodate a godless agenda, have been systematically and blatantly twisted so that the meaning of the original framers of the Constitution has now been disputed and ridiculed, accusing the Founding Fathers who wrote it, of being ignorant of its true intent when they drafted it.

Once that was accomplished, and the uproar died down sufficiently, there was no stopping evil from sucking the life out of our country. This plague has gotten so out of hand that laws and morality are virtually non-existent in this country. But the right to be as immoral as we please, and to impose that immorality on our neighbor is protected by various civil rights groups. They will defend anyone's rights as long as they are not pro-church, pro-religion or pro-God. And these organizations are funded by our government. *What can we do?*

**Put them out of business!**
†Next time you vote, vote your conscience, your Catholic conscience.
†*Stop supporting* violent and immoral films. Don't go to them and don't let your children see them. Protest to your congressman.
†*Stop supporting* violence, sex and immorality on television. Find out who the sponsors of these programs are,[2] and write to them, telling them you will boycott their products as long as they support those type of programs. Then if that doesn't help, stop buying their

---

[2]Contact American Family Association - Tupelo, MS for names and addresses of sponsors of objectionable TV programs.

products and tell your friends not to!

†*Stop supporting* violence and immorality in songs, musical groups and rap groups.

   †Do not buy their products.

   †Do not give your children money to support these groups.

   †Do not go to their concerts.

   †Do not watch these types of music video programs; contact the sponsors and tell them why you're boycotting them.

†*Vote your conscience! Stop supporting* politicians and public officials whose voting record is anti-Christian, anti-life, pro-violence.

†Don't keep voting a favorite son/daughter into office whose voting record is not Christian.

†Don't buy into the philosophy that his/her personal life does not affect his/her performance in office.

†*Campaign against* godlessness.

†Speak up when decisions are made under the cloak of being constitutional and they are not.

†Vote for reform.

†Insist that these Constitutional rights which have been taken away from us be given back to us; make your voice heard by your franchise as an American, to vote!

†Insist on laws governing material being put on the Internet.

   †Does your child have his/her own website? Does he or she go online without any supervision?

†Are they getting into violence - neo-Nazism?

†Is your child hiding para-military material in his rooms, including weapons?

†Are your children taking drugs?

†Are they adopting secretive habits?

†Are they blocking you out of their lives?

†Be aware of what your child is doing.

†Support your child.

†Offset the godlessness which is being taught,
   with the truths of God.
                *Most importantly, pray!*
                   *Pray, as a family,*
                  *pray as a community,*
                  *pray as a country!*
                  *Pray! Pray! Pray!*
                  *Pray constantly!*

**Take Back Your Country - Take Back Your World!**

We are a part of the whole. All the evil that man does echoes throughout the atmosphere, reverberating, affecting the entire world. Mother Nature has joined her Creator, bringing about vengeance upon the world, throughout the history of our universe. In the "*Roaring Twenties,*" the height of decadence in 1927, men and women in the United States were wildly enjoying a false prosperity - no limit to recklessness, irreverence, decadence, amorality - their souls decaying into wastelands where flowers of purity once bloomed.

Churches were being closed, priests murdered, martyrs by the tens of thousands piling one on top of the other, our cousins to the South in Mexico pleading for help; and we did nothing! The Lord was angry! Something had to be done about it! It had to be stopped - this wanton waste of lives and more importantly souls. Mother Nature joined her Creator and in 1927, the Mississippi River, which is usually *one mile* wide flooded, causing its banks to stretch to *three hundred miles* wide, flooding most of Arkansas and all of Mississippi.

Flappers kept dancing wildly, men kept drinking intemperately, and husbands and wives continued sinning against their Sacraments of Matrimony, adultery an accepted *given!* Something had to be done! 1929 came and with it the Stock Market on Wall Street crashed! Suddenly the frenzy halted; the never-ending flow of money, drink, drugs, dancing, infidelity, and immorality were no more! Yes, and irreverence became reverence!

The mask was off!    Satan had exposed his ugly countenance. There was an air of desperation and despair in the air; the banks failed, the stocks were not worth the paper they were written on and bread lines started to form! Those who remembered there was a God Who loved them, returned to church, and *fell on their knees.* Those who had sold out their souls, to the gods of power, wealth, licentiousness, and wanton evil, *jumped out of windows*; their gods had betrayed them.

We came out of the Depression; things began to slowly look up. Then twenty years later, we had World War II and with it more jobs and more money; too much time and too much money, service men came home to wives who had found others to help them in their loneliness. All those who had gone to church daily began to go only on Sundays; and then not knowing they still needed God, they stopped going altogether. Again prosperity and all that goes with it.

Our world has gone through two world wars and we have lost young lives in countless others! God has spared our country from attack on our land. And what have we done, we have stood by and allowed Him to be slighted, maligned, and forgotten! And with Him, we have forsaken all that we once held dear - new gods filling our lives! Do you wonder, for one moment if the Lord is angry with the world and especially the United States, a country He has plainly favored with untold gifts and mercy? Never has a people had so much opportunity, and means, to spread the Good News to the world; and we citizens of the last decades of the Second Millennium, have said, *We are too busy...Later Lord, I have to work seven days a week to live in the best neighborhood, to give my family what I never had.* Was what you never had - murder in schools, children killing each other, mothers killing their own flesh and blood in their wombs, grandparents who were once the story-tellers and passers-down of tradition and heritage being locked away in homes?

**What can we do?  We can change the world!**

How can we abate or lessen the tribulation and chastisement that is sure to come?  We can pray; we can beg Jesus to "*change His Mind.*"  Many of us have been told intercessory prayer is not worth anything.  God has already made up His Mind.  Nothing we do is going to change it. But the Lord teaches us differently, in His Word....

†††

*"**Have faith in God.**  In truth I tell you, if anyone says to this mountain 'Be pulled up and thrown into the sea' with no doubt in his heart, but believing that what he says will happen, it will be done for him.  I tell you, therefore, everything you ask for, believe that you have it already and it will be yours.  And when you stand in prayer, forgive whatever you have against anybody, so that your Father in Heaven may forgive your failings too."*[3]

†††

*"Ask, and it will be given to you; search, and you will find; knock and the door will be opened to you.  Everyone who asks receives; everyone who searches finds; everyone who knocks will have the door opened."*[4]

†††

*"Then He told them a parable about the need to pray continually and never lose heart.*

*"'There was a judge in a certain town,' He said, 'who had neither fear of God nor respect for anyone.  In the same town there was also a widow who kept on coming to*

---
[3]Mk 11:22-26
[4]Mt 7:7-9

*Him and saying, 'I want justice from you against my enemy!'*

*"'For a long time he refused, but at last he said to himself, 'Even though I have neither fear of God nor respect for any human person, I must give this widow her just rights since she keeps pestering me, or she will come and do me harm.'*

*"And the Lord said, 'You notice what the unjust judge has to say? Now, will not God see justice done to His elect if they keep calling on Him day and night even though He still delays to help them? I promise you, He will see justice done to them, and done speedily."*[5]

†††

We've been in churches where St. Luke's Gospel, above, was proclaimed, and right after it, in the homily, the priest discredited the very Gospel he had just read, by saying God has already made up His Mind. Yet, St. Paul tells us, *"Pray, without ceasing!"*[6] *"...we do not cease praying for you..."*[7]

**Pray and believe! There is hope! We can change the world!**

This brings us to the heart of this chapter, and of this book. While we believe that all the prophecies we have written about in this book are true, and there will be chastisement and tribulation, it can be lessened and minimized by our fasting, our prayers - especially before the Blessed Sacrament, and our supplications.[8]

Whereas Jesus predicts the Last Days, He also assures us of hope in the wake of hopelessness, Light to cut through the darkness:

*"...He said to them, 'Nation will rise against nation and kingdom against kingdom. There will be powerful*

---

[5]Lk 18:1-8
[6]1Thes 5:17
[7]Col 1:9
[8]offering our suffering

*earthquakes, famines, and plagues from place to place;
and awesome sights and mighty signs will come from the
sky.'"*

*"Then they asked Him, 'Teacher, when will this
happen? And what sign will there be when all these things
are about to happen?' He answered, 'See that you are not
deceived, for many will come in My name, saying 'I am
He' and 'The time has come.' Do not follow them! When
you hear of wars and insurrections, do not be terrified; for
such things must happen first, but it will not immediately
be the end."*[9]

Jesus prophesied the Second Coming, speaking of the
fright before His Coming and the joy which would follow:

*"There will be signs in the sun, the moon, and the stars,
and on earth nations will be in dismay, perplexed by the
roaring of the sea and the waves.*

*"'People will die of fright in anticipation of what is
coming upon the world, for the powers of the heavens will
be shaken.*

*"'And then they will see the Son of Man coming in a
cloud with power and great glory. But when these signs
begin to happen, stand erect and raise your heads because
your redemption is at hand."*[10]

Basically, everything you read in the Bible regarding
tribulation and chastisement, you can pretty well count on
happening, if it has not already. By the same token,
however, all the benefits Our Lord has given us through
Scripture and Tradition, especially with regard to praying for
intercessory help, Angelic intercession and Our Lady's help
are also there for us.

However, even prophecies which are Scriptural, can be
conditional. The punishment can be lessened, or completely

---

[9]Lk 21:7-11
[10]Lk 21:25-28

eliminated by the actions of the Faithful. A perfect example would be:

**Jonah and the people of Nineveh.**

The Lord told Jonah to walk through the city of Nineveh, and preach a chastisement against it. At first, Jonah fled from the Lord and wound up in the belly of a whale for three days. *Then* he set out to fulfill the Lord's command. He walked through the city of Nineveh, proclaiming *"Forty days more and Nineveh will be destroyed."* Nineveh was a big city, and it took three days to walk through the entire city. Now this was not a situation where the Lord had Jonah say to the people of Nineveh, *"If you don't repent, I'll do this. But if you change your ways, I'll do that."* No. It was a straight statement. *"Forty days more and Nineveh will be destroyed."*

But without any bargain from the Lord, the people of Nineveh reacted to the Lord's Word as given them by the prophet Jonah. They proclaimed a fast, and every one of them put on sackcloth and ashes.

Word got to the king of Nineveh. He tore his clothes, a sign of repentance, and made a proclamation:

*"Neither man nor beast, neither cattle nor sheep, shall taste anything; they shall not eat, nor shall they drink water. Man and beast shall be covered with sackcloth and call out loudly to God; every man shall turn from his evil ways and from the violence he has in hand. Who knows, God may relent and forgive, and withhold His blazing wrath, so that we shall not perish.*

*"When God saw by their actions how they turned from their evil way, He repented of the evil that He had threatened to do to them; He did not carry it out."*[11]

Now this is amazing! They believed in God's anger and punishment, as witnessed by how seriously they took the

---

[11]Jon 3:6-10

word of His prophet that Nineveh would be destroyed. But they also had great faith in God's Love and Mercy. There were no guarantees. As far as they knew, the punishment was coming. But they trusted that *maybe* God would relent and forgive, and in so doing withhold His wrath. And that's just what happened.

So here's a situation, where the Lord did not make any commitment to the people of Nineveh, but He did reward them for turning away from their evil ways.

✝✝✝

There are prophecies of the end times which cause us to cringe - chastisements resulting from man's cold, callous, stubborn, hard heart, but on the other hand, there are prophecies speaking of God's Mercy, as a result of man relinquishing control of his destiny, softening his heart, converting and coming back to the Lord. As man's actions can be the catalyst for destruction of himself and the world, a reversal of those actions can bring about peace and harmony, Redemption of body and soul as was planned for us, by God, in the Garden of Eden:

"*But a shoot shall sprout from the stump of Jesse, and from his roots a bud shall blossom.*

"*The Spirit of the Lord shall rest upon him, a spirit of wisdom and of understanding.*

"*A Spirit of counsel and of strength, a spirit of knowledge and of fear of the Lord,*[12] *and his delight shall be the fear of the Lord.*[13]

"*Then the wolf shall be a guest of the lamb, and the leopard shall lie down with the kid; the calf and the young lion shall browse together with a little child to guide them.*

"*The cow and the bear shall be neighbors, together their young shall rest; the lion shall eat hay like the ox. The*

---

[12]Fear in this context means awe of the Lord
[13]Is 11:1-2

*baby shall play by the cobra's den, and the child lay his hand on the adder's lair.*

*"There shall be no harm or ruin on all my holy mountain; for the earth shall be filled with knowledge of the Lord, as water covers the sea."[14]*

✝✝✝

We prayed a great deal writing this book. We had an urgency to write it and get it to you. *Be not afraid, God is with us!* As we bring to an end this book on Prophecies and Promises, we would like to quote St. Paul's letter to the Romans. It has to do with *remnant*, the key word in this prophecy and in this book. We believe that we all are called to be that *raggedy remnant* of the Lord, of which St. Paul and Isaiah before him, spoke. The Lord has called us, at this time and place, to be heralds of His coming, and with our words and actions, to help bring others to the Kingdom on the Last Day; because, remember and believe my brothers and sisters, we have truly been chosen; the responsibility is ours to spend each waking moment carrying out this mission.

*"...Isaiah cries out, referring to Israel, 'Though the number of the Israelites should be as the sands of the sea, only the remnant will be saved, for quickly and decisively will the Lord execute sentence upon the earth.'*

*"It is just as Isaiah predicted: 'Unless the Lord of Hosts had left us a remnant, we should have become as Sodom, we should be like Gomorrah.'"[15]*

Remember we are called to be that remnant! See you on the battlefield! *We can change the world! We will change the world!* And then, we'll see you in Heaven...

---

[14]Is 11:6-9
[15]Rom 9:26-29

# Bibliography

Barton, David - *Original Intent*
    Wallbuilders Press Aledo, TX 1996
Birch, Desmond A. - *Trial, Tribulation & Triumph*
    Queenship Publishing - Santa Barbara CA 1996
Bosco, St. John - *Dreams, Visions & Prophecies*
    Don Bosco Publications - New Rochelle, NY 1986
Cumbey, Constance - *The Hidden Dangers of the Rainbow*
    Huntington House, Shreveport, LA 1983
Culleton, Rev. Gerald - *The Prophets and our Times*
    Tan Publications - Rockford, IL 1974
Dirvin, Fr. Joseph I. - *Saint Catherine Labouré*
    Tan Publications - Rickford, IL 1984
DuPont, Yves - *Catholic Prophecy*
    Tan Publications - Rockford, IL 1970
England, Randy - *Unicorn in the Sanctuary*
    Tan Publications - Rockford, IL 1990
EWTN - On Line Library
Kowalska, Sr. Faustina Bl. - *Divine Mercy in my Soul*
    Marian Helpers Press - Stockbridge, MA 1987
Lord, Bob & Penny
*Many Faces of Mary, a love Story 1987*
*We Came Back to Jesus 1988*
*Scandal of the Cross and Its Triumphs 1992*
*Visionaries, Mystics and Stigmatists 1995*
*Visions of Heaven, Hell and Purgatory 1996*
*Treasures of the Church 1997*
    Journeys of Faith - Fair Oaks, CA
John Paul II - *Speeches and Encyclicals*
    Vatican Printing Office - 1991-1999

## Publishers of the Good Newsletter

Published 4 times per year
Special articles on our Faith,
and information on our community.

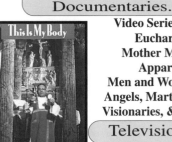

## Lectures

**Bob and Penny
travel to all parts of the
world to spread the** Good News.

## Over 150
## Videos & On-Site
## Documentaries.

Video Series on the
Eucharist,
Mother Mary's
Apparitions,
Men and Women Saints,
Angels, Martyrs, Mystics,
Visionaries, & Stigmatists.

*Bob and Penny Lord speaking
at a National Conference*

This Is My Body
    This Is My Blood
Miracles of the Eucharist

Bob and Penny Lord

## Television Series

These series are shown on
Mother Angelica's Eternal
Word Television Network.

## Pilgrimages

To the Shrines of Europe,
the Holy Land, and the Shrines of Canda and Mexico.

*Bob and Penny Lord
with Mother Angelica*

*Bob and Penny Lord
with Pope John Paul II*

THE FOCUS OF THEIR MINISTRY IS
EVANGELIZATION THROUGH COMMUNICATION